Pre-intermediate Student's Book

ASPIRE

Discover
Learn
Engage

Jon Naunton and Robert Crossley

NATIONAL GEOGRAPHIC LEARNING | CENGAGE Learning·

Australia • Brazil • Japan • Korea • Mexico • Singapore • Spain • United Kingdom • United States

Contents

**Aspire Pre-intermediate
Student's Book**
Jon Naunton and Robert Crossley

Publisher: Jason Mann

Commissioning Editor: Alistair Baxter

Editorial Project Manager: Karen White

Development Editor: Kathryn Eyers

Editorial Technology: Debie Mirtle and
   Melissa Skepko

Project Editor: Amy Smith

Production Controller: Tom Relf

Senior Marketing Manager: Ruth McAleavey

National Geographic Liaison: Leila Hishmeh

Art Director: Natasa Arsenidou

Cover Designer: Sofia Ioannidou

Text Designer: Natasa Arsenidou

Compositor: eMC Design Ltd.

Audio: the Soundhouse Ltd.

Acknowledgements

The publisher would like to thank the following
for their invaluable contribution: Sandra Frith
and James Greenan.

© 2013 National Geographic Learning, a part of Cengage Learning

For permission to use material from this text or product, submit all
requests online at **cengage.com/permissions**.

Further permissions questions can be emailed to
permissionrequest@cengage.com.

ISBN: 978-1-111-77068-6

National Geographic Learning
Cheriton House, North Way, Andover, Hampshire
SP10 5BE United Kingdom

Cengage Learning is a leading provider of customised learning
solutions with office locations around the globe, including Singapore,
the United Kingdom, Australia, Mexico, Brazil and Japan. Locate our
local office at **international.cengage.com/region**

Cengage Learning products are represented in Canada by Nelson
Education Ltd.

Visit National Geographic Learning online at **elt.heinle.com**
Visit our corporate website at **cengage.com**

Printed in China by RR Donnelley
1 2 3 4 5 6 7 8 9 10 – 17 16 15 14 13 12

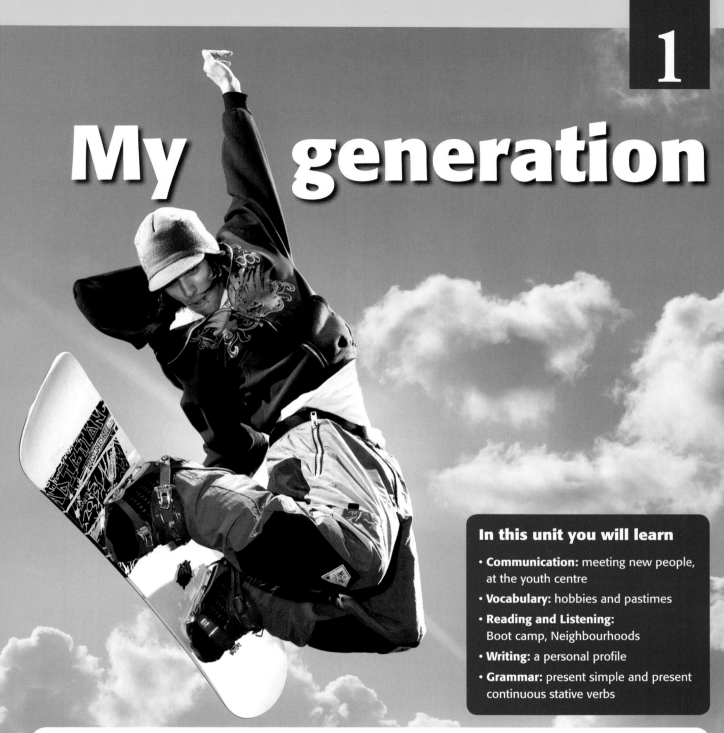

My generation

In this unit you will learn

- **Communication:** meeting new people, at the youth centre
- **Vocabulary:** hobbies and pastimes
- **Reading and Listening:** Boot camp, Neighbourhoods
- **Writing:** a personal profile
- **Grammar:** present simple and present continuous stative verbs

Let's get started

1 Describe the picture and answer the questions.

   1 Why is the young person in the picture doing this kind of sport?

   2 What is your favourite hobby? Why?

Vocabulary

2 Decide whether each of the adjectives in the box best describes your generation or your parents' generation. Write each one in the column you decide.

> careful with money   conservative   creative
> fashion-conscious   generous   hardworking
> law-abiding   open-minded   optimistic
> prejudiced   selfish   sociable

My generation	My parents' generation

3 Compare your list with a partner. Explain your decisions.

4 What is the relationship between different generations in your country? Do different generations understand each other? What makes you think so?

1A A helping hand

Reading

1 Study the pictures. How are these teenagers helping other people?

2 Read the interview with Melinda Bradley and answer the questions.

1 Who is the shelter for? 2 What are Melinda's reasons for volunteering? 3 Is she a typical teenager?

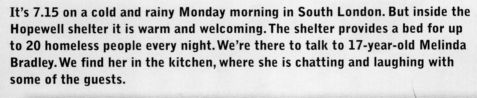

It's 7.15 on a cold and rainy Monday morning in South London. But inside the Hopewell shelter it is warm and welcoming. The shelter provides a bed for up to 20 homeless people every night. We're there to talk to 17-year-old Melinda Bradley. We find her in the kitchen, where she is chatting and laughing with some of the guests.

Hi Melinda. Something smells good. So what are you cooking?

Well, I'm making a cooked breakfast for everyone. It's important that they have something warm inside their stomachs.

What do you do when you're not at the shelter?

Well, I live with my parents and I go to school in Croydon. I'm studying for my A levels*.

I see. How often do you come down here?

I usually work here on Tuesday, but I'm working here today because another volunteer is ill. Sometimes I come two or three times a week if we are short of helpers.

Do the guests appreciate your help?

Yes, they do. A lot of the homeless people are young. They usually want to speak to someone of their own age.

Why do you do it?

Because I want to do something to help the community. It doesn't take up much of my time, but it makes a big difference to the people here.

What do you get out of it on a personal level?

Well, it makes me feel good about myself and I never regret the time I spend here. It's really rewarding to do a little to help and I have a good time too – honestly!

*A levels are exams students take before they finish school at age 18.

It's eight o'clock. She's saying goodbye as the final guests leave. She finishes tidying up the kitchen and quickly changes into her school uniform. Then it's off to school for the rest of her busy day.

Grammar: present simple and present continuous

3 Sentences a–c use the present simple. Match sentences a–c to uses 1–3.

a I usually work here on Tuesday.

b The shelter provides a bed for up to 20 homeless people every night.

c I live with my parents and I go to school in Croydon.

1 ☐ a general fact

2 ☐ a piece of personal information

3 ☐ a routine / something that happens regularly

4 Complete the table using *do, don't, does* and *doesn't.*

The present simple

Affirmative statements
I/You/We/They live in London.
He/She/It lives in London.

Negative statements
I/You/We/They don't live in London.
He/She/It (1) _____ live in London.

Wh- questions
Where (2) _____ I/you/we/they live?
Where (3) _____ he/she/it live?

Yes / No questions
(4) _____ I/you/we/they live in London?
(5) _____ he/she/it live in London?

Short answers
Yes, I/you/we/they (6) _____.
Yes, he/she/it (7) _____.
No, I/you/we/they (8) _____.
No, he/she/it (9) _____.

See Grammar Reference, page 146

5 Complete the questions and answers below using the present simple. Use verbs from the text.

1 How often _____ Melinda _____ at the shelter?
   She _____ there once a week.
2 How many people _____ Melinda _____ breakfast for? Eighteen.
3 Where _____ Melinda _____ to school?
   In Croydon, South London.
4 What _____ a lot of the homeless people _____? Someone to talk to.
5 _____ Melinda _____ she makes a difference? Yes, she _____.
6 _____ Melinda _____ the time she spends at the shelter? No, she _____ _____ a second.

6 Sentences a–c use the present continuous. Match sentences a–c to uses 1–3.

a I'm studying for my A levels.
b I'm making a cooked breakfast.
c I'm working here today because another volunteer is ill.

1 ☐ an action we can see right now
2 ☐ an action which is a change to the usual routine
3 ☐ an action in progress over a longer period of time, around now

7 Complete the table.

We make the present continuous with
be + verb + -*ing*:
She (1) _____ (2) mak____ breakfast.
They (3) _____ (4) eat____ breakfast.
To make the question we swap the order of the subject and *be*:
What (5) _____ she (6) mak____?
(7) _____ they (8) eat____ breakfast?

See Grammar Reference, page 146

8 Which adverbs of frequency and time expressions do we use with the present continuous and which do we use with the present simple?

always   at the moment   currently   never occasionally   often   right now   sometimes this morning   usually   today

9 Complete the sentences by changing the verbs into the present simple or the present continuous.

1 Hey, why _____ (**you / touch**) my computer? Stop what you _____ (**do**) right now!
2 She usually _____ (**play**) handball on Tuesday evenings, but at the moment she _____ (**finish**) her homework.
3 The children _____ (**make**) so much noise that I can't hear what you _____ (**say**).
4 We _____ (**not go**) to restaurants often, but today we _____ (**celebrate**) my exam results.
5 How often _____ (**Ian and Anne / visit**) you?
6 They usually _____ (**come**) on Friday, but they _____ (**come**) today for a change.

10 1.2 Listen to the three ways of pronouncing verbs ending in –*s*, then listen again and repeat:
/s/ as in *stops*   /z/ as in *is*   /ɪz/ as in *wishes*

11 Work in pairs. As part of a school project, you want to write about a visitor to your country. Use the prompts below to make questions. Ask your partner …

• his/her name.
• where he/she is from.
• about his/her background.
• what he/she does back home.
• what he/she is doing at the moment.
• what he/she likes doing in his/her free time.
• about his/her ambitions.

Student A turn to page 142, Student B turn to page 144

1B What we like doing

Listening

1 Look at the pictures. What do the people do in their free time?

2 ⊙ 1.3 Listen and complete the table.

Name	Hobbies or pastimes	Amount of time
Sally		
Justin and Alex		
Mark		
Hannah		

3 Complete the sentences with a preposition from the box.

> about   by   into   in   of   on

1 I'm really keen _____ handball.
2 I love travelling and I'm interested _____ other cultures.
3 I'm fond _____ arts and crafts and making things with my hands.
4 I'm fascinated _____ the Ancient Egyptians – I can write my name in hieroglyphs.
5 I'm totally crazy _____ Manchester United. I'm their biggest fan.
6 I'm _____ skateboarding. I practise about two hours a day.

Pronunciation

4 ⊙ 1.4 When a word ending in a consonant comes before a word beginning with a vowel, we usually make a 'link'.

a I'm really keen‿on handball.
b I'm‿interested‿in‿other cultures.

What other links can you make in Exercise 3?

Grammar: stative verbs

5 Read the information about stative verbs, then put the verbs in the box into the correct list.

Stative verbs

There is a group of verbs that we don't usually use in the continuous form. These verbs usually refer to states or to the senses and emotions.

> believe   belong   hate   have   hear   know
> like   love   need   own   seem   smell   taste
> think   understand   want   wish

States		Senses and Emotions	
knowledge and belief	possession	senses	emotions
believe			

6 Work in groups. Tell your group about …
- a hobby you have.
- an unusual hobby that someone you know has.

Reading

7 Study the picture at the bottom of the page. Discuss what you think these boys are doing, and why.

> **Spotlight**
>
> **on reading and listening skills:** prediction
>
> Before you read or listen to a text, look at the picture and read the title. This can often give you an idea of what the text is about and help you listen or read more effectively.

8 Read the first paragraph of the text 'Boot Camp' and check your predictions.

9 Read the rest of the text and find out what these figures refer to.

1 90 per cent
2 30 per cent
3 12 days
4 one hour
5 17 hours

10 Read the text again. Decide which sentences are true and which are false. Put a tick (✓) in the correct box.

1 The camp emphasises practical and physical activities.
   True ☐   False ☐

2 There is one girl in the programme.
   True ☐   False ☐

3 The camp is in Seoul.
   True ☐   False ☐

4 Lee Yun-hee thinks many Koreans live in an unreal world.
   True ☐   False ☐

5 Lee Chang-hoon's school work is suffering.
   True ☐   False ☐

6 Lee Chang-hoon will reduce the hours he spends gaming.
   True ☐   False ☐

Speaking

11 Discuss the questions.

1 Do you think you need a camp like this in your country?

2 What do you think is a healthy amount of time to spend on the Internet each day?

3 What do you use the Internet for?

Boot Camp

THE WORLD'S first ever boot camp for teenagers addicted to the Internet is in South Korea. It provides a mixture of military-style physical exercise and rehabilitation. The teenagers climb over assault courses and learn how to ride horses as well as participate in workshops such as pottery and drumming.

The aim is to cure them of their obsessive use of computers in a country with almost universal internet access. Concern over compulsive internet use is growing in South Korea where 90 per cent of homes have high-speed broadband connections and some online games players die from exhaustion after playing for days on end. Psychiatrists estimate that up to 30 per cent of South Koreans are at risk of internet addiction. The rescue camp in woodland near the capital Seoul treats the most severe cases – they're all male. During the 12-day sessions participants can't use a computer and can only use their mobile phones for one hour a day.

Lee Yun-hee, a counsellor, says that the priority of the camp is to provide them with a lifestyle that has its roots in the real world – not the Internet. She says, 'Young Koreans don't know what this is like.'

One participant, Lee Chang-hoon, regularly spends 17 hours a day in front of the screen, surfing Japanese comics and playing a roleplay game called 'Sudden Attack'. He usually plays all night and misses school to catch up on sleep. Three days into the physically challenging programme he says, 'I don't have a problem – 17 hours a day online is fine.' A few days later he seems to change his mind. 'I'm not thinking about games now. Maybe five hours a day online is enough.'

Listening and speaking

1 ⊙ 1.5 Lucy is staying with some relatives in Cambridge. She is speaking to Rebecca, their neighbour's daughter. Listen to their conversation and tick (✓) the topics they mention.

family ☐   friends ☐   pets ☐
hobbies ☐   studies ☐   sport ☐
ambitions ☐   home town and country ☐
favourite books / films ☐

2 ⊙ 1.5 Listen again and fill in the gaps.

S = Sam, R = Rebecca, L = Lucy

S Hello, Rebecca. **(1)** _____ introduce you to Lucy. She's from Scotland. She's staying with us over the summer.

R **(2)** _____ to meet you, Lucy.
(3) _____ visit to England?

L **(4)** _____ it isn't. But it is my first stay in Cambridge.

R And how **(5)** _____ so far?

L I'm **(6)** _____. It's a lovely city.

R So **(7)** _____ home?

L Well, I'm still at school – I have another two years at high school.

R And what do you **(8)** _____ in your free time?

L Well, I **(9)** _____ to music, and I really love playing tennis.

R So do I. **(10)** _____ to play tomorrow afternoon?

L Yes, please. **(11)** _____.

3 Make questions about the topics they didn't mention.

4 You are talking to a French student at a language course. Introduce yourself, ask them about their interests, and tell them about yours.

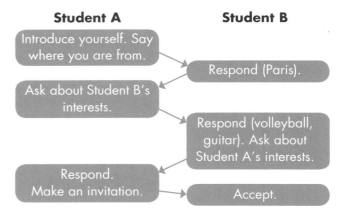

Student A	Student B
Introduce yourself. Say where you are from.	
	Respond (Paris).
Ask about Student B's interests.	
	Respond (volleyball, guitar). Ask about Student A's interests.
Respond. Make an invitation.	
	Accept.

USEFUL EXPRESSIONS

Saying what you enjoy
I like / love playing tennis.
I enjoy listening to music.

Giving your own reaction
That sounds interesting.

Making invitations
Would you like to play tennis?

Accepting and refusing
Yes, please. I'd love to.
I'd love to, but I'm busy.
Sorry, I can't.

Introducing questions
And how are you finding it so far?
So what do you do back home?

Introducing an answer
Well, I'm still at school.

Correcting or adding information
Is this your first visit? Actually, / In fact, it's my second.

Reading and writing: a personal profile

5 Read about these three students. Which one do you have most in common with?

Hi, I'm called Sarah and I'm from near Nottingham. I'm 16 and I live with my mum and sisters. I'm in year ten at my local school. I'm really interested in science and maths. When I leave school, I'd like to study medicine because I'd like to work in a poor country for a few years. In my free time I go ice-skating. I'm crazy about medical dramas like *Grey's Anatomy* and *House M.D.* I enjoy most kinds of music but I don't like opera or rap!! My favourite colours are pink and purple.

Hi everybody! We are Marion and Tara. We're 15 and 16 years old. We're crazy about everything Japanese. We'd like to go to Japan one day so we're learning Japanese from a CD. It's hard work but fun. We both like Manga and think the characters and stories are really cool. Our favourite series is *Streetfighter Girl*. We've got a cat we call Tomoko after the heroine. We're also into heavy metal music and we're big fans of old heavy metal bands. We also spend a lot of time surfing the Internet and looking for stuff on Manga and games.

Hello there, my name's Marcus, but my friends call me Waldo. I come from Holloway which is in North London. I live with Beth, my younger sister, and my mum and dad. I'm captain of my school football team and would like to be a professional player – my teachers think I am good enough. My favourite team's Arsenal, but tickets are so expensive I don't see them very often. I am also into music and am learning the saxophone. I really like jazz so my mates think I'm weird. I spend my time listening to old vinyl records of the great jazz artists – they sound better than on CD.

Spotlight

on writing skills: linkers (1)

and

*I am interested in chess **and** history.*

or

*I don't enjoy listening to classical music **or** going to the cinema.*

but, because and *so (that's why)*

*I enjoy tennis **but** I don't like squash / **but** not squash.*

*I'm learning English **because** I want to study in Canada one day.*

*I want to study in Canada one day, **so** (that's why) I'm learning English.*

6 Look at the Spotlight box. Join the sentences using the words in **bold**.

1 I am a keen tennis player. I am a keen swimmer.
2 William hates watching TV. He likes listening to pop music.
3 I like to keep fit. I play a lot of sport.
4 I am crazy about American TV series. I am crazy about sudoku.
5 I love visiting monuments. I love reading about my country's history.
6 Katie wants to be a doctor. She is working hard for her exams.
7 Andy loves snowboarding. He doesn't like ice hockey.
8 I don't enjoy listening to classical music. I don't enjoy going to the theatre.

7 Find examples of these ways of linking in the three profiles above.

8 Use the three example profiles, and *but, and, because* and *so* to write your personal profile for a blog page. Make yourself sound interesting! Use some or all of the categories below.

name age where you live nickname where exactly you are from

free time family situation studies ambitions

favourite subjects likes and dislikes favourite animals

Reading

1 Look at the pictures of three cities. Which one do you think is …

- Berlin?
- San Francisco?
- London?

2 Match the words in the box to definitions 1–5.

> multicultural ☐ immigrant ☐ refugee ☐
> neighbourhood ☐ community ☐

1 a group of people who are similar in a special way and often live in the same area

2 a person who has come to live in a country from another country

3 with people of many different cultures and traditions

4 an area of a town or city with a clear identity

5 a person who leaves their own country as the result of a war or persecution

3 Read about different neighbourhoods in the three famous cities and answer the questions by writing *B* for Berlin, *L* for London and *S* for San Francisco. Which city …

1 has one person in three from another country? ☐

2 is home to a large Bangladeshi community? ☐

3 has lots of street paintings? ☐

4 welcomes immigrants from its ex-colonies? ☐

5 holds two annual events that are famous worldwide? ☐

6 has three remarkable districts? ☐

7 has lots of Spanish-speaking new arrivals? ☐

4 Which of the cities would you like to visit? Why?

5 Do any cities in your country have areas that are similar to the ones described?

The new Berlin

These days, Berlin is one of the most exciting multicultural cities in Europe. A third of its 3.5 million people aren't originally from Germany. They come from 185 different countries, and many of them live in communities with other people from their homelands. These neighbourhoods are great places to visit and each one has its own very different look and atmosphere. We're here in the Kreuzberg area where many people from Turkey now live. People are buying special foods from Turkey and eating in Turkish restaurants. We can find clubs here, too. In these clubs people from many different cultures come together to play music and dance. Another area is the Art Mile which is the city's lively art centre. Every year it has two international festivals that attract visitors from around the world. People also love the area called Prenzlauerberg. Its streets are jumping with the energy of its musicians, artists and designers.

> "Its streets are jumping with the energy of its musicians, artists and designers."

A London welcome

The whole world lives in London. Fifty nationalities with communities of more than 50,000 live in the city, and speak 300 languages. Most of these Londoners are the second- and third-generation descendants* of subjects* of the old British Empire. I am with Annas Ali, a 17-year-old Londoner of Bangladeshi descent, and we are pushing through the crowds filling Brick Lane in London's East End. People are celebrating the Bangladeshi festival of Baishakhi Mela. The British flag flies alongside the green and red flag of Bangladesh. Nowadays people call the neighbourhood 'Banglatown' and the annual Brick Lane Festival attracts visitors from all over the world, all eager to experience the multi cultural mix of fashion, cuisine and art.

> "The whole world lives in London."

Destination San Francisco

The Chinatown area of San Francisco is one of the largest chinatowns outside Asia. It originally sprung up with the arrival of Chinese immigrants in the early 1800s. After further waves of immigrants from Ireland, Germany and Italy, it is now the turn of new arrivals from Mexico and Central and South America.

> "It isn't just the music that is full of life and colour, but the art of the district, too."

It is easy to see the style that these recent additions give the neighbourhood. You can see it in the art on the walls, taste it in the food and hear it in the music. It isn't just the music that is full of life and colour, but the art of the district, too. The local art community stays close to the area's culture and tradition. A local art organisation often leads people on walks through the district. They visit streets which are famous for their murals. These murals reflect the interests of the communities that live in the district.

descendants a person's descendants are the people in later generations who are related to them

subjects people who live in or belong to a particular country, usually ruled by a king or queen

San Francisco

Berlin

BRICK LANE E.L.
ব্রিক লেন

Brick Lane, London

At the youth centre

Listening and speaking

1 Look at the pictures of young people enjoying their free time. Describe the pictures and answer the questions.

1 Why are the young people in the pictures spending their free time in this way?

2 Do you prefer indoor or outdoor activities? Why?

2 Look at the choice of activities at the youth centre. Which one do you think is the most interesting?

BETTER THAN TV!

Look at the activities you can do at the Stanhope Youth Centre. It doesn't matter if you're an indoor or an outdoor person, there is something for you. There are physically-challenging activities that build your self-confidence, and activities that help you find the hidden artist or computer wizard inside you. Come along and find out more.

Sam Walsh – Youth Centre Coordinator

Wall-climbing   Kayaking
Theatre   Mural painting
Film making   Building a PC

3 1.6 Cindy is talking to a youth centre officer about the wall-climbing classes. Listen to their conversation and answer the questions.

1 What is Cindy worried about?
2 What safety precautions do they take?
3 What special equipment do people need to buy?
4 What is the price of the course?
5 When is the course?
6 What two documents do you need to do a course?
7 When is registration?
8 How many places are there?

4 1.6 Study the Useful expressions box, then listen again. Tick (✓) the expressions you hear.

USEFUL EXPRESSIONS: asking for information

1 a *Have you got a moment?* ☐
 b *Do you have a minute?* ☐

2 a *Yes, of course.* ☐
 b *Yes, sure.* ☐

3 a *I'd like to find out …* ☐
 b *I'd like to know…* ☐

4 a *What do you want to know?* ☐
 b *What would you like to know?* ☐

5 a *Do I need to …?* ☐
 b *Do you have to …?* ☐

6 a *How much does the course cost?* ☐
 b *What's the price of the course?* ☐

7 a *Which day of the week is it?* ☐
 b *When is it?* ☐

8 a *It's on Tuesday evening.* ☐
 b *It takes place on Tuesday evening.* ☐

9 a *from 6.30 to 7.30* ☐
 b *between 6.30 and 7.30* ☐

5 Work in pairs. Student A go to page 144. Student B go to page 146.

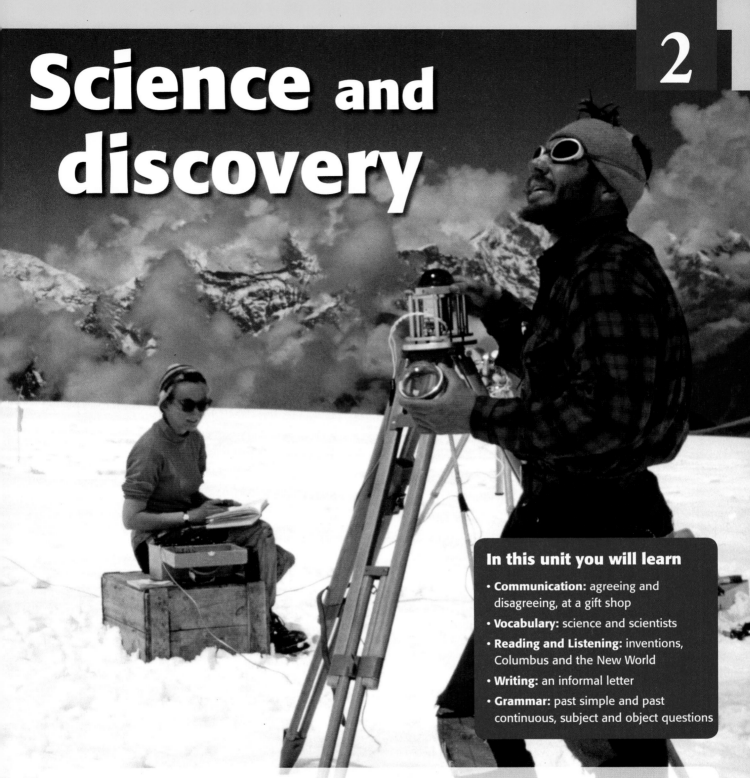

Science and discovery

In this unit you will learn

- **Communication:** agreeing and disagreeing, at a gift shop
- **Vocabulary:** science and scientists
- **Reading and Listening:** inventions, Columbus and the New World
- **Writing:** an informal letter
- **Grammar:** past simple and past continuous, subject and object questions

Let's get started

1 Describe the picture and answer the questions.

1 What kind of research are these scientists doing? Why do you think so?

2 Would you like to do this kind of work?
Why / Why not?

Vocabulary

2 Match the jobs in the box with the definitions 1–6.

astronomer ☐ engineer ☐ physicist ☐
biologist ☐ inventor ☐ mathematician ☐

1 An ... **creates** new ideas or things.
2 An ... **designs** and **constructs** things like bridges and roads.
3 A ... studies the **physical** world and the forces that rule it.
4 An ... studies the stars and planets.
5 A ... studies numbers and **calculations**.
6 A ... studies **living** things.

Reading

1 Look at the pictures. What do you think the story is about?

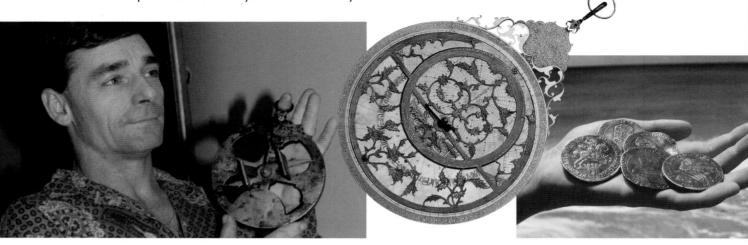

2 Check you know the meaning of these words.

> ship   diver   anchor   sailor   navigation

3 Read the story quickly and answer the questions.

1 Where was Wayne Mushrow diving?
2 What was the name of the mystery object?
3 How old was it?

4 Read the story again and answer the questions.

1 Where was Wayne from?
2 Was he a professional diver?
3 Did he discover the mystery object immediately?
4 What did he do with the object?
5 How did he find out what it was?
6 What was it used for?

Wayne Mushrow was a milkman from Canada. In his free time he was a keen diver and liked to look for sunken ships and interesting objects. On 26 November 1981 he made an important discovery near an island off the coast of Newfoundland. He and his friends were enjoying themselves as usual. Wayne was swimming along the seabed when he discovered an old ship's anchor. Before long the team also found some French coins from 1618.

This proved that the ship was old. Then Mushrow discovered something much more special. While he was looking around, he saw a small shiny object in the sand. He dug down and rescued it. The rest of the object was black so he took it home, washed it and removed the rest of the dirt. He then tried to identify it. What was it? Where did it come from? He searched through encyclopedias and navigation books and eventually learned it was an instrument called an astrolabe, which Greek astronomers invented in medieval times to calculate the position of the stars. It was the only way sailors had to measure latitude*, and was therefore vital in the race to discover new lands and new sources of wealth. Mushrow's astrolabe was 350 years old and probably came from Portugal. Few have survived, and Mushrow's was especially valuable because it was in perfect condition and even still worked!

> **latitude** a ship's position north or south of the equator

Grammar: past simple

5 Look at these sentences from the text. Match them to their uses (1–3).

a He **made** an important discovery.

b Wayne Mushrow **was** a milkman from Canada.

c He **took** it home, **washed** it and **removed** the rest of the dirt.

1 ☐ a past state

2 ☐ a single completed action in the past

3 ☐ a series of completed actions in the past

6 Complete the table using the words in the box.

> created   went   did   didn't

The past simple

Affirmative statements

He (1) _created_ a new invention last year.

We (2) _went_ to Canada a month ago.

Negative statements

She (3) _didn't_ create a new invention.

You (4) _didn't_ go to Canada.

Yes / No questions

(5) _did_ he/she create a new invention?

(6) _did_ they go to Canada?

Short answers

Yes, he/she (7) _did_. / No, they (8) _didn't_.

Wh- questions

What (9) _did_ he create?

Where (10) _did_ they go?

7 Complete the sentences using the words in the box. You can use a verb more than once.

> find   did   do   saw   see   was   were

1 What _was_ Wayne's job? He _was_ a milkman.

2 What _did_ he _do_ in his spare time? He _was_ scuba diving.

3 Where _were_ Wayne and his friends? They _were_ off the coast of Newfoundland.

4 What _did_ Wayne _find_ first? An anchor.

5 _did_ they _find_ anything else? Yes, they _did_.

6 What _did_ Wayne _find_ sticking out of the sand? He _saw_ a small shiny object.

8 1.7 Listen to the –ed ending in *played*, *watched* and *waited*. Then listen to the verbs in the box and put them in the correct column.

/d/ play**ed**	/t/ watch**ed**	/ɪd/ wait**ed**
showed		

> ~~showed~~   liked   decided   removed
> washed   cleaned   tried   rescued   searched

Grammar: past simple and past continuous

9 Match sentences a–c with uses 1 and 2.

a Wayne **was swimming** along the seabed when he **discovered** an old ship's anchor.

b Wayne and his friends **were diving** near Canada.

c While he **was looking** around, he **saw** a small shiny object.

1 ☒ ☒ a past action that interrupted an activity

2 ☐ a background to the story

10 Name the tense used for each verb in sentences a–c.

11 Complete the rule for forming the past continuous.

The past continuous

We form the past continuous with the past simple of the verb (1) _be_ + base form + (2) _ing_

See Grammar Reference, page 149

12 Choose between the past simple and past continuous form of the verbs.

Natural rubber is difficult to use in its original state. It melts in the heat and breaks when it is cold. For many years Charles Goodyear (**1**) **tried / was trying** unsuccessfully to transform natural rubber into a substance that stayed strong and flexible at different temperatures. He (**2**) **worked / was working** in his workshop one cold winter's evening when he (**3**) **made / was making** an amazing discovery. He (**4**) **stood / was standing** near his stove because of the cold. He (**5**) **examined / was examining** a piece of sulphur-covered rubber when by accident he (**6**) **dropped / was dropping** it onto the hot surface. The rubber (**7**) **melted / was melting** and (**8**) **became / was becoming** a small flat disk that was both strong and flexible. He (**9**) **put / was putting** it outside in the freezing cold. The following morning he (**10**) **noticed / was noticing** that the disk still (**11**) **had / was having** the same qualities it had the night before.

2B A piece of luck

Reading

1 Thomas Edison, the inventor of the light bulb, said that invention was 'one per cent inspiration and ninety-nine per cent perspiration'. What did he mean?

   a All you need is luck.

   b You never succeed without hard work.

   c It's easy to have an idea.

2 Read the introduction, 'Inspiration or perspiration?', to the articles about two unusual inventions. How does the author answer the question in the title?

3 Work in pairs. Student A read the text about the Slinky, and Student B the text about Velcro. Complete the table for your text, then exchange information with your partner.

Inspiration or perspiration?

Where and how do inventors make their discoveries? Do they spend days, weeks or even years working on a particular theory or invention? Or can it happen another way? Scientists and inventors work hard, but sometimes their ideas and hard work can take them in an unexpected direction. Chance and their observation of something unexpected often play an important part.

Slinky

An American engineer called Richard James was working in a shipyard in Philadelphia. He was searching for a way to make ships more stable in bad weather, so he was doing some experiments with hundreds of different springs. While he was working, he put the springs on his desk. One day, one of them fell off his desk and 'walked' down some books onto the floor. James was so surprised that he took the spring home for his children. They were delighted. Soon all the children's friends wanted one, too. His invention didn't work for ships so he decided to turn it into a toy. His wife came up with the name 'Slinky' for the spring and they decided to go into business. They created their own company but never imagined it would be so successful. When a department store demonstrated the Slinky to the public, they sold 400 of them in 90 minutes. Nowadays the firm still makes between three and four million Slinkys each year.

Velcro

The problem with the old-fashioned zip fastener was that it often broke. Georges de Mestral experienced this when a broken zip fastener on his wife's dress spoilt an evening out for the couple. It took a country walk and careful observation for him to have the clever idea for an alternative. On his return he noticed that he and his dog were covered with 'burrs' from a type of plant. They were so difficult to take off that he decided to find out why.

When he looked at one under a microscope, he found out it had hundreds of small hooks that allowed it to stick to anything it touched. He immediately understood how he could use the hook idea to create a better alternative to the zip fastener. With the help of his business partner Jakob Muller he developed 'Velcro'. Velcro has one side with thousands of very small loops, and another with thousands of little hooks. It is such a part of everyday life now that it is difficult to imagine how we managed without it. The name Velcro comes from the beginnings of two French words – *velours* (velvet) and *crochet* (hook).

	Slinky	Velcro
1 Who invented it?		
2 What problem did they want to solve?		
3 What did they observe?		
4 What happened next?		
5 How successful were they?		

4 Which was more important in each discovery – chance or observation?

Listening

5 Look at the picture of the scientist Alexander Fleming. Which of the following words would you associate with him?

> slide   radioactivity   bacteria
> astronomy   culture   penicillin   infections
> exploration   research   laboratory

6 1.8 Listen to the interview and answer the questions. Circle A, B or C.

1 During the war, Fleming worked as …

   A a soldier.   B a doctor.

   C a researcher into infections.

2 After the war he became a professor of …

   A bacteriology.   B biology.   C medicine.

3 Fleming discovered penicillin in …

   A 1908.   B 1918.   C 1928.

4 Fleming's discovery was …

   A the result of hard work.

   B a mixture of luck and experience.

   C the result of a lucky mistake.

5 What happened with the Nobel prize?

   A Fleming received it for later work.

   B Fleming never received it.

   C Fleming shared the prize with other scientists.

Speaking

7 Discuss the question with a partner.

Which discovery or invention discussed in this lesson was the most important / surprising / interesting for you? Explain your answer.

Grammar: subject and object questions

8 Study sentences a–c and identify the subject, verb and object.

   a De Mestral invented Velcro.

   b Fleming noticed something interesting.

   c Several scientists shared the Nobel prize.

9 Look at questions and answers a–d.

   a What **did** de Mestral **invent**?
   answer: Velcro

   b What **happened** to his dog?
   answer: He got covered in burrs.

   c Who **understood** the importance of the hooks?
   answer: De Mestral

   d Who **did** de Mestral **work** with?
   answer: Jakob Muller

   1 Which questions use *did*? Is the answer to these the subject or the object?

   2 In which questions are *who* and *what* the subject of the question?

10 Complete the rule by choosing the correct alternative.

Subject / Object questions

When *who* or *what* is the subject of the question in the present or past simple, we **(1) use / don't use** the auxiliary verb *do / does*.

When *who* or *what* is the object of the question in the present or past simple, we **(2) use / don't use** the auxiliary verb *do / does*.

See Grammar Reference, page 147

11 Read the text and create questions.

> In 1904 Henry Royce made his first car, the Royce 10. He showed it to Charles Rolls, a car dealer. Charles Rolls decided to sell Royce's cars. In 1906 Rolls and Royce opened a car factory in Manchester. Soon Rolls-Royce cars became known all over the world.

1 Who / make / the Royce 10? Henry Royce did.
2 What / Royce / make in 1904?
   His first car, the Royce 10.
3 Who / open / a car factory?
   Rolls and Royce did.
4 What / Rolls and Royce / do?
   They opened a car factory.
5 What / happen / to Rolls-Royce cars?
   They became known all over the world.

2C Good luck

Listening and speaking

1 Richard Wiseman, a professor of psychology, believes there is a connection between being observant and having good luck. Do you agree?

2 Read the questionnaire and circle A, B or C.

> **ARE YOU LUCKY?**
> **1** We get the luck we deserve.
>   **A** I agree   **B** I disagree   **C** I don't know
> **2** I trust my inner feelings and do what I think is right.
>   **A** I agree   **B** I disagree   **C** I don't know
> **3** I am usually positive, even when things go wrong.
>   **A** I agree   **B** I disagree   **C** I don't know
> **4** We can learn to be luckier and more successful.
>   **A** I agree   **B** I disagree   **C** I don't know
> **5** I am a lucky person.
>   **A** I agree   **B** I disagree   **C** I don't know

3 Turn to page 147 and find out what your answers say about you.

4 ⊙ 1.9 Frank, Megan and Simon are discussing the first two questions of the questionnaire. Listen and guess their answers.

5 Read their conversation. Match the highlighted expressions to the other similar expressions in the Useful Expressions box.

F = Frank, M = Megan, S = Simon

F Megan, did you see the questionnaire about luck in this weekend's magazine?

M Oh, yes, 'Are you lucky?' Yes, I looked at it, but I didn't do it. What does it say?

F Well, basically, it claims that we get the luck we deserve. Do you think that's true?

M Yes, by and large, I do. I believe that people who are positive and who work hard tend to be the ones who are lucky.

S There's some truth in that, but sometimes you can see an opportunity but you can't afford to take a chance. So I can't make up my mind. Anyway, what's your view on this, Frank?

F Personally, I think you can create your own luck if you trust your feelings.

S I hear what you're saying, Frank, but what happens if our feelings are wrong? We can end up losing everything. As far as I'm concerned, it's better to be safe than sorry.

F I totally disagree, Simon. As I see it, all successful people take risks.

M On the whole I agree with you, Frank, but I can see Simon's point of view, too.

6 Work in groups and discuss the questionnaire. Practise using different expressions from the Useful Expressions box.

USEFUL EXPRESSIONS: exchanging opinions

> **Giving your opinion**
> *In my opinion, …*
> *From my point of view, …*
>
> **Agreeing and disagreeing**
> *I think you're right.*
> *I don't agree. / I disagree.*
>
> **Asking for someone's opinion**
> *What do you think?*
>
> **Mentioning what someone else says**
> *According to …*
>
> **Recognising what another person thinks or says**
> *I understand / hear what you're saying.*
> *I see what you mean.*
>
> **Saying you're uncertain or undecided**
> *I can't decide / make up my mind.*
>
> **Saying what is usually true**
> *In general, …*

Pronunciation

7 ⊙ 1.10 Listen to these introductory phrases. Mark the words that are stressed.

1 In my opinion, …
2 As far as I'm concerned, …
3 From my point of view, …
4 Personally, I believe …

8 Continue the sentences from Exercise 7 in your own words. Choose from these topics:

1 The best thing about learning English
2 The advantages or disadvantages of new technology
3 The most useful invention of the past 20 years

Writing: an informal letter

9 Marie is in London with her parents. She is writing to her Spanish friend Pilar. Read her letter and answer the questions.

1 What coincidence happened?

2 Which places in London did Marie visit?

Thursday evening

Hi Pilar,

Just a quick word from London! We are staying near the British Museum. The weather isn't great, but we're having a good time. On Sunday, after we unpacked, we explored Covent Garden. Then on Monday morning we had breakfast and visited the Natural History Museum — the dinosaurs are incredible! After that we walked to Oxford Street and did some shopping. I came across a beautiful cashmere pullover for 50 pounds! Yesterday morning we went to Buckingham Palace, and guess who we bumped into — Sally Dixon, our old summer camp leader! Afterwards we took the bus to Baker Street and went to Madame Tussaud's — they even have Pablo Picasso in there.

See you in the summer.

Lots of love,
Marie
P.S. We're going to see 'Mamma Mia' tomorrow.

10 The letter is difficult to read because she doesn't use paragraphs. Divide the letter into three paragraphs.

11 Improve this short story about a perfect day by adding linkers where appropriate.

Last weekend I went out with my friends to celebrate my birthday. It was sunny. and we We went to the park. We played softball. We rested. We walked in the park. I met my uncle and aunt and my cousin. We went to the cinema to see an action film. We had a pizza in an Italian restaurant. We had an ice cream. We ate and laughed a lot. My friends paid the bill because it was my birthday. It was a really perfect day.

12 Write a short letter to a friend about a holiday or trip, or a perfect day you had. Think of something unusual or lucky that happened. Follow the steps below.

- Begin with *Hi* or *Dear* and your friend's name.
- Say where you are writing from.
- Say when you arrived.
- Talk about the weather and how you feel.
- Describe a full day of your visit.
- Describe a coincidence or something unusual that happened.
- End with *Lots of love,* or *Best wishes,* and your name.
- Add a *P.S.* with a plan.

Reading

1 Read the text 'Columbus and the New World' on page 23 and check your answers.

1 Where was Columbus born?

2 Which continent did Columbus discover?

3 Which country supported his voyage?

4 Which country was Columbus trying to go to when he made his discovery?

a Spain   b the USA   c India   d Italy

2 Read the text again. Match the headings A–F with the paragraphs 1–5. There is one extra heading.

A The reason for Columbus's voyage

B An unachieved aim

C A new colony

D Beliefs and support

E Who was Columbus?

F The voyage

3 Read the text again and decide which sentences are true and which are false. Put a tick (✓) in the correct box.

1 Columbus was in his early thirties when he made the voyage.
True ☐   False ☐

2 Food without spices often had a bad taste.
True ☐   False ☐

3 Columbus decided to sail west because he wanted to reach Asia.
True ☐   False ☐

4 The King of Portugal gave Columbus money for the voyage.
True ☐   False ☐

5 Columbus took four ships on his voyage.
True ☐   False ☐

6 Columbus and his crew knew what land they could see.
True ☐   False ☐

7 Columbus eventually found a way to India.
True ☐   False ☐

8 Da Gama succeeded where Columbus failed.
True ☐   False ☐

Listening

4 🔊 1.11 Listen and complete the text below.

Did you know ...?

1 The price of pepper in the late 1400s

In India a kilo of pepper cost one gram of silver. In Alexandria its price was (1) _____ grams, and in Venice (2) _____ grams. Final customers in Europe paid (3) _____ grams of silver per kilo!

2 Was Columbus really the first?

Yes and no. Leif Ericsson was the first to go across the Atlantic to North America in (4) _____ AD. He called the land he discovered Vinland.

An early map of America   *Amerigo Vespucci*

3 What's in a name?

America is named after the (5) _____ explorer Amerigo Vespucci. The man who drew the map of America called the continent after his master.

4 Two languages

In nearly all of Latin America people speak Spanish. The exception is in (6) _____, where they speak (7) _____. This is because Spain and Portugal wanted to avoid (8) _____. The two countries agreed that Portugal could explore (9) _____ and Africa, and Spain could explore everywhere else!

Project

Work in groups. Think of another explorer or inventor. Perhaps there is someone with connections to your town or region. Research and prepare a short description about them. You can include maps and diagrams as necessary, plus some *Did you know ...?* facts. Say how people today remember his/her life and achievements.

 Watch a video about uncovering the past. Turn to page 138.

Columbus and the New World

(1) ___ Different countries claim Columbus as their own. In fact, he was born in Italy in 1451. However, he made his discoveries while serving the King and Queen of Spain.

(2) ___ At that time, food often tasted bad, so people used spices from India and China to improve the taste. However, it cost too much money to carry the spices from the East using the traditional land and sea routes, so Columbus wanted to find a new sea route from Europe to Asia.

(3) ___ In common with other educated people, Columbus knew the Earth was round. Because of this, he thought he could reach India and the East by sailing west. However, he needed a lot of money for his voyage. He asked people to help, but his idea seemed unrealistic to many people at that time. He asked the King of Portugal to help him, but he refused. Eventually he persuaded King Ferdinand and Queen Isabella of Spain to give him the money for the voyage and to buy three ships – the *Santa Maria*, the *Pinta* and the *Santa Clara*.

(4) ___ The boats set off on 3 August 1492 and sailed west. The voyage was very long and, as they continued west, his crew became more and more frightened. After two months, Columbus agreed to return to Europe if they didn't find land soon. Fortunately on 12 October 1492 a sailor saw land, but they didn't know where they were. Columbus thought they were near the coast of the East Indies, but in fact it was a small island in the Bahamas. Columbus later returned to Spain with gifts from the 'New World' for the King and Queen.

(5) ___ Columbus made three more voyages to the New World but he never found the route to bring spices from Asia to Europe. In the same decade that Columbus discovered America, in 1498 the Portuguese navigator Vasco da Gama sailed round the Cape of Good Hope, opening a direct sea route to India and beyond. Through his explorations, Columbus changed our knowledge of the world. But on a personal level he died a disappointed man.

Christopher Columbus

> ‘Through his explorations, Columbus changed our knowledge of the world.’

Columbus's ship the *Santa Maria*

A recent recreation of Columbus's voyage

Case Study 1 ⟩ Finding your way around

GPS

Thousands of years ago, travellers on land and sea could navigate half way round the world using just the Sun and the stars as a guide. This seems incredible when so many of us today depend on a satellite navigator or GPS receiver to help us find our way around our own town or city! GPS, which stands for Global Positioning System, helps us do many things today. But how much do you really know about it?

The history
The launch of *Sputnik I*, the first artificial satellite, in 1957 marked the start of an important age of space exploration. People soon realised that 'artificial stars' would be a good way to help with orientation here on Earth, since they knew exactly where they were at any time. In 1993, the United States launched the 24th satellite in what was originally a defence system. The number 24 is important because that is exactly the number of satellites needed to cover the whole world – in other words, for it to be truly global.

How does it work?
A receiver, such as the one in your car or on your mobile phone, uses radio signals to communicate with the satellites orbiting the Earth. For a GPS system to give you reliable information about your location, your receiver has to be able to 'see' at least four satellites. Although we can't really see these satellites, there must be nothing in between the satellite and the receiver, so you usually point your receiver towards the sky.

A question of time
For GPS to work properly, we need to know the exact time. Many years before space travel, physicists were looking for answers to questions about the universe. They invented the atomic clock – a clock that is accurate to within one billionth of a second. They had no idea that this would later help other scientists to create GPS!

Some uses for GPS
- Police and fire services can find the location of a crime or a fire.
- Rescue services can find ships lost at sea.
- Transport companies know exactly where their vehicles are.
- Pilots know their position even in the dark or bad weather.

---

1 Match the words from the text to the definitions.

1	navigate	a	worldwide
2	satellite	b	knowing which way is east, for example
3	receiver	c	a device for picking up signals
4	global	d	something which circles the Earth
5	artificial	e	which you can trust
6	orientation	f	find your way around
7	communicate (with)	g	man-made
8	reliable	h	contact

2 Choose the correct answers, *A* or *B*.

1 In the first paragraph, the writer suggests that
   A we can easily get lost.
   B we can now travel great distances.

2 How is *Sputnik I* connected to the subject of GPS?
   A It carried the first GPS system into space.
   B It made people think of other uses for satellites.

3 What happened in 1993?
   A We found the exact location of the Earth in space.
   B We had enough satellites in space for a GPS system.

4 What needs to happen before we can find out where we are?
   A Our receiver must be in contact with three or more satellites.
   B We need to have at least three receivers.

5 What does the writer say about the atomic clock?
   A Physicists were trying to make it more accurate.
   B Physicists invented it while they were looking for something else.

Review 〉 Unit 1

Vocabulary

1 Complete the sentences with an adjective.

1. People who are **s**_____ only care about themselves.
2. A **g**_____ person always gives more than is expected.
3. Someone who is **s**_____ enjoys meeting and talking to other people.
4. A person who is **p**_____ has an unreasonable dislike of a certain type of people.
5. Somebody who is **c**_____ has the ability to invent and create original ideas.
6. We say a person is **c**_____ if they find it hard to accept change or new ideas.

Grammar

2 Complete the sentences by changing the verbs into the present simple or present continuous.

P = Peter, J = Jason

P That (1) _____ (**smell**) good, Jason! What (2) _____ (**you / do**)?

J Well, I (3) _____ (**cook**) the evening meal for me and my friends. Everybody (4) _____ (**take**) turns to prepare something. We (5) _____ (**always / try**) to eat together twice a week. The other evenings (6) _____ (**be**) free.

P That (7) _____ (**be**) a nice arrangement. So, how often (8) _____ (**you / prepare**) the meal?

J Well, I (9) _____ (**usually / make**) it on Wednesdays, but I (10) _____ (**cook**) today because Tim (11) _____ (**study**) for an exam.

P It (12) _____ (**taste**) really good.

J Well, why (13) _____ (**you / not / stay**)? There's enough for everyone.

Pronunciation

3 Decide whether the words end in (a) /s/, (b) /z/ or (c) /ɪz/. Write a, b or c.

1 catches ☐	5 guests ☐	9 volunteers ☐
2 teenagers ☐	6 difference ☐	10 hobbies ☐
3 understands ☐	7 celebrates ☐	11 exercise ☐
4 homeless ☐	8 washes ☐	12 changes ☐

Functions

4 Write the conversation by making complete sentences.

A = Alex, P = Philip, M = Marco

A Philip, I / like / introduce you / Marco. He / stay / here / three months / improve his English.

_____

P Hi, Marco, I / be / pleased / meet you. So, where in / Italy you be / from?

_____

M I / be from Milan, in / north.

_____

P You have two really great football teams. Which one you / support?

_____

M I / be *Inter* fan. I / be really crazy / them. What about you?

_____

P Well, I / be more interested / rugby, but I like / watch / football, too. you go / to the matches?

_____

M I sometimes go, but / tickets / be / so expensive. I usually watch them / big screen / café.

_____

P There / be / Champions' League match / TV tonight. you like / come / my house / watch it.

_____

M Yes, please, I / love to, but I need / check / Alex first.

_____

Now I can ...

☐ agree and disagree.
☐ introduce myself to new people.
☐ talk about my hobbies and pastimes.
☐ write a personal profile.
☐ use the present simple and present continuous.

Review › Unit 2

Grammar

1 Change the verbs in brackets into the simple past.

A couple of years ago, when Jessica Evans was 12, she (1) _____ (**be**) at a party. As part of the fun she (2) _____ (**tie**) a label with her name and address to a helium-filled balloon and (3) _____ (**release**) it into the air. She (4) _____ (**watch**) as it (5) _____ (**float**) into the sky and (6) _____ (**disappear**) from view. Some days later, and 200 kilometres away, the balloon finally (7) _____ (**land**) in another 12-year-old girl's garden. Believe it or not the second girl's name (8) _____ (**be**) Jessica Evans, too. The second Jessica (9) _____ (**contact**) the first and they (10) _____ (**decide**) to meet. They (11) _____ (**discover**) they (12) _____ (**have**) other things in common: they (13) _____ (**be**) both red-haired and (14) _____ (**own**) a dog, a goldfish and a rabbit!

2 Complete the questions and answers based on the story.

1 Where _____ the first Jessica?

Answer: At a party.

2 _____ Jessica lose the balloon?

Answer: No, she _____. She released it.

3 What _____ the balloon do when she released it?

Answer: It _____ away and _____ from view.

4 How far _____ the balloon go?

Answer: 200 kilometres.

5 Who _____ the balloon?

Answer: Another Jessica Evans!

6 Who _____ a dog?

Answer: They both _____ one.

3 Complete the story by changing the verbs in brackets into the past simple or the past continuous.

A lucky discovery

A few years ago Jen Cullen from Park Avenue, New York, and her husband (1) _____ (**travel**) around Europe. As part of their trip they (2) _____ (**go**) to Italy. One day they (3) _____ (**walk**) through Rome when they (4) _____ (**see**) a second-hand bookshop. They (5) _____ (**decide**) to go inside for a look. While Jen (6) _____ (**look**) at the books she (7) _____ (**find**) a title that (8) _____ (**remind**) her of her childhood: *The Hungry Caterpillar.* She (9) _____ (**open**) it and to her surprise she (10) _____ (**find**) the words 'Jen Cullen, Park Avenue, New York'.

Functions

4 Put the different ways of exchanging opinions into the right order.

1 my / in / research / money / opinion / on / space / waste / travel / is / a / of

In _____, _____.

2 my / of / from / the / exist / point / view / life / must / in / somewhere / universe

From _____.

3 according / years / the / about / to / Earth / is / five billion / old / scientists

According _____, _____.

4 exist / as / far / I'm / don't / concerned / as / aliens

As _____, _____.

5 proof / hear / what / saying / but / I / enough / we / you're / don't / have

I hear _____,

_____.

6 your / space exploration / view / what's / on

What's _____?

Now I can ...
☐ agree and disagree.
☐ talk about science.
☐ write an informal letter.
☐ use the past simple and past continuous.
☐ ask subject and object questions.

Law and order

Miss Marple

Hercule Poirot

In this unit you will learn

- **Communication:** making and accepting an apology
- **Vocabulary:** law and order
- **Reading and Listening:** Cluedo, Sherlock Holmes
- **Writing:** a letter of apology
- **Grammar:** past perfect, *used to / would*

Let's get started

1 Look at the pictures of two of fiction's most famous detectives.

1 Do you know anything about them?
2 Who was their creator?
3 Have you ever read any books or seen any films or TV programmes about these detectives?
4 Do you think they are like modern detectives?

2 Continue these descriptions.

1 Well, she is a sweet-looking old lady. She must be in her sixties. She …
2 He is extremely well dressed. He doesn't look English. He looks very pleased with himself. I think he must be …

Vocabulary

3 Complete the story with the words from the box.

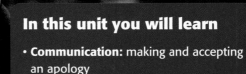

> investigation cell burglary misunderstanding evidence
> suspect alibi witness fingerprints clue crime statement

1 The police got a phone call to report a _____ at the house next door.
2 The _____, a neighbour, saw someone climbing through the kitchen window. The police came and took her _____.
3 They found an important _____ in the garden, it was a button from a coat.
4 There were no _____ on the window to point to the criminal …
5 … so they went into the house to continue their _____ but there was no _____ of a break in.
6 The police interviewed the main _____ but he had a perfect _____. He had been in a police _____ at the time of the incident!
7 Later that day they got a phone call from the owner. He said no _____ had been committed and that it was a _____ – he had climbed through the window because he had lost his house keys.

Reading

1 Read the two stories. Which criminal was clever, and which one was not so clever?

An unfortunate call

When the Green family went shopping, a young thief called Brian Fortune got into their house through an open window. He was looking for things to take when he heard their car come back. Brian escaped the way he had come in. While the police were looking for clues they heard the sound of a mobile phone coming from a flower bed. Detectives found the phone under some flowers where Brian had dropped it. It was his friend, Dermot, who was still waiting for him outside. He didn't realise that he'd dropped his phone.

A clean getaway

A prisoner escaped from jail in Germany in a box of laundry. The man hid in the laundry room when the other prisoners had finished work. He climbed into a large box and wrapped himself up in bed sheets. The box was then loaded onto a van and driven through the gates of the prison. While the driver was picking up another delivery, the prisoner got out of the box and escaped into nearby woods. The driver understood what had happened when he saw the empty box. He also noticed that someone had opened the lock from the inside.

Grammar: past perfect

2 Study this sentence from the first story and answer the questions underneath by ticking (✓) the correct box.

Detectives found the phone under some flowers where Brian had dropped it.

1 What happened first?

    a Detectives found the phone. ☐

    b Brian dropped the phone. ☐

2 Which part of the sentence uses …

    a the past simple?   1st ☐ 2nd ☐

    b the past perfect?   1st ☐ 2nd ☐

3 Complete the rule about when we use the past perfect with examples from the sentence in Exercise 2.

The past perfect
We use the past perfect (for example (1) _____) to make it clear that something happened before something else in the past.
We use the past perfect for the thing that happened first, and the past simple (for example (2) _____) for the thing that happened next.
The past perfect is 'two steps back' into the past.

4 Study the diagram for sentence 1. Then write the actions for sentence 2 under the correct part of the diagram.

1 Detectives found the phone under some flowers where Brian had dropped it.

2 The man hid in the laundry room when the other prisoners had finished work.

	the past		**now**
	1st action	2nd action	

1 Brian dropped the phone.   Detectives found the phone.

2 _____   _____

See Grammar Reference, page 150

5 🎧 1.12 When we speak, we often contract *had* to *'d* or we use its weak pronunciation /həd/. Listen to the sentences. Which one uses the weak form of *had*? Which one uses a contraction?

a Detectives found the phone under some flowers where Brian had dropped it.

b He didn't realise that he'd dropped his phone.

6 🎧 1.12 Listen and repeat the sentences.

7 Complete the sentences by putting the verbs in brackets into the past perfect.

1 They caught the burglar because he _____ (**not wear**) gloves.

2 They noticed that the thief _____ (**break into**) the flat through the bathroom window.

3 She was upset because her sister _____ (**borrow**) her sunglasses without asking.

4 He left the police station after the detective _____ (**take**) his statement.

5 When she went to the cash machine, she discovered someone _____ (**empty**) her bank account.

6 The detective _____ (**see**) her talking to the main suspect after he _____ (**interview**) her.

8 Match sentences 1–3 with pictures A–C.

1 ☐ When the police arrived, the suspect escaped through the window.

2 ☐ When the police arrived, the suspect was escaping through the window.

3 ☐ When the police arrived, the suspect had escaped through the window.

A

B

C

Where's the proof?

Reading

1 Look at the board game. Do you have a version of this game in your country?

Do you know the names of the different characters in your country?

Do you enjoy games like this, or do you think that they are too old-fashioned?

Spotlight

on reading skills: matching missing sentences

- Always begin by reading the text all the way through for a general understanding.
- Never try to fill the gaps as you go along.
- Study the words directly before and after the gaps.
- Look carefully at pronouns (*he, her, its, they*, etc.) to help you make your choice.
- Make sure your choice follows the logic of the text.
- Be systematic. Try each sentence in each gap to make sure.
- Deal with the easier questions first. Leave the more difficult ones to later.

2 Read the article. Which do you think is the best title?

a My brother Jamie

b Innocent pastimes

c Mysteries can be fun

3 Match sentences A–G to gaps 1–6. There is one extra sentence you don't need.

A You used the clues to help you work out who the culprit was.

B The house was divided up into a big hallway with rooms that led off to places like the library, conservatory and billiard room.

C Even though I have now grown up I haven't lost my enthusiasm for Cluedo or similar games.

D I think this is because while everyone else just treated it as a fun, I was much more competitive.

E I have never really seen the point of computer games that you play on your own.

F Afterwards everyone said how much they had enjoyed it and what a success the weekend had been.

G But I never really minded because it meant that we would take out some of the board games we always brought with us.

When I was growing up we used to spend two weeks by the sea every summer. We never seemed to have much luck with the weather as it always seemed to rain for a few days while we were away. (1) ☐ My favourite game of all was Cluedo, the detective game where you have to find the murderer in a country house. (2) ☐ The suspects were a group of characters with names like Professor Plum, Miss Scarlett and Colonel Mustard. I now know that these names are different according to which version around the world is being played. The murder weapons were the kind of thing you would find in an Agatha Christie mystery, a candlestick or rope and so on. With a throw of the dice you could make your way to a room or travel through one of the house's secret passages to collect clues. (3) ☐ The most exciting part was when you accused the person you thought was guilty. Looking back, perhaps the reason I used to enjoy it so much was that I usually seemed to win. (4) ☐ My brother Jamie used to have a terrible temper when he was young and he really hated losing. When he got upset he would throw the board in the air or run away for an hour. I suppose I had an unfair advantage as I was three years older than Jamie! (5) ☐ In fact, I sometimes organise murder mystery weekends in hotels where people actually come and play one of the roles in the story. It's great fun and a good way of getting to know people better. I even organised an event for the place where I work as a kind of team-building event. (6) ☐ All the same, I have never been able to convince Jamie to come along.

Grammar: *used to / would*

4 Study the sentences from the text and answer the question.

When I was growing up we used to spend two weeks by the sea.

… the reason I used to enjoy it so much was that I usually seemed to win.

Do they describe something that happened once, or on a regular basis?

5 Read the rule, then rephrase sentences 1–4 using *used to* + base form.

> **used to**
>
> We use *used to* + base form to talk about past states or actions that happened regularly in the past but which no longer happen.

1 When I was a child I belonged to a chess club. I don't any more.

2 They invited friends to play Scrabble every Saturday evening. They stopped a long time ago.

3 My grandmother took only ten minutes to do the crossword. She no longer does.

4 I never played football when I was younger. Now I play twice a week.

6 Study the grammar note and find similar examples of *would* in the reading passage.

> **would / used to**
>
> We can use *would* + base form instead of *used to* to talk about repeated actions and events:
> *When he got upset he would (=used to) throw the board in the air.*
> However, we **cannot** use *would* to talk about states:
> *My brother Jamie ~~would~~ used to have a terrible temper when he was young.*

See Grammar Reference, page 150

7 Study these sentences. In which sentence are both *would* and *used to* correct?

1 She *would / used to* have long hair when she was young.

2 She *would / used to* brush it for hours.

Pronunciation

8 (1.13) Listen to the sentences. In which one is *used* pronounced /juːzd/ and in which one /juːst/?

a You **used** the clues to help you work out who the culprit was.

b We **used to spend** two weeks by the sea.

9 (1.13) Listen again and repeat the sentences.

Vocabulary

10 Group the words in the box into verbs, adjectives and nouns. Some words can appear in two columns. Use a dictionary to help you.

> innocent   jury   confess   law   witness
> forensic   alibi   trial   oath   guilty   judge
> lawyer   sentence   evidence   proof

11 Make sentences that contain two or more words from the box.

Example:

There wasn't enough evidence to find him guilty.

Listening

12 What kind of thing do forensic scientists do?

13 Read about *CSI: Crime Scene Investigation.*

> The TV series *CSI: Crime Scene Investigation* began in 2000 in Las Vegas and has been expanded to include Miami and New York. You can see it in over 200 countries in the world and there is an estimated global audience of two billion people.

14 Do you watch *CSI: Crime Scene Investigation* or a similar programme? Are you a fan? Why?

15 (1.14) Dr Mortimer is a forensic scientist. Listen to the interview with her and answer the questions.

1 When did forensic science start to be used in a serious way?

2 When did the police begin using fingerprints?

3 What were the next major developments?

4 When was DNA testing first used successfully?

5 What two things did the DNA test achieve?

6 How reliable is DNA evidence?

7 What do investigators need to establish about the DNA at the crime scene?

8 What does Dr Mortimer think about the techniques shown on *CSI: Crime Scene Investigation*?

9 What do American juries now expect?

10 How can TV series like this help criminals?

3C Lost and found

Listening and speaking

1 🔘 1.15 Simon has lost his suitcase. Listen to his conversation with a police officer in part A and answer the questions.

1 Choose the picture that describes his case. Circle A, B or C.

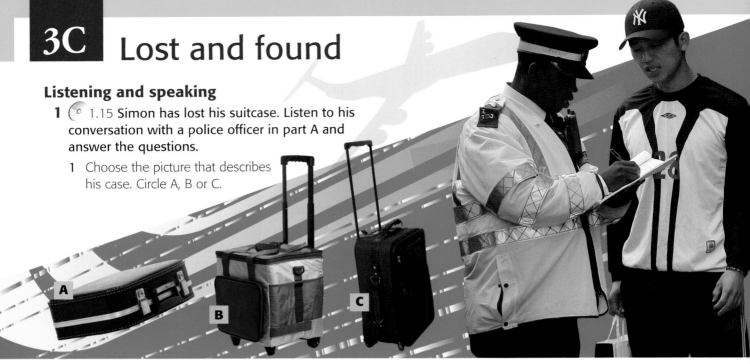

2 What was in the case?

3 What does the police officer tell Simon to do?

2 🔘 1.15 Listen again and complete the sentences.

1 What _____ the problem?

2 Oh dear! What _____?

3 What _____ when you last saw it?

4 I see. _____ anyone suspicious?

5 _____ pity.

6 Oh no! What _____!

3 Read Simon's conversation with a boy. Put the missing words from the box into the conversation.

> you'll forgive me   so sorry   an accident
> on purpose   thank goodness   a relief
> by mistake   mean to

B = Boy, S = Simon

B Excuse me, are you looking for this?

S Oh, _____ – it's my case. Where did you find it?

B I took it _____. I'm _____! I've got one that's exactly the same. Mine's over there. I hope _____ – I didn't _____ take it.

S Please don't worry about it. It was just _____. You didn't do it _____. What _____!

4 🔘 1.16 Listen to part B and check your answers.

USEFUL EXPRESSIONS: making or accepting an apology

Expressing surprise or disappointment
Oh dear!   *What a disaster!*
Oh no!   *What a pity!*

Apologising
I'm so sorry.   *I didn't mean to take it.*

Forgiving
Please don't worry about it.
It was just an accident.
You didn't do it on purpose.

Pronunciation: stress on key words

5 🔘 1.16 We show we are very sorry by using strong stress on key words and a wide voice range. Listen to Simon's conversation with the boy again and copy what the boy says as closely as you can.

6 Work in pairs. Decide what to say in these situations and respond. Be sympathetic and forgiving!

1 **Student A:** You borrowed Student B's dictionary and you spilt coffee on it.

2 **Student B:** Student A lent you his/her homework but you forgot to bring it back.

3 **Student A:** Student B let you borrow his/her tennis racquet but someone took it by mistake.

4 **Student B:** Student A gave you a calculator but you accidentally broke it.

Writing: a letter of apology

7 Ben Haynes is writing to a hotel where he stayed. Read his letter and answer the questions.

1 Why is Ben writing to the hotel?

2 What mistake did he make?

Nettles Hotel   23 Carpenter's Lane
Park Road   Rickwood
Cardiff   WD3 7HG
CF12 7GH

                  19th February 2____

Dear Sir or Madam,

I am writing to see if you can help me resolve a problem concerning a piece of luggage I took by mistake. I would also like to apologise in advance for any inconvenience I have caused another guest at your hotel. When I returned home last Sunday I discovered that I had accidentally taken the wrong suitcase.

I have an identical suitcase and picked the wrong one up without checking, leaving my own suitcase at the hotel. I am afraid that there is no label or other form of identification on the suitcase I took. Is there a way I can return it to its rightful owner and pick up my own missing luggage?

Once again, please accept my apologies for what has happened and any trouble it has caused.

Yours faithfully,
Ben Haynes

---

8 Study the layout of Ben's letter and answer the questions.

1 Where does he put the hotel's address? / his address? / the date?

2 What punctuation mark comes after *Madam* and *Yours faithfully*?

3 Does he use small or capital letters for titles?

Opening and closing more formal letters

When we don't know the other person's name:
Dear Sir or Madam … Yours faithfully + your name

When we know the other person's name:
Dear Mr Haynes … Yours sincerely + your name

Titles

In British English we do not usually put a full stop after titles.
Mr Jones, Mrs Green, Dr Brown

In American English, titles are followed by a full stop.

Dates

In British English, the order is **day / month / year**.
In American English, the order is **month / day / year**.
Example: *28 / 12 / 99* (UK), *12 / 28 / 99* (US)

---

9 Read the reply from the Nettles Hotel. How does the manager feel about Ben's mistake?

10 What differences do you notice in the layout of the two letters?

11 Underline the expressions that are used to apologise in the first letter and those that are used to forgive the customer in the reply.

Nettles Hotel | Park Road | Cardiff

23 Carpenter's Lane
Rickwood
WD3 7HG
23 / 02 / 2____

Dear Mr Haynes,

Thank you very much for your letter. I have told the guest in question who took the news well. She is relieved that she is going to see her suitcase again. Our driver is going to be in your area tomorrow morning, so would it be possible to arrange a time for him to make an exchange?
Do not worry as this kind of mistake can happen to anyone. I appreciate that you have taken the trouble to inform me of the matter.

Yours sincerely,
Trudi Marks
Trudi Marks, Manager

---

12 Read the situation and write a letter apologising for what happened.

You were working on a school computer when you received an email offering you some free games. The games are usually very expensive so it was an offer you weren't able to resist. After you downloaded them you realised that you had imported a virus into the system. A lot of people who use the school network are extremely angry with you. They have complained to the head of the school about what you did.

In your letter:

- Explain exactly what you did and when you decided to do it.
- Give at least two reasons why you did it.
- Say when you realised that it wasn't a good idea, and say what you think of your actions now.
- Apologise for any upset you have caused.

3D The detectives

Listening

1 Sherlock Holmes is the world's most famous fictional detective. Have you ever read one of his adventures, or seen a film or TV programme with him in? Do you remember anything about the story?

2 Before you listen to an interview about Holmes, work in pairs or groups and discuss what you already know about him. Make notes about …

- his creator.
- his physical appearance.
- his clothes.
- objects associated with him.
- where he lives.
- his closest friend and associate.
- his greatest enemy.
- his favourite expression.

3 1.17 Sally Whistler is a keen Sherlock Holmes fan and has written a book about him and his creator. Listen to part A of the interview and answer the questions.

1 Why did Conan Doyle start writing the Holmes stories?
2 In what year was the first Holmes story published?
3 Where did the stories appear?
4 How many short stories and novels feature Holmes?
5 What is Holmes's address and who is his flatmate?
6 What three reasons does Sally give for the popularity of the Holmes stories?
7 Who was the inspiration for Conan Doyle's hero?

4 1.18 Listen to part B of the interview and answer the questions.

1 What does the picture above show?
2 What happened after it?
3 How is the picture of Holmes on page 35 different from Holmes in the stories?
4 Where is the headquarters of the Sherlock Holmes Society? How does it celebrate its hero's life?

Reading

5 Read the introduction to one of the Sherlock Holmes mysteries. Can you think of an explanation for *The Red-headed League*?

Introduction

One of Sherlock Holmes's most mystifying cases is *The Red-headed League*. Jabez Wilson, a shopkeeper with bright red hair, answers a job advertisement which his new assistant, Vincent Spaulding, has shown him. The advertisement is for a job for someone with red hair! Wilson gets a job in an office where he is well-paid simply to copy the pages of the *Encyclopedia Britannica*. His employer is an unknown rich American who wants to help people with red hair. Every day for two months Wilson goes to an office where he carries out his duties. Then one day later, when he arrives at work, Wilson discovers that the office is closed and the Red-headed League no longer exists. He goes to Holmes to see if he can find out more about the League and who is behind it.

6 In the extract from the novel, Holmes and Watson meet Mr Wilson for the first time. Holmes demonstrates his powers of observation and deduction. Read the extract and answer the questions.

1 What evidence shows that Mr Wilson …
   a has worked with his hands?
   b is a member of a secret society?
   c has been to China?
   d has done a lot of writing?
2 How does Mr Wilson react when Holmes first tells him about himself?
3 How does this change after Holmes's explanation?

7 Are you a good detective? Here is some more information that Holmes discovers during the story. Can you guess the solution to the story and explain *The Red-headed League*?

- Holmes hit the pavement outside Wilson's shop and noticed that it made an empty sound.
- Vincent Spaulding, Wilson's assistant, had only worked for Mr Wilson for a few months.
- Holmes noticed that the knees of Spaulding's trousers were dirty.
- Holmes knew that there was a lot of gold in a nearby bank.

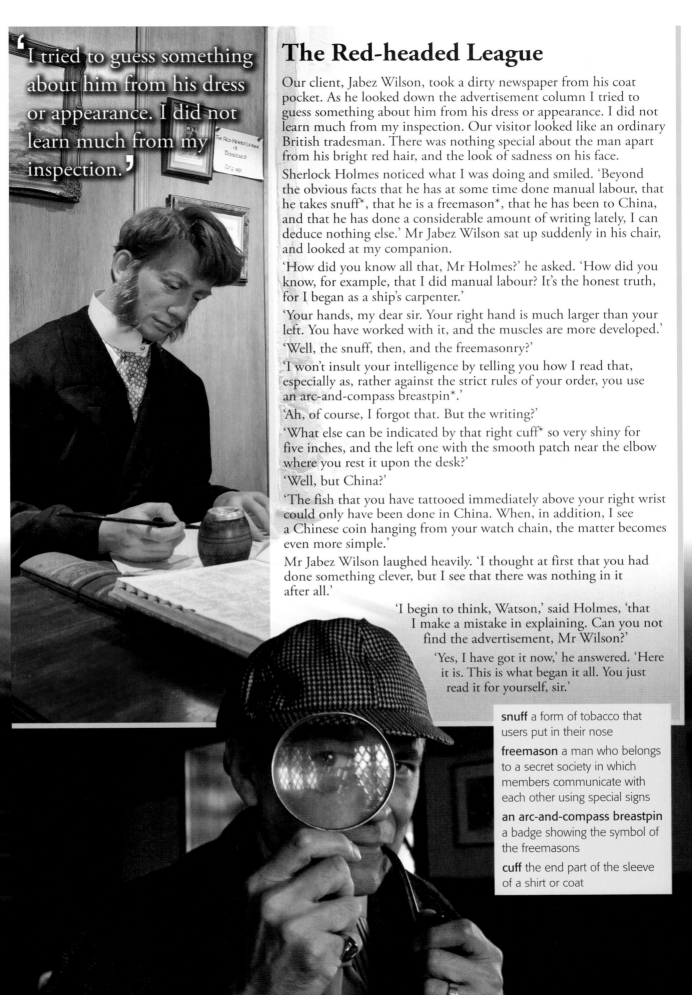

> 'I tried to guess something about him from his dress or appearance. I did not learn much from my inspection.'

The Red-headed League

Our client, Jabez Wilson, took a dirty newspaper from his coat pocket. As he looked down the advertisement column I tried to guess something about him from his dress or appearance. I did not learn much from my inspection. Our visitor looked like an ordinary British tradesman. There was nothing special about the man apart from his bright red hair, and the look of sadness on his face.

Sherlock Holmes noticed what I was doing and smiled. 'Beyond the obvious facts that he has at some time done manual labour, that he takes snuff*, that he is a freemason*, that he has been to China, and that he has done a considerable amount of writing lately, I can deduce nothing else.' Mr Jabez Wilson sat up suddenly in his chair, and looked at my companion.

'How did you know all that, Mr Holmes?' he asked. 'How did you know, for example, that I did manual labour? It's the honest truth, for I began as a ship's carpenter.'

'Your hands, my dear sir. Your right hand is much larger than your left. You have worked with it, and the muscles are more developed.'

'Well, the snuff, then, and the freemasonry?'

'I won't insult your intelligence by telling you how I read that, especially as, rather against the strict rules of your order, you use an arc-and-compass breastpin*.'

'Ah, of course, I forgot that. But the writing?'

'What else can be indicated by that right cuff* so very shiny for five inches, and the left one with the smooth patch near the elbow where you rest it upon the desk?'

'Well, but China?'

'The fish that you have tattooed immediately above your right wrist could only have been done in China. When, in addition, I see a Chinese coin hanging from your watch chain, the matter becomes even more simple.'

Mr Jabez Wilson laughed heavily. 'I thought at first that you had done something clever, but I see that there was nothing in it after all.'

'I begin to think, Watson,' said Holmes, 'that I make a mistake in explaining. Can you not find the advertisement, Mr Wilson?'

'Yes, I have got it now,' he answered. 'Here it is. This is what began it all. You just read it for yourself, sir.'

snuff a form of tobacco that users put in their nose

freemason a man who belongs to a secret society in which members communicate with each other using special signs

an arc-and-compass breastpin a badge showing the symbol of the freemasons

cuff the end part of the sleeve of a shirt or coat

At the police station

Listening and speaking

1 Look at the picture of a police control room. Describe the picture and answer the questions.

1 Lots of public places in the UK now have CCTV (closed-circuit television). Do you think these cameras reduce crime?

2 Would you like to see these cameras introduced in the public places where you live? Are there dangers for ordinary citizens? Why?

2 1.19 A teenager is making a report at the police station. Listen to his conversation with a police officer and complete the report.

Time: _____
Place: _____
Description of supect: _____
_____
Age: _____
Height and build: _____
Dress: _____
Distinguishing features: _____
Item(s) taken: _____

Contents:
cash ☐   keys ☐
credit cards ☐   documents ☐
mobile phone ☐   ID card ☐
computer ☐   passport ☐
Other: _____

3 1.20 Study the Useful expressions box, then listen again. Tick (✓) the expressions you hear.

USEFUL EXPRESSIONS: describing a person's appearance

1 a *So, what exactly happened?*	☐
b *Can you tell me what happened?*	☐
2 a *What did he look like?*	☐
b *Can you describe him?*	☐
3 a *He was about 20.*	☐
b *He was around 20 years old.*	☐
4 a *He was tall and skinny.*	☐
b *He was tall with a slim build.*	☐
5 a *He had jeans on.*	☐
b *He was wearing jeans.*	☐
6 a *There was a small scar under his right eye.*	☐
b *He had a small scar under his right eye.*	☐
7 a *He had short dark hair.*	☐
b *His hair was short and dark.*	☐

4 Work in pairs. Take it in turns to be the person reporting an incident and the police officer.

Student A

You are a police officer. You are talking to a man/woman who is reporting a missing friend. Find out as much information about the missing person as possible.

Student B

Your friend Jim is missing. He left home at 10 am this morning for a bike ride and he has not come back. Here are some notes on his appearance:

1 tall, slim, dark hair, 25 years old

2 wearing jeans, trainers, yellow T-shirt

3 small scar on left cheek

4 green mountain bike, red and black helmet

4

Travel and adventure

Let's get started

1 Describe the picture and answer the questions.

1. This woman spent millions of dollars on her trip into space. Do you think it was money well spent?
2. What unusual places would you like to visit? Why?

Vocabulary

2 Complete the sentences with a word from the box.

> historic scenery statue birthplace souvenir
> sightseeing guidebook tourism museum
> Gallery festival monument

1. There is some beautiful _____ in the Alps.
2. Rebecca bought a model of the Eiffel Tower as a _____ of her visit to Paris.
3. Don't forget to buy a _____ – it will tell you which places to visit and how to get around.
4. When my uncle went to New York on business, he took the opportunity to go _____.
5. I think that _____ has spoilt Venice – far too many people go there nowadays.
6. It's a really strange _____ – each year in this Spanish town they have a huge fight with tomatoes.
7. The Uffizi _____ in Florence has probably the most important collection of Renaissance paintings in the world.
8. The shipyards in Gdańsk witnessed some _____ events in the struggle for democracy.
9. Stratford-upon-Avon is famous as the _____ of William Shakespeare.
10. The _____ has an amazing collection of dinosaur fossils.
11. The _____ of the Bronze Horseman is the symbol of St Petersburg.
12. This strange tower is a _____ to the Great Fire of London.

3 Work in pairs. Think of the following in your country:

- the birthplace of a famous person, for example an artist or scientist
- a famous statue or monument
- an important museum or gallery
- a typical souvenir
- the three most important historic events
- a strange tradition or festival
- a place of outstanding natural beauty
- five places you expect to see in a guidebook

4 Tell another pair what you have chosen, and why.

Reading

1 Read the text 'A family affair' about explorers David and Camilla Hempleman-Adams, then discuss the questions.

1 What different adventures has David had?
2 What do you think motivates him?
3 What do David and Camilla have in common?
4 What is special about Camilla?
5 What risks did Camilla face on the trip?
6 What did she think was the worst thing about it?

A family affair

David Hempleman-Adams is one of Britain's most famous explorers and adventurers. He has taken many risks in his long career. He has climbed the highest mountains on each continent and has been to both Poles. In 1984 he completed a solo expedition to the North Pole.

His adventures also include hot-air ballooning. He has flown over the North Pole, and in 2003 he flew across the Atlantic in an open basket. David is not alone in his love of danger. He and his friends have eaten dinner around a table suspended from a balloon! It was an extremely memorable event.

This love of excitement and adventure runs in the family. David and his daughter Camilla have been on an expedition together. At the age of 15 she became the youngest British woman to ski to the North Pole. She spent a week in temperatures as low as minus 60 degrees Celsius. During the trip she risked death and attacks from polar bears. For her, the worst thing was putting up with David's snoring in the tent!

Grammar: present perfect or past simple

2 Study the sentences and complete the rule about how we form the present perfect.

*He **has taken** many risks in his long career.*

*They **have eaten** dinner around a table suspended from a balloon!*

The present perfect

We form the present perfect with the auxiliary verb (1) _____ followed by the **past participle** of the main verb. Remember, the **past participle** is the third form of the verb:

base form	past simple	past participle
eat	(2) _____	(3) _____

3 Study the table and answer questions 1–4 below.

Affirmative	He has taken many risks.	They have eaten dinner.
Negative	He hasn't taken many risks.	They haven't eaten dinner.
Yes/No questions	Has he taken many risks?	Have they eaten dinner?
Short answers	Yes, he has. / No, he hasn't.	Yes, they have. / No, they haven't.
Wh- questions	Why has he taken many risks?	Where have they eaten dinner?

1 How do we make *yes / no* questions with the present perfect?
2 How do we make the short *yes / no* answer?
3 How do we make negative statements?
4 What is the difference between the *I/we/you/they* form and the *he/she/it* form?

See Grammar Reference, page 151

4 Study the sentence then choose the best answer to the questions below.

*He **has flown** over the North Pole, and in 2003 he **flew** across the Atlantic in an open basket.*

1 Do we know when he flew over the North Pole?
yes no ☐

2 Which tense is used to refer to his North Pole flight?
present perfect ☐ past simple ☐

3 Do we know when he flew across the Atlantic?
yes ☐ no ☐

4 Which tense is used to refer to his Atlantic flight?
present perfect ☐ past simple ☐

5 Complete the rules in the box about when we use the past simple and the present perfect by <u>underlining</u> the correct alternative.

> **Past simple or present perfect?**
>
> 1 When we place an event at a specific time in the past we use the **past simple / present perfect**.
>
> 2 When we talk about a past event or experience in a general way with no specific time we use the **past simple / present perfect**.

6 With a partner, go through the reading passage and find …

- other examples of general experiences using the present perfect.
- specific events in the past using the past simple.

7 1.20 Listen and repeat. What happens to the pronunciation of *have / has* in the present perfect?

a **He's** (= He has) flown over the North Pole.

b **They've** (= They have) been on an expedition together.

Practise reading other sentences from the text, pronouncing the contractions.

> **Learning irregular verbs**
>
> With regular verbs, the past simple and past participle are the same:
>
> | base form | past simple | past participle |
> | --- | --- | --- |
> | *climb* | *climbed* | *climbed* |
>
> With irregular verbs, this is not necessarily true. Study some different types of irregular verb. Can you add any verbs to these categories?
>
> | A A A | *cut* | *cut* | *cut* |
> | A B B | *spend* | *spent* | *spent* |
> | A B C | *fly* | *flew* | *flown* |

See the Irregular Verb List, page 137

8 Work in pairs. Look at Marina's pictures. Talk about her experiences.

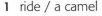

1 ride / a camel   2 swim / in the Indian Ocean

3 be / a girl guide   4 go / bungee jumping

5 speak to / someone famous   6 see / the Taj Mahal

7 fly / in a hot-air balloon   8 write / a job application

9 Now rewrite the sentences using the extra information. What does this mean for the tense we use?

1 ride a camel / when she visited Tunisia
2 swim in the Indian Ocean / she went to India on holiday
3 be / a girl guide between the ages of 14 and 17
4 be terrified / when she went bungee jumping
5 speak to the Prime Minister / when he came to her school
6 see the Taj Mahal / for the first time in 2009
7 fly round the world / two years ago
8 write a job application / last summer

> Watch a video about the future of a fishing village in Morocco. Turn to page 139.

Keep moving!

Reading

1 Read the introduction to the article 'Blog trotter'. What are the two main reasons for Rebecca's non-stop journey?

2 Read the article. Match questions A–F to paragraphs 1–5. There is one extra question.

A How many forms of transport have you used altogether?

B Why do you communicate with other bloggers?

C Have you ever written a blog?

D Hi, Rebecca. Why do you want to visit 15 countries in 33 days?

E So how do you keep moving even while you're asleep?

F Have you done much sightseeing?

Spotlight

on reading skills: matching

- Read the text through quickly.
- Read the statements or questions and highlight key words which will help you match them with the paragraphs.
- Match the questions with the correct paragraph.

Grammar: present perfect with *ever*

3 Study example conversations A and B.

1 How can you ask if someone has had a particular experience?

2 What tense do you use?

3 What short answers can you give?

4 What tense do you use when you want to ask for or give more detail?

A

L = Lisa, R = Rob

L Have you ever spoken to a famous person?

R Yes, I have, I've spoken to the Prime Minister.

L Wow, when was that?

R When she visited our school. She asked me about my plans for the future.

B

R Have you ever been to Ireland?

L No, I haven't.

Blog trotter

Australian Rebecca Campbell, 26, has taken on a non-stop round-the-world tour that includes 15 countries. Why? To raise money for charity and to publicise a new kind of mobile phone. As part of the challenge, Rebecca has to eat and sleep on the move. The one place where she can sit and have a normal meal is in a revolving restaurant in Singapore! We catch up with her and her progress.

1 ☐
Well, I have always wanted to discover the world. As I love writing, I am keeping a blog so everyone can follow my progress. That way I can combine my two great loves – writing and travel.

2 ☐
I have prepared my itinerary very carefully so that I travel mostly at night. I sleep in whatever means of transport I'm taking, like the train or boat, so I can move and rest at the same time.

3 ☐
Goodness! A lot! I've travelled by plane, train and car but I've also used more unusual forms of transport like a rickshaw, helicopter, gondola, camel and hot-air balloon.

4 ☐
As I travel alone through countries at high speed, meeting other bloggers gives me a quick introduction to the life of a country. They give me advice and act as guides, and through their blogs I can pass on the appeal for donations to Motivation, a charity that provides wheelchairs for handicapped people in developing countries. Without the help of this charity they wouldn't be able to get around. It's for this reason that I haven't stopped moving.

5 ☐
This trip is incredible as I'm seeing lots of towns and countries in a short space of time. The downside is that I don't have the time to stop and take advantage of anything. That's really frustrating. Sometimes I only stay two hours in a town, which means I don't see very much. That's why I'd really like to go back to certain cities and do some sightseeing. But that's another story and another trip!

Pronunciation

4 🔊 1.21 Listen to the recording and copy the intonation as closely as possible.

  a Have you ever spoken to a famous person?

  b Have you ever been to Ireland?

5 Make *Have you ever …?* questions. In pairs, ask and answer your questions. If your partner answers *yes*, ask for more details.

  1 speak to someone from an English-speaking country?

  2 go abroad?

  3 fall off a bicycle?

  4 miss a train or bus?

  5 eat foreign food?

Listening

6 🔊 1.22 Listen to these six speakers and answer the questions. Write A–G in the correct box. There is one extra question.

In which situation …

  A has someone lost an important document?

  B do two friends argue?

  C does someone get information about a day trip?

  D does someone have a very big disappointment?

  E does someone receive advice on getting around a city?

  F do two travellers receive a warning?

  G does someone need a visa?

Speaker 1 ☐   Speaker 4 ☐

Speaker 2 ☐   Speaker 5 ☐

Speaker 3 ☐   Speaker 6 ☐

Vocabulary

7 Complete the sentences with a word from the box.

> travel   flight   itinerary   journey   excursion
> voyage   trip   cruise

  1 The train _____ through Siberia to Vladivostok seemed endless.

  2 How was your _____ to Lublin? Was it successful?

  3 Does your father often _____ abroad for his job?

  4 The sea _____ to India used to take a month.

  5 While I was staying in London, I went on an _____ to the famous castle at Windsor.

  6 The _____ to Sydney took eighteen hours – I couldn't wait to get off the plane.

  7 They are going on a ten-day _____ around the Mediterranean. Their _____ includes visits to Naples, Malta and Athens.

8 Match the verbs in box A with the nouns in box B. Some verbs can combine with different nouns.

> **A**
> catch   hire   take   lose   miss

> **B**
> a taxi   a bus   a train   a connection   a bicycle
> a passport / an ID card

9 Work in pairs. Ask and answer questions beginning with *Have you ever …? / When was the last time you …?* based around the collocations in Exercise 8.

Examples:

Have you ever hired a bicycle?

When was the last time you took a taxi?

Listening and speaking

1 1.23 Abbie, Becky and Caroline want to go to Edinburgh for a long weekend. They are discussing the best way to get there. Listen to the conversation and answer the questions.

1 How long does it take to fly?
2 Why don't they want to go by train?
3 How long does the coach take?
4 How far is Edinburgh?
5 Why does it take so long?
6 How do they finally decide to travel? Why?

2 1.23 Try to complete the conversation with two words in each space, then listen again and check.

A = Abbie, B = Becky, C = Caroline

A So how _____ get there? Does _____ any suggestions?

B Why _____ fly? It only takes an hour.

C Yeah, but flying is incredibly expensive.

A That's true. We _____ by train, but that's expensive, too.

B I know. How _____ the coach? That's really cheap.

C That's not a bad idea. How _____ it take?

B About eight hours I think.

A Eight hours! How _____ it?

C Only five hundred kilometres, but there's a lot of traffic.

A I see. What _____ take the overnight coach?

C Yes, that way we can sleep a few hours.

B … and have an extra day for sightseeing.

A OK. The coach it is! _____ have a look on the Internet at prices.

3 Work in groups of three. Practise the conversation. Take it in turn to change roles.

4 Imagine that you are the three friends. Study the information about accommodation, and continue their conversation.

5 Work in small groups. A group of students of your age is coming to your town for three nights and three days. They arrive on Friday evening and leave on Monday morning. Discuss a three-day programme that includes the following:

- some sightseeing in town
- an excursion to a place of historical interest or natural beauty
- a sporting event or festival
- a meal with typical food from your region

6 When you have finished, present your programme and itinerary to the rest of the class.

Castle Lodge
Guest house and Bed & Breakfast
Double room £80 a night, single £60
Breakfast included
Five minutes from the castle on foot
Comfortable family hotel

Heron Hotel
Large room for three people
£60 a night
Breakfast extra (£6 per person)
30 minutes by bus
from the city centre
Part of the City Traveller hotel group

Youth Hostel
£20 per person
Bring a sleeping bag
Help with housework
Doors close 10 p.m.
Three kilometres
from the city centre

Writing: a formal letter or email

7 Abbie, Becky and Caroline are trying to organise their accommodation in Edinburgh. Read Caroline's email and the reply.

  1 How many nights do they want to stay?
  2 What time are they arriving in Edinburgh?
  3 What time can they check in?

Dear Sir or Madam,

I am writing to enquire if you have a room available for the nights of 18 to 20 September. According to your website, you offer double and single rooms. Would it be possible for me and my two friends to stay together in a double room? If so, we would like to book for the above dates. Please could you tell us if you have a room, giving details of its price?

We have one further question. We are planning to take the overnight coach from London, which arrives at seven o'clock in the morning. Could you tell me the earliest time we can check in?

I look forward to hearing from you.

Yours faithfully,

Caroline Henquist

Dear Ms Henquist,

Thank you for your enquiry. We can put an extra bed in a large double room for the dates you mentioned. The price is £110 a night including breakfast. I have made a provisional booking that I can keep open until tomorrow evening. Please could you send me your credit card details to confirm your booking.

Check-in is from 2 p.m. This gives us time to prepare the room for our next guests. However, you are welcome to leave your luggage at the guest house when you arrive. We can look after it until the room becomes available.

Yours sincerely,

Stephanie McDougall (Mrs)

8 Study the formal expressions used in the emails. How do they differ from those in your language?

USEFUL EXPRESSIONS

Stating the purpose of the letter / email
I am writing to …
We would like to …

Asking for information / Requesting
What is the earliest time we can check in?
Could you tell me the earliest time we can check in?
Would it be possible to check in in the morning?

Referring to previous correspondence
Thank you for your enquiry …
Further to your question …
Many thanks for agreeing to …

9 You are organising a visit to the Lake District from 15 to 22 July next year. Write a letter to Kendal Youth Hostel.

  • You want to book places for ten people.
  • You have seen that accommodation is available in dormitories.
  • You want to know if there is a safe place to park your hired minibus.
  • Ask if there is a special rate for large groups.

10 Create a suitable reply from the youth hostel. Use the information below.

> July – a popular period
>
> Separate dormitories for female and male guests
>
> Car park at your own risk
>
> Special rate only available for groups of 15 or more

4D The Edinburgh Festival

Reading

1 Quickly read the information about the Edinburgh Festival on page 45 and decide which part of the festival you would most like to visit.

on page 45

Spotlight

on reading skills: multiple-choice questions

- Always read the text all the way through to get a general idea of what it is about.
- Read the questions carefully.
- Do not jump to conclusions – sometimes an answer that seems obvious is a trap.
- Mark the parts of the text that refer specifically to the question.
- Eliminate obviously wrong answers.
- Find supporting evidence for your answer in the passage.

2 Study the Spotlight box and then answer questions 1–7. Circle A, B, C or D.

1 Which of the statements is true?
- **A** There is only one event called the Edinburgh Festival.
- **B** It lasts less than a month.
- **C** It happens at exactly the same time every year.
- **D** It begins with a firework display.

2 Altogether the article mentions … festivals that take place in August.
- **A** five **B** six **C** seven **D** eight

3 If you want to perform at the Edinburgh International Festival, you have to …
- **A** know the director.
- **B** be from another country.
- **C** have an international reputation.
- **D** be invited.

4 At the Fringe …
- **A** anything can happen.
- **B** performers have to pass a tough audition.
- **C** you don't need to book tickets.
- **D** everything is perfectly organised in advance.

5 The Fringe is best known for …
- **A** poor-quality acts.
- **B** TV stars.
- **C** comedy acts.
- **D** its size.

6 At the Edinburgh Military Tattoo you can see …
- **A** soldiers marching and playing music.
- **B** over 2,000 performers.
- **C** the inside of the castle.
- **D** demonstrations of body art.

7 The Tattoo is popular with …
- **A** Americans who live in Scotland.
- **B** Americans who have Scottish ancestors.
- **C** American regiments who are serving in Scotland.
- **D** American soldiers.

3 Is there a similar arts festival in your country? If so …
- where and when is it held?
- what kind of events can you see?

Each summer in Scotland's capital, Edinburgh, there is an explosion of events that is known collectively as the Edinburgh Festival. However, there is no single event called the Edinburgh Festival. For about three weeks from August to early September the city hosts several different festivals. Before making travel arrangements and booking accommodation visitors should check exact dates, as these do vary. The Edinburgh Festival phenomenon started life in 1947 and continues to grow.

The Edinburgh International Festival

This lasts three weeks and has some of the world's top international artists participating in this prestigious* season. It is a carefully organised event where performers are individually invited by the director. The International Festival focuses on classical music, opera, dance and theatre. It stages some marvellous productions each season.

The Edinburgh Fringe Festival

This is an alternative to the International Festival. It is now the biggest arts festival in the world. Performers on the Fringe don't get an invitation from the director, and aren't checked in any way. This means it is an exciting, sometimes anarchic event which is full of unexpected pleasant surprises, and the occasional disappointment. Among the general public it is famous for its comics. The stars of many of today's TV comedy shows were first noticed at the Fringe.

The Edinburgh Military Tattoo

This is the highlight of the festival for many visitors and is held in the marvellous grounds of Edinburgh Castle itself. Spectators can watch and listen to the best military bands from Britain and the Commonwealth countries*. This amazing spectacle of performers in traditional regimental* dress marching and playing music delights over two hundred thousand spectators every summer. If you want tickets for this you'd better book well in advance, as it sells out* very quickly. It is particularly popular with visitors from the USA, Canada, New Zealand and Australia who are keen to re-establish contact with their Scottish roots*.

Other festivals

If the three festivals we have described aren't enough, there is also the International Book Festival where famous writers and poets read and talk about their work. The novelist JK Rowling, creator of the Harry Potter books, has appeared here. There is also the Edinburgh Annual Art Festival and the People's Festival, and the International Film Festival, which takes place in June. The latest arrival on the Edinburgh festival scene is the New Comedy Festival which made its first appearance in 2008.

' The Edinburgh Festival phenomenon started life in 1947 and continues to grow. '

Commonwealth countries a group of 53 nations, which used to be part of the British Empire

prestigious *(adjective)* (used about an institution, a job, an activity, etc.) respected and admired by people

regimental *(adjective)* of a regiment (= a large group of soldiers that is commanded by a colonel)

sell out *(verb)* If a performance, sports event or other entertainment sells out, all the tickets for it are sold.

roots the place or culture that a person or their family came from originally

Case Study 2 〉 An adventurer

KIT DESLAURIERS

Kit DesLauriers was born in 1969 and spent her childhood in Massachusetts and Long Island before moving to Arizona, where she studied at university.

Kit has achieved many things in her life. By the time she was 14, she had already mastered cross-country skiing. She then turned her attention to downhill skiing. She has been the women's world freeskiing champion twice. The first time she won, in 2004, she had only been in the sport for two years.

Through her love of skiing, Kit has spent a great deal of time climbing in the mountains. Her first major **expedition** was to India in 1998. While she was there, Kit wished she had taken her skis with her. After that trip, she **devoted** more time to ski mountaineering, and she soon knew what she wanted to do.

Climbing to the top of a high mountain is a major **achievement** for anyone. Most climbers would only be **concerned about** climbing down safely. But, in 2006, after she had climbed to the top of Mount Everest, Kit came back down on skis – the first American, and the first woman, to do so. Over the previous two years, she had climbed up, and skied down, the 'Seven Summits' – the highest mountains in each of the seven continents. Kit was the first person ever to do this.

Kit has also worked in search and rescue teams, and has been a member of a helicopter crew. This side to her career began in 1995, when she helped to rescue a woman who had fallen while climbing.

In addition to all this, Kit has run camps which aim to teach women some of the skills she has learned. She hopes to **pass on** to these women the message that you can achieve your dreams. In 2006, she helped to start an organisation called *Pursue Balance*. Its aim is to motivate people and to encourage them to **respect** the environment. These days, she lives in Wyoming with her husband and two children.

Kit DesLauriers

Kit's record-breaking skis down the Seven Summits

- McKinley – highest mountain in North America – May 2004
- Elbrus – highest mountain in Europe – June 2005
- Kosciusko – highest mountain in Australia – September 2005
- Vinson Massif – highest mountain in Antarctica – December 2005
- Aconcagua – highest mountain in South America – December 2005
- Kilimanjaro – highest mountain in Africa – May 2006
- Everest – highest mountain in Asia (and the world) – October 2006

1 Read the text and list the main things Kit DesLauriers has done.

2 What do you understand by these words and phrases in bold?

  1 expedition _____

  2 devoted _____

  3 achievement _____

  4 concerned about _____

  5 pass on _____

  6 respect _____

3 Look at the prompts below. With a partner, take turns telling each other the information. Use the present perfect, the past simple and the past perfect.

  1 Kit / spend / time / Long Island / , / she / move / Arizona
    After Kit *had spent* some time in Long Island, she *moved* to Arizona.

  2 After Kit / win / freeskiing championship / . / The first time / be / 2004

  3 When Kit / go / India / , / she / wish / she / take / her skis with her

  4 After Kit / climb / Mount Everest / , / she / come / down on skis

  5 Kit / rescue / injured people / . / The first time / be / 1995

  6 Kit / work / *Pursue Balance* / . / It / start / 2006

Review 〉 Unit 3

Grammar

1 Complete the paragraph about a famous detective by underlining all the correct choices.

Some of my favourite films of all time are in the *Pink Panther* series. Each film (1) **was beginning / began** with the famous cartoon character. The equally famous theme tune (2) **used to accompany / was accompanying** the introduction. The incompetent Inspector Clouseau, played by Peter Sellers, (3) **used to / would** be very clumsy and even though he (4) **wasn't / didn't use to be** very clever he always managed to solve crimes through a mixture of good luck and accident. This (5) **was making / made / had made** his boss mad. By the end of the series Clouseau (6) **had risen / rose / was rising** to the rank of Chief Inspector.

2 Complete the sentences by underlining the correct form of the verbs.

1 I **was travelling / travelled** to work when someone knocked me off my bike.

2 They **managed / were managing** to get into the house because I **had forgotten / forgot** to close an upstairs window.

3 The suspects **were trying / had tried** to escape when they suddenly **realised / were realising** that the manager **had locked / locked** them in the strong room.

4 The police **caught / were catching** the burglar because he **had not worn / didn't wear** gloves and **had left / was leaving** his fingerprints on the window.

5 When I **turned on / had turned on** my computer I **noticed / was noticing** that someone **had accessed / accessed** my private data.

Vocabulary

3 Read the clues and reorder the letters in brackets to make words.

1 What you leave if you don't wear gloves: _____ (NFIGRERNPIST)

2 A room in a police station: _____ (LECL)

3 Someone who saw what happened: _____ (ITESNWS)

4 What the police perform: _____ (IVNTENSIGTOAI)

5 3's declaration: _____ (TNAETMEST)

6 What the police look for: _____ (SCULE) and _____ (VDEIENEC)

7 A story that proves someone wasn't there when a crime took place: _____ (LABII)

8 Someone the police think committed a crime. _____ (SCSUPET)

9 The opposite of innocent: _____ (ULGYIT)

10 Hercule Poirot's profession: _____ (EETDVCIET)

Functions

4 Complete the conversation in a police station by writing questions for the answers. You have some 'clues' to help you.

P = police officer, M = man

1 P Good evening. _____? (**help**)

  M Yes, I'd like to report an incident.

2 P _____? (**happen**)

  M Well, I was crossing Silver Street Bridge when I saw a young man breaking into a car. He smashed the window and took a briefcase from the back seat.

3 P _____? (**look**)

  M Well, it happened so quickly, but he was tall and skinny with short dark hair.

4 P I see, and _____? (**wear**)

  M He had on a pair of dark green shorts and was wearing a red T-shirt.

5 P _____? (**old**)

  M About 20 I would say.

Now I can ...

- ☐ apologise.
- ☐ talk about law and order.
- ☐ write a letter of apology.
- ☐ use the past perfect.
- ☐ use *used to* and *would* to talk about past habits.

Review 〉 Unit 4

Vocabulary

1 Complete the sentences with words from the box.

> balloon trip voyage transport excursion
> souvenirs connection gondola cruise
> sightseeing missed flight itinerary

1 When Grandad went on an _____ to Cardiff, he got lost and _____ the coach to come back home.

2 They took a _____ in a hot-air _____ to watch the animal migrations.

3 The _____ is the type of boat they use in Venice.

4 What is the _____ of the school _____ to Italy? How many nights do we spend in Rome?

5 Your train needs to arrive at Reading on time if you want to make the _____.

6 When they retired they went on a _____ round the Mediterranean. It was an interesting _____. They did a lot of _____ and bought lots of _____.

Grammar

2 Expand the prompts to make 'have you ever' questions.

1 you ever / fly / in a plane _____?

2 you ever / forget / an address _____?

3 you ever / lose / an important document _____?

4 see / a shooting star _____?

5 swim / the Baltic _____?

6 wear / a traditional costume _____?

7 win / a prize _____?

8 write / a foreign pen-friend _____?

3 Complete the passage about extreme swimmer Lewis Pugh by changing the verbs into the past simple or the present perfect.

Swimming with icebergs

Extreme swimmer Lewis Pugh (1) _____ (travel) all over the world and (2) _____ (swim) in some of the most dangerous seas in his search for challenge and adventure. He specialises in swimming in very cold water. He (3) _____ (do) all his swims wearing goggles and a swimming costume. He (4) _____ (train) himself to raise his body temperature to 38 degrees Celsius just by thinking about it. In December 2005 he (5) _____ (swim) for 35 minutes in water of two degrees

Celsius in Antarctica. There are dangers in addition to the cold, such as sharks and leopard seals. So far nothing serious (6) _____ (attack) him, but the last time his team (7) _____ (see) penguins, they (8) _____ (pull) him out of the water because they (9) _____ (know) that penguins, are the leopard seal's favourite food, so one is never far away! Pugh tries to forget about the dangers by doing mental arithmetic. He said, 'That (10) _____ (work) for me so far!'

Functions

4 Steve, Jeff and Mark are discussing a holiday in the Lake District. Put their conversation in the right order. The first and last lines are done for you.

S = Steve, M = Mark, J = Jeff

S So **where shall we stay**? Does anyone have any suggestions?

a ☐ **M** I don't like the sound of that. **How about taking** our tents? That way we can stop when we want.

b ☐ **S** No, they're about half the price. But **how far is it** between them?

c ☐ **J** Yes, that's not a bad idea. **What if we spend** a couple of nights camping and the rest of the time in hostels?

d ☐ **J** Yes, but we can't afford that, it costs at least 40 pounds a person a night.

e ☐ **M** **Why don't we stay** in bed and breakfast accommodation? That's the most comfortable.

f ☐ **J** About 40 miles, I think. **How long does that take** by bike?

g ☐ **S** Yes, that's true. B&B is out. **We could stay in youth hostels**. That's not as expensive, is it?

h ☐ **S** All day if there are a lot of hills in between.

M OK, that sounds like a good solution. **Let's have a look** at where the campsites and hostels are, shall we?

Now I can …

☐ make arrangements.
☐ talk about travel.
☐ write a formal letter or email.
☐ use the present perfect with *ever*.

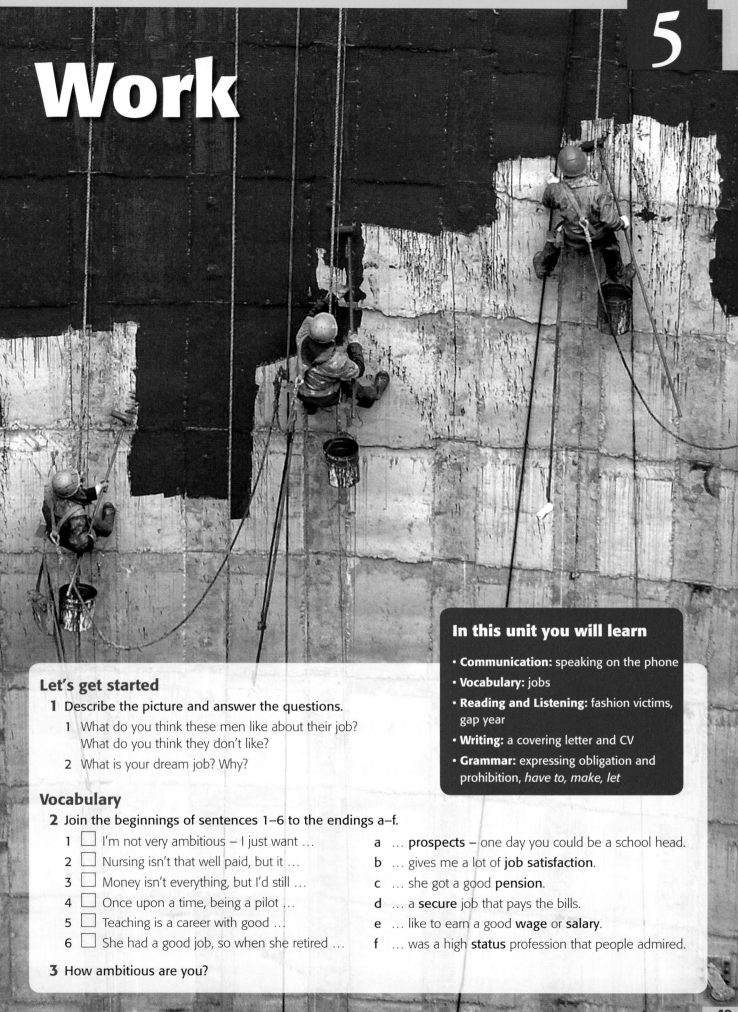

Work

5

In this unit you will learn

- **Communication:** speaking on the phone
- **Vocabulary:** jobs
- **Reading and Listening:** fashion victims, gap year
- **Writing:** a covering letter and CV
- **Grammar:** expressing obligation and prohibition, *have to, make, let*

Let's get started

1 Describe the picture and answer the questions.

1 What do you think these men like about their job? What do you think they don't like?

2 What is your dream job? Why?

Vocabulary

2 Join the beginnings of sentences 1–6 to the endings a–f.

1 ☐ I'm not very ambitious – I just want …
2 ☐ Nursing isn't that well paid, but it …
3 ☐ Money isn't everything, but I'd still …
4 ☐ Once upon a time, being a pilot …
5 ☐ Teaching is a career with good …
6 ☐ She had a good job, so when she retired …

a … **prospects** – one day you could be a school head.
b … gives me a lot of **job satisfaction**.
c … she got a good **pension**.
d … a **secure** job that pays the bills.
e … like to earn a good **wage** or **salary**.
f … was a high **status** profession that people admired.

3 How ambitious are you?

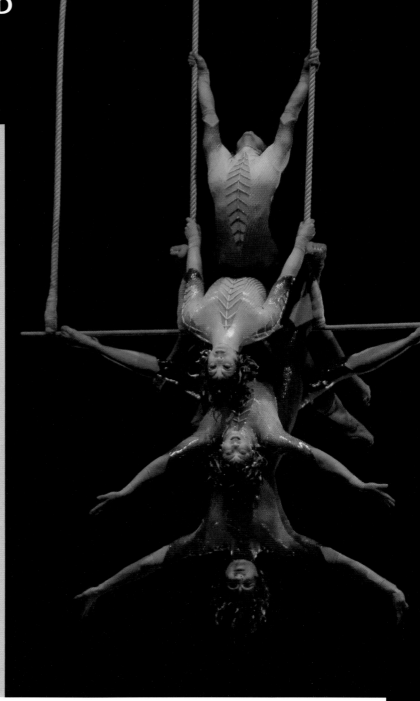

Reading

1 Look at the picture. What do you think they do for a living?

2 Read the introduction to an article about Pauliina Räsänen. How did she become a trapeze artist?

> Pauliina Räsänen is a trapeze artist from Finland. She did gymnastics and ballet as a child before joining a youth circus at the age of 14. She performs with the French-Canadian circus *Cirque du Soleil*.

3 Read the article quickly. How important are talent (= natural ability) and skill (= ability that is the result of training and experience) in her profession?

4 Read the interview and match headings A–F with paragraphs 1–5. There is one extra heading.

A What's the salary and career path like?

B How dangerous is it?

C What is hard about it?

D What skills do you need to be a trapeze artist?

E Why do you love your job?

F What's a day at work like?

1 ☐
I perform in the evenings, but luckily I don't have to get up early. So in the mornings I sleep in, then practise on stage for 45 minutes. I perform my act nine or ten times a week. Before each show I put on my make-up and costume and warm up for half an hour. I have to do a lot of strength and flexibility exercises.

2 ☐
It's like a dream of flying. When you do a great performance on the trapeze it's an incredible feeling.

3 ☐
Working at such a high level every day. Sometimes you wake up with a stomach ache but you have to perform.

4 ☐
You have to be talented and also need to be strong to deal with the intense physical training. You mustn't be heavy. If you are, your partner can't catch you easily. You can't be at all nervous when there are 5,000 people watching you.

5 ☐
We get paid per show and the amount depends on how you have negotiated your contract. I've only met two trapeze artists in their late thirties or early forties.

Grammar: expressing obligation and prohibition

5 🔊 1.24 Listen carefully to these sentences and answer the questions.

a *You **have to** perform.* — Do we say *have* to with a /v/ or a /f/?

b *You **need to** be strong.* — Which sound almost 'disappears'? Is it the /d/ or /t/?

c *You **mustn't** be heavy.* — Which letter **don't** we pronounce in **mustn't**?

6 Read the ways Pauliina describes the duties and requirements of her job and find them in the text.

Obligation and prohibition

Things it is necessary to be or do
*You **have to** perform …* (= a duty / an obligation)
*You **have to** be talented. / You **need to** be strong.*
(= a requirement)

Things it is necessary NOT to be or do
*You **mustn't** be heavy. / You **can't** be nervous.*
(= a prohibition)

Things that aren't necessary
*She **doesn't have to** / **doesn't need to** get up early.*
(= lack of necessity)

See Grammar Reference, page 152

7 Read the note about *must* and *mustn't*. Then answer questions 1–5 by choosing the correct verbs.

---

must / mustn't

Only use **must** for …
- strong recommendations:
  You must see her new show – it's amazing!
- orders to yourself:
  I must revise for my exam before it's too late!
- prohibitions:
  You mustn't touch that switch.

Note: The past of **must** is **had to**, and the future is **will have to**.

---

1 At the beginning of the lesson **I have to / must** check the register and find out who is absent.

2 I'm a receptionist – I **have to / must** answer the phone and welcome visitors.

3 You **don't have to / mustn't** play with matches, kids – it's dangerous!

4 You **don't need to / mustn't** buy a uniform – the restaurant provides one.

5 I absolutely **need to / must** finish my homework this evening!

---

8 Work in pairs. Student A, study the information on page 144. Student B, turn to page 146. Ask and answer questions about …

a the salary and career path.

b the skills and talents that the job requires.

c a typical day at work.

d the good and bad things about it.

Vocabulary

9 Work in pairs or groups and check that you know the meanings of the professions in box A and the adjectives and expressions in box B.

A

actor   lawyer   salesperson   teacher
professional footballer   doctor or nurse   soldier
waiter   hotel receptionist

B

skilful   brave   fit   honest   self-confident
hardworking   efficient   a good listener   fair
kind   enthusiastic   well-organised
good with people   persuasive   polite   patient

---

10 Choose five of the professions from box A. For each one, choose three or four qualities from B that they need in order to be successful.

11 Use the framework to give some careers' advice.

If you want to be a(n) _____
then you need to be _____.
You have to know _____.
Someone who wants to be a _____
has to be good at _____ and be
_____.
You mustn't _____ or
_____.
You don't have to _____.

Reading

1 'Cheap fashion' means low-cost clothes. Before you read the article, discuss the questions.

1 How popular is cheap fashion in your country?
2 Where are the best shops to find cheap clothes?
3 Where do these cheap clothes come from?
4 What do you know about the lives of the people who produce them?

The real price of fashion

A group of young people from the UK have taken part in an interesting social experiment for the BBC. All of them were fans of the cheap clothes that you can buy in any shopping centre. The young women went to India for four weeks to work in the factories that produced the fashions they liked to wear. Mark Rubens, the programme's producer, said that as clothes have become cheaper people buy more and more items and throw them away without thinking. 'We wanted to see how these young people would react if they could not only see how their clothes were made, but actually experience what it was like to make them.'

Georgina Briers, aged 20, went to work in a New Delhi workshop where employees work up to eighteen hours a day, six days a week, for a tiny wage. Their supervisors didn't let them get up and leave their machines without permission, even to go to the toilet.

Everything was timed and controlled. The pace of work came as an enormous shock to the youngsters. After their training, they were expected to sew on collars or sleeves at a rate of two a minute. They earned less than £2 a day – the same pay as their Indian colleagues. Georgina was too slow at all her tasks so they gave her more and more basic and less demanding jobs. Sewing was too difficult so she was sent to do ironing. She wasn't able to iron fifty shirts an hour and so was given the lowest position in the factory – putting buttons on shirts.

As part of the experiment they had to sleep on the factory floor, and even went to pick the cotton used to make the clothes under the hot sun. Stacey Dooley (21, a shop assistant) went to a sweatshop in Mumbai, whose low-paid workers included many children.

For Georgina, the turning point was when she met a worker who described how hard he had to work to support his family on the salary he made. She realised how selfish her behaviour back home in Britain was.

2 Read the article 'The real price of fashion'. Use the information from the text and decide which sentences are true and which are false. Put a tick (✓) in the correct box.

1 The British girls only liked expensive clothes.
True ☐ False ☐

2 Mark Rubens wanted to question the 'throw-away' culture.
True ☐ False ☐

3 The British girls were treated the same as their Indian colleagues.
True ☐ False ☐

4 The manager gave Georgina more difficult tasks.
True ☐ False ☐

5 Georgina seems ashamed of the way she used to behave.
True ☐ False ☐

6 Georgina went back to her love of cheap fashion.
True ☐ False ☐

Georgina claims that she had a life-changing experience in India. 'Before, I was worried about how I looked all the time. The people I talked to had so many dreams and they were willing to work hard, while I have thrown away so many opportunities. Now I owe it to them to work hard and make something of myself.' Now she also writes to high-street stores to find out where and how the clothes they sell are made. These days she is more interested in fair trade than in finding a bargain. Since their return to Britain, the young women have raised money for a refuge in Mumbai.

Vocabulary

3 Go through the article again and find words associated with …

- making clothes.
- money.

4 In groups or as a class, discuss the questions.

1 What do you think of the experiment?
2 Was it a life-changing experience for the girls? Why?
3 Do you know who makes your clothes?

Women working in an Indian clothes factory.

Grammar: *have to, make* and *let*

5 Look at sentences a and b. Which sentence describes …

1 an obligation in the past? _____   **a** She had a life-changing experience.
2 a past fact / event? _____   **b** They had to sleep on the factory floor.

6 Study sentences a and b. In which sentence does *made* mean …

1 forced / obliged? _____   **a** They *made* clothes in a factory.
2 created? _____   **b** They *made* them work 18 hours a day.

7 Study sentences a and b. Which one …

1 is a suggestion? _____   **a** *Let's* watch TV.
2 talks about permission? _____   **b** They didn't *let* them leave their machines.

See Grammar Reference, page 152

8 Imagine that you are Georgina. Answer these questions using *had to, make* and *let*, and the prompts at the end of the answers.

I = Interviewer, Y = you

1 **I** How many hours a day did you have to work?
  Y It was hard. We _____18 hours / day.

2 **I** Did you get lots of tea breaks?
  Y The supervisor was really strict. She didn't even _____ go / toilet.

3 **I** Did you stay in a nice hotel?
  Y A nice hotel! They _____ sleep / floor by our machines.

4 **I** Did the jobs you did become more interesting?
  Y Quite the opposite. They didn't _____ do anything difficult.

5 **I** Did you enjoy going to pick the cotton?
  Y You must be joking! They _____ work in the hot sun!

9 Work in pairs and tell each other about your upbringing. What were the things your parents / grandparents / teachers *made* you do and *let* you do? What were the things you *had to* do? Discuss …

- clothes and fashion.
- hairstyles and make-up.
- bedtime.
- going out with friends.
- sleeping late.
- homework.
- family meals and occasions.

British children in the 19th century

 Watch a video about weavers in Peru. Turn to page 140.

Vocabulary

1 Complete the sentences with the words in the box. Use your dictionary to help you.

> covering letter   candidate   interviews
> qualifications   apply for   recruit   references
> CV   application form   vacancy

1 She went for three _____ before she got the job.

2 We have a _____ for a student this summer.

3 You don't need lots of _____ for this job – personality is more important.

4 You can't even _____ this job without lots of experience.

5 Have you got a recent _____ you could send us?

6 Some businesses like the _____ to be written by hand.

7 Please fill in the _____ on our website.

8 We generally _____ and train fifty school-leavers each autumn.

9 We always check _____ before we make a job offer to a _____.

Speaking

2 Look at the advertisement. Would this kind of opportunity interest you?

> ## Blunt's department store
> **is recruiting shop staff for the January sales.**
> We also have vacancies for storeroom assistants.
> Candidates do not need previous experience.
> Please call us for further information
> and an application form on
> **01207 876998.**

Listening: making a phone call

3 1.25 Bernadette Miller is calling Blunt's for more information. Listen to her first call in part A. Why can't Bernadette speak to anyone? What does the receptionist give her?

4 1.26 Bernadette is speaking to Mark Dean from Human Resources. Listen to part B and answer the questions.

1 What does Bernadette hope to do next year?

2 Where would she prefer to work?

3 What experience does she have?

4 What does she need to do now?

5 1.25–26 Study the expressions in the Useful expressions box, then listen to the two phone calls again. Tick (✓) the expressions you hear.

USEFUL EXPRESSIONS: phoning about a job

1	**a** *I'm phoning about …*	☐
	b *I'm calling about …*	☐
2	**a** *I'll put you through to Human Resources.*	☐
	b *That'll be Human Resources.*	☐
3	**a** *Could you hold the line, please?*	☐
	b *Please hold.*	☐
4	**a** *I'm afraid there's no one to take your call.*	☐
	b *I'm sorry – there's no answer.*	☐
5	**a** *Would you like to leave a message?*	☐
	b *Can I take a message?*	☐
6	**a** *I'll call back later.*	☐
	b *I'll try again later.*	☐

Pronunciation: *Could you* and *Would you*

6 🔊 1.27 **Listen and repeat the pronunciation of *Could you* and *Would you*. Then repeat the sentences, paying attention to their intonation.**

Could you … /ˈkʊʤuː/   Would you … /ˈwʊʤuː/

Could you hold the line, please?

Would you like to leave a message?

7 🔊 1.28 **Listen to the sentences and practise saying them.**

1 Would you like to call back later?

2 Could you put me through to Paola Harper?

3 Would you tell her that Mel called?

4 Could you spell that for me, please?

Writing: a covering letter and CV

8 **Julia is looking for work in a hotel in Brighton. Read her letter to the manager of the Pavilion Hotel. Which paragraph (1, 2 or 3) …**

a describes her experience? ☐

b talks about her personal qualities? ☐

c introduces her and talks about her ambitions? ☐

d asks about a job? ☐

e says what she can offer an employer? ☐

Dear Sir or Madam,

1 Please allow me to introduce myself. My name is Julia Giorgi. I am an eighteen-year-old high-school student from Italy. I am writing to enquire if you have any vacancies for summer staff. I would like to gain further experience of hotel work and improve my English. My ambition is to train in hotel management, where English will be essential.

2 I already have some experience of the hotel business. For two summers I worked as a waitress and a chambermaid in my aunt's guest house and restaurant in Florence.

3 I am a friendly and honest person who understands the meaning of hard work. I get on well with the public and colleagues. I also hold a certificate in first aid which could be useful in a busy tourist season. Please find enclosed an up-to-date CV for your consideration.

I look forward to hearing from you.

Yours faithfully,

Julia Giorgi

9 Julia begins her letter with *Dear Sir* or *Madam*, and ends it with *Yours faithfully*. How would she have to finish her letter if she began it with *Dear Mrs Jones*?

10 Read Julia's CV and write the headings in the correct section.

> Hobbies and interests   Education
> Skills and qualifications   References
> Languages   Personal details   Work experience

Curriculum vitae

Julia Giorgi

Date of birth	14 / 12 / 1994
Address	Via Calzaivoli 6 50122, Firenze
Telephone number	+39 555 212666
Mobile	0 602 15 45 00
Email	juliag@wizserve.it
_____	Da Vinci High School, Firenze. I am currently in my final year of high school.
_____	Basic computer skills, Microsoft® Word. I hold a certificate in first aid.
_____	Italian: mother tongue English: pre-intermediate A2 German: elementary A1
_____ Summer seasons 2009/2010	Florence Guest House, Zakopane: chambermaid and waitress
_____	flute, volleyball, snowboarding
_____	Mr Manfredi, Mrs Nencioni

11 **Create your own CV using Julia's as a model.**

Reading

1 How common is it for people in your country to do something different between school and university, or some other kind of training?

2 Charlotte Hindle is a travel writer and photographer. She has written *The Gap Year Book*. Read the interview on page 57 and match questions A–I to answers 1–8. There is one extra question.

  A Of all the gap year ideas you list in the book, which is the most unusual?

  B Tell us a bit about your own travel experiences.

  C What advice would you have for someone taking a gap year?

  D What are your three favourite travel memories?

  E Tell us a little about your book, Lonely Planet's *The Gap Year Book*.

  F And which one would you most like to do yourself?

  G Of the people you spoke to, did anyone have a particularly unusual gap year?

  H Do you regret not taking a gap year?

  I What's 'new' in gap years?

3 Read the interview again and answer the questions.

  1 Which part of Charlotte's book has information on studying in your gap year?

  2 Are people these days taking a gap year earlier or later than before?

  3 How many companies in the UK can you learn to sail with?

  4 Which of Charlotte's best experiences took place on a boat?

4 Choose two activities mentioned in the interview, one that you would most like to do, and one that you would least like to do.

5 Compare your choices with a partner's. Explain your choices.

6 Do you think taking a gap year is a good idea? What advantages or disadvantages does it have?

Listening

7 ⊙ 1.29 You will hear Cindy and Felix talking about their gap year. Answer questions 1–5 from the information you hear and put a tick (✔) in the correct box.

Who …	Cindy	Felix
1 knew what they wanted to study before their gap year?	☐	☐
2 spent their gap year in Europe?	☐	☐
3 built something?	☐	☐
4 did not make any money?	☐	☐
5 learnt a language during the gap year?	☐	☐

8 Work in groups. Tell each other about your ideal gap year.

1 ☐ There are three sections to the book – Part I is all about planning your gap year, Part II looks at the regions of the world that the gapper* might travel to and Part III investigates all the activities that gappers can do.

2 ☐ I was surprised at the increase in gappers taking their gap year between school and university. When I researched the last edition there seemed to be many more going after higher education. As for new gap year options, this edition of *The Gap Year Book* features a paragliding school in the French Alps, travel photography courses in Greece and Zanzibar, an option to teach drama in Ghana, and a number of placements to teach soccer, rugby, tennis, basketball or boxing to under-privileged children* in Costa Rica, Ghana or South Africa.

3 ☐ Probably working for a yacht deliverer. This is a fantastic deal. You sign up with one of two UK companies and work your passage to wherever the yachts need delivering. If you want to crew around the world then this is a good way of starting off.

4 ☐ I'd probably most like to train to become a cruise ship photographer. You don't need any experience, all your expenses are paid, you get to travel the world, and you learn everything about taking photos on board.

5 ☐ I spent my gap year travelling overland to Australia, where I stayed for four years. I now have children and much of my travelling is within Europe, but we rarely go to your run-of-the-mill* destinations. This year we've visited Iceland, Finland and the Faroe Islands, to name but a few places.

The Northern Lights

6 ☐ 1) Buying a sari in Mysore, India.
2) Walking around Ayers Rock and then watching it change colour in the sunset.

Name: Charlotte Hindle
Age: 41
Occupation: Freelance travel writer and photographer

3) Seeing the Northern Lights on a steamer off the coast of Norway. It was the middle of the night, we were in the Arctic Circle and I was out on deck.

7 ☐ One of the gappers travelled abroad for half of his gap year and then spent the other half in the UK doing work experience in the Houses of Parliament. He intended to study politics at university and thought he'd get a good insight into its workings first. Smart thing to do, I thought.

8 ☐ I'd advise anyone taking a gap year to do a safety course in the UK before going away.

gapper a person who stops studying for a year between school and university to do a particular activity

under-privileged children children from very poor families

run-of-the-mill usual, ordinary

Ayers Rock / Uluru

A job for the summer

Listening and speaking

1 Describe the picture and answer the questions.

1 Why are the children wearing identical T-shirts?

2 What kind of personal qualities and skills do people need to work with children? Why?

2 Read the advertisement from the activity holiday company English Realm. Do you find this opportunity attractive?

> English Realm is looking for camp counsellors to work with kids at summer camps throughout Europe. Candidates are expected to be able to speak basic English and to have a skill to offer such as being able to play a musical instrument or teach a sport. Candidates with medical or first-aid experience preferred.

3 (°) 1.30 Pete Velios from English Realm is following up an application from a young woman called Margie Greenaway. Listen and decide if she is a good candidate for the advertised job. Why? / Why not?

4 (°) 1.30 Listen again and complete the sentences.

1 Can you spare me a _____ of minutes?

2 Have you got any experience of _____ with older kids?

3 I see from your _____ that you are keen on sport.

4 Do you have any other _____ we could use?

5 Is there _____ you'd like to ask?

6 How many children would I be in _____ of?

7 Are you _____ then?

8 And what are the _____?

9 And can you tell me something about the _____ hours?

10 And how much do you _____?

5 Imagine that you are a candidate for a job at a Kidcamp activity centre.

1 Write down three or four special skills you have – or invent them!

2 Write a list of three or four questions that you would like answers to.

3 When you are ready, take it in turns to interview your partner.

6 Work in pairs. Student A, turn to page 144. Student B, turn to page 146.

Nature and the environment

In this unit you will learn

- **Communication:** presenting information, in an emercengy
- **Vocabulary:** natural disasters
- **Reading and Listening:** water, story of a young lion
- **Writing:** a letter to the editor
- **Grammar:** *will* and *be going to*, the definite article

Let's get started

1 Describe the picture and answer the questions.

1 What is going to happen in a minute?

2 What kind of help do people need after a disaster like this?

Vocabulary

2 Match the words in the box to the disasters described in the sentences.

> flood ☐   tornado ☐   volcanic eruption ☐
> drought ☐   pollution ☐

1 Oh no – it's coming towards us! We'd better go now before it catches us!

2 It hasn't rained here for years. We can't grow anything – not even grass.

3 I couldn't believe my eyes – there were people in canoes going down the street!

4 All the dirt the factory pumps out is destroying the atmosphere.

5 It was like fireworks lighting up the sky. All the same, we were taking a big risk by standing there.

3 Which of the disasters in Exercise 2 are natural? Which are man-made?

4 Which of these events happen in your country?

6A Storm chasers

Twister hunters

Sunday evening and I am half asleep when the phone rings. 'Jeff? Hi, Hannah Klein here. I'm going to hunt twisters tomorrow. Are you still interested?' she asks.

I'm immediately fully awake. 'Sure,' I say, trying to sound calm and confident, 'That's wonderful news.'

'Be at the centre at seven tomorrow,' she answers.

'I'll be there,' I promise as she puts down the phone.

In ten hours I am going to be part of the team in one of the most dangerous activities in the world – twister-hunting. I am going to join Professor Hannah Klein – a legend in her profession. I watch the news on the TV and listen carefully to the weatherman: 'Tomorrow there will be an orange alert for people living in the following towns and …'. The weatherman lists the places where they think the twisters will strike. 'This is where I'll be tomorrow,' I think to myself. I set the alarm for six, but find it hard to sleep. I hope I won't be too frightened tomorrow.

It's eight in the morning, and Hannah and Lester – one of her research students – are studying aerial maps and reports.

'I think one will form over there,' Hannah says. Lester nods his agreement. 'I'll drive – you put down the probes*,' Hannah says. So Lester is going to put probes directly in the path of the tornado to record its speed and other details. They believe that at least one will work.

We drive across the vast open space towards the tornado. It's heading straight for a farm. It's going to destroy it. The farm looks tiny compared with the enormous twister. We watch as buildings and machinery fly into the air. There is nothing left. How terrible – a lifetime's work gone in a couple of seconds. We take another road that puts us directly in its path. Hannah stops the car and Lester jumps out and puts the last probe down. Over my shoulder I can see its huge angry shape – I feel terrified. Hannah accelerates – 60, 70 miles per hour, but the twister keeps getting closer. I shut my eyes, and have an awful feeling inside me. It's going to catch us and we're all going to die. At the last moment it moves away and we are safe. 'That was close,' I say. 'That was nothing,' Hannah replies.

> **probe** a scientific instrument for recording measurements

Reading

1 Jeff O'Leary is a journalist who hunts tornadoes – commonly called 'twisters'. Read his story, 'Twister hunters' and complete his notes.

Sunday
9 p.m. I get a call from
(1) _____, who invites me to go
(2) _____.
I promise to be at the centre at
(3) _____ the following morning.
The weather forecast warns that it will be
(4) _____. I feel
(5) _____.
Monday
8 a.m. I meet Hannah and a
(6) _____ of hers called Lester.
Hannah says she'll (7) _____ while
Lester (8) _____.
We drive towards the tornado. We see it destroy
(9) _____. Lester
(10) _____ and we leave. Then
the twister comes after us! I think we are going to
(11) _____. Just before it reaches us
it (12) _____.

Grammar: *will* and *be going to*

2 Match the beginnings and endings of the sentences to form definitions of the words in *italics*.

1 When we make a *prediction*, we … ☐
2 An *intention* is something we … ☐
3 If we make a *spontaneous decision*, we … ☐

a plan to do or have decided to do.
b make it at the moment of speaking.
c say what we think can happen in the future.

3 Match examples a–d of *will* and *be going to* to their uses 1–4.

a I'm *going* to *hunt* twisters tomorrow.
b I *think* one will *form* over there.
c I'll *drive* – you put down the probes.
d It's *heading* straight for a farm. It's *going to destroy* it.

1 ☐ a future prediction – something in the future you can see happening
2 ☐ a future prediction – something in the future you guess or imagine (often after verbs like *hope*, *think* and *believe*)
3 ☐ a spontaneous decision made at the moment of speaking
4 ☐ an intention – something already planned or decided

4 Remember: we also use *will* for promises. Go through the story and find an example of this use.
See Grammar Reference, page 153

5 Study these other examples of *will* and *be going to* from the story and say why they are used.

1 Lester is going to put probes directly in the path of the tornado.
2 'I'll be there,' I promise as she puts down the phone.
3 I am going to be part of the team in one of the most dangerous activities in the world.
4 The weatherman lists the places where they think the twisters will strike.
5 'This is where I'll be tomorrow,' I think to myself.
6 I hope I won't be too frightened tomorrow.

6 Match sentences 1–6 with a replies a–f.

1 What are you going to do this evening? ☐
2 What do you want to do when you finish school? ☐
3 I haven't done my homework. ☐
4 Do you know the times of buses to the station? ☐
5 Hurry up and get dressed. ☐
6 It's getting late. ☐

a Oh, are we going to be late?
b Don't worry about that. I'll take you there.
c Yes, I hope she'll be here soon.
d I'm going to be a chef.
e I think I'll stay at home.
f Your teacher isn't going to be happy with you!

7 1.31 **Work in pairs. Listen to the sounds. Take turns to say what you think is going to / will happen next.**

8 **Work in groups. Exchange ideas based on the situations.**

Situation 1

Look out of the window and make a prediction about the weather. Decide what to wear based on your prediction. Now tell someone else about your decision.

Situation 2

Make a prediction about the climate of your region in 20 and 50 years' time.

Say what you think and hope, and what you're worried about.

6B The blue planet

Reading

1 Work in pairs and try to answer the questionnaire.

> 1 How much of the Earth's surface is covered by water?
>
>   **a** 50 per cent   **b** 60 per cent   **c** 70 per cent
>
> 2 How much of the human body is water?
>
>   **a** 20 per cent   **b** 40 per cent   **c** 60 per cent
>
> 3 How much water does a person need to survive in an average climate each day?
>
>   **a** 1 litre   **b** 5 litres   **c** 15 litres
>
> 4 How much of the planet's water is fresh (= not salty)?
>
>   **a** 3 per cent   **b** 13 per cent   **c** 33 per cent
>
> 5 How many people haven't got enough water to grow food?
>
>   **a** 1 billion*   **b** 2 billion   **c** 3 billion
>
> **billion** a thousand million (1,000,000,000)

2 Read the text 'H₂0 – this precious liquid' quickly and check your answers.

3 Read the text again and complete it with sentences A–G. There is one extra sentence.

A Such extreme weather, and rising sea levels from the melting ice caps and glaciers, threaten some cities and countries.

B The last century was about oil, and this century will be about water – water is the new oil.

C So far the charity has provided 22,500 people with access to fresh water.

D This is why it is more important than food for our short-term survival.

E It was launched in 2004 to raise money to drill wells in Africa, and in particular in Sudan.

F This is equal to ten times the annual flow of the Nile.

G By contrast, people in rich countries refuse to drink the water from their taps, choosing bottled water that is 200 times more expensive.

4 What can countries and individual people do in their everyday lives to save water? Look at the pictures.

H₂0 – this precious liquid

Water is everywhere. It covers 70 per cent of the world's surface and makes up 60 per cent of the human body. (**1**) ☐ According to the United Nations, we need five litres of water a day just to survive, and another 50 litres for cooking, washing and sanitation. Yet only three per cent of the planet's water is fresh – and most of this is frozen in the Antarctic and Greenland. Even so, there is still enough water for the Earth's 6.5 billion people. In fact, there are ten million cubic kilometres of water available each year. (**2**) ☐ Now, that's a lot of H₂O!

Global warming is having some strange effects on weather and rainfall, and causing an increase in the number of hurricanes. (**3**) ☐ What's more, rain is falling in the wrong places, with serious consequences – Australia now has a permanent drought, and in parts of Africa people have to dig deeper wells as the underground lakes that supply them are running dry. As usual, it is the poorest people in the world who suffer the most. One billion people worldwide are hungry because they don't have enough water to grow food. Polluted drinking water is the main cause of infant mortality.

(**4**) ☐ Fortunately, there are people who believe that access to clean water is a basic human right. The other day a friend gave me a key ring. The key ring was from the Polish humanitarian organisation 'I Collect Water'. (**5**) ☐ 'I Collect Water' organises workshops for students, provides teachers with educational materials, sells 'Water for Africa' key rings and T-shirts, and collects donations from people and businesses. (**6**) ☐ Before, the idea of this precious liquid being easily available was just a dream, but the campaign 'I Collect Water' has given many people access to clean water for the first time.

Grammar: the definite article

5 Match the uses of the definite article (= *the*) to examples a–f taken from the text.

a ... there is still enough water for **the** Earth's 6.5 billion people.

b ... for **the** first time.

c ... a friend gave me **a** key ring. **The** key ring ...

d ... it is **the** poorest people in the world who suffer the most.

e According to **the** United Nations ...

f ... most of this is frozen in **the** Antarctic ...

We use the definite article ...

1 ☐ when we mention something or someone for the second time.

2 ☐ when we are talking about something that there is only one of.

3 ☐ for organisations.

4 ☐ for plural place names, names with *Republic* and *Kingdom*, and names of some of the geographical regions.

5 ☐ with a superlative.

6 ☐ before ordinal numbers.

See Grammar Reference, page 153

6 Read the text again and explain why the definite article is used.

7 Complete the passage about Janina Ochojska by choosing *a*, *the* or *Ø* (= no article).

Janina Ochojska-Okońska is probably (**1**) **a / the / Ø** best-known social activist in Poland. In 1989 she opened (**2**) **a / the / Ø** first branch of the Equi-Libre foundation, (**3**) **a / the / Ø** foundation that provides humanitarian aid for (**4**) **a / the / Ø** people in need. She is also President of (**5**) **a / the / Ø** humanitarian campaign 'I Collect Water'. She understood that the right to drink (**6**) **a / the / Ø** water is a basic human right. (**7**) **A / The / Ø** water many people have to consume in (**8**) **a / the / Ø** world's poorest countries is polluted. (**9**) **A / The / Ø** Sudan has been terribly affected by some of (**10**) **a / the / Ø** most serious water shortages in the world. In 1993 (**11**) **a / the / Ø** European Commission awarded her the title of European Woman of the Year.

Pronunciation: *the*

8 📀 1.32 Listen to the way *the* is pronounced in these words and phrases.

1 the Earth   3 the poorest people

2 the main cause   4 the Antarctic

What difference do you notice? How do we say *the* ...
- before consonants?
- before vowels?

Vocabulary

9 Match the words in the box to their definitions.

glacier ☐   global warming ☐
atmosphere ☐   fossil fuel ☐
greenhouse ☐   polar ice caps ☐

1 the layer of air and gas that lies around the Earth

2 an increase in the world's temperature

3 coal, oil and natural gas

4 a glass building where you can grow tomatoes

5 the areas at the top and bottom of the Earth

6 a mass of ice in a mountain valley

Listening

10 An expert on the environment is talking about global warming. Before you listen, tell each other what you think the causes are.

11 📀 1.33 Listen to part A of the talk and answer the questions.

1 Why is some global warming good for us?

2 How does the Earth's atmosphere help us?

3 What is meant by 'global warming' these days?

4 According to the speaker, what is the main cause of global warming?

5 What is 'the greenhouse effect'?

12 📀 1.34 Listen to part B and complete the summary.

We can blame global warming for the (**1**) _____ weather of recent years. (**2**) _____ and the polar (**3**) _____ are melting. Countries like the (**4**) _____ and the Maldives are threatened by rising sea levels. In Western Europe global warming could make the (**5**) _____ Stream stop. This is a (**6**) _____ current that flows across the (**7**) _____. Without it, Britain could be as cold as (**8**) _____!

Listening and speaking

1 1.35 Charlene, Henry and Melanie are giving a poster presentation to their class about practical ways of saving the environment. Listen to Charlene and complete her poster.

Tips for making memorable presentations

Use questions to help your talk along
So what can we do?

Use contrasts
*Many people believe that they can do nothing, **but** we strongly believe each one of us can make a difference.*

Use groups of three
Our message is recycle, save water, and turn off appliances.

Use memorable examples
It can take one thousand years for a plastic bag to disappear.

Say you're sincere
I strongly believe …
I sincerely think …

SAVING THE PLANET

Our message is
- (1) _____
- (2) _____ water
- Turn off (3) _____

Rubbish – three methods of disposal:
- Bury it
- (4) _____ it
- Dump it

What can we do? Three suggestions:
- Sort out household rubbish
  - *(5) _____ bottle bank
  - *separate (6) _____ from plastic
  - *take (7) _____ paper bank
- (8) _____ and appliances to collection points
- Shopping. Ask supermarkets to (9) _____
- Use (10) _____

USEFUL EXPRESSIONS: giving a presentation

Stating the purpose and organisation of the talk
Today we are going to talk about … / make three suggestions …

Referring to visual aids
As you can see from my poster, …
As you can see on the screen, …

Listing points
First of all … Next … Last but not least / Finally …

Talking about consequences
This means that …

Summarising
To sum up … I have given you some advice …

Introducing another speaker
I'm now going to hand you over to …, who is going to …

2 Work in pairs or groups. Group A, turn to page 144 for ideas for Henry's presentation. Group B, turn to page 146 for ideas for Melanie's presentation.

3 When you are ready, give your talk.
Remember to …

- introduce your objectives.
- list your points.
- have at least one list of three.
- use concrete examples, not just dry statistics.
- use questions to help your talk along.

Writing: a letter to the editor

4 Have you ever written a letter to a newspaper or magazine? What was it about?

5 Read Brenda McVitty's letter to the editor of her local newspaper and find out why she wrote it. Do you agree with what she says?

> Dear Sir or Madam,
>
> Last week the council sent every home a brochure about the importance of recycling. Everybody is talking about what we can do to reduce waste and help the environment, **so** I was very happy to read it.
>
> It was a very interesting brochure and contained a lot of useful advice. **However**, my nearest bottle bank is four kilometres away, so I have to drive there – this is not very 'green'. I am sure that many people who want to recycle throw everything away because it is easier.
>
> I also did some research and found out that the average British family throws away 330 glass bottles each year, and 40 kilos of newspapers. This is a huge amount of waste, **but** there are simply not enough bins to deal with this sort of volume if everyone follows the advice in the brochure.
>
> **Although** I'm sure the council is sincere about recycling, it should think of ways of making this a practical reality. It should increase the number of recycling areas and place them within walking distance of most people's homes.
>
> Yours faithfully,
> Brenda McVitty

6 Study these sentences from the text. What do *however* and *although* mean in your language?

a *It was a very interesting brochure and contained a lot of useful advice.* ***However****, my nearest bottle bank is four kilometres away.*

b ***Although*** *I'm sure the council is sincere about recycling, it should think of ways of making this a practical reality.*

7 Rewrite sentence a using *although* and b using *however*.

8 Contrast these ideas using *although* and *however*.

1 The documentary was interesting. It made me worried.
2 Nuclear power doesn't produce CO_2. Its waste is dangerous for the environment.
3 It was winter. People were walking around without coats.
4 We have insulated our house. Our gas bill is still high.

9 <u>Underline</u> other linkers in Brenda's letter.

Spotlight

on writing: a letter to the editor

- Open your letter with *Dear Sir or Madam,* or *Dear Editor,* and close it *Yours faithfully,*
- Organise your letter in paragraphs, for example:

paragraph 1: the event or article that you are writing about, and how you feel about it

paragraph 2: the reason why you feel that way

paragraph 3: points about the topic

paragraph 4: your conclusions; what you think should happen

---

10 Write a letter to the editor of a magazine or newspaper about the following situation or another topic that interests you. Include sentences with *however* and *although*.

> A recycling centre in your town is going to close because the company that owns it says the land is needed for another activity. Even though you know it belongs to a private company, you believe that the town council should find a way of helping it to stay.

6D Born to be wild

Vocabulary

1 Work in pairs. Try to identify the six animals and name the regions where they are found. Then turn to page 145 to check your answers.

2 Complete the sentences using the words in the box. Use your dictionary to help you.

> breed   conservation   endangered
> extinct   wildlife

1 Bison were hunted until they became _____, so now there are none left.

2 The giant turtle is an _____ species – only a few now remain.

3 There's a lot of _____ around here, such as foxes, deer, eagles and owls.

4 Experts try to _____ pandas in zoos, but very few young are born.

5 Wildlife _____ aims to protect species that are in danger of disappearing.

3 All the animals in Exercise 1 are *endangered*. What is the reason for this?

Reading

4 Look at the pictures on page 67 about the extraordinary story of a lion cub called Christian. Can you predict what the story will be about?

5 Read the story and put paragraphs A–E in the correct order.

1 ☐   2 ☐   3 ☐   4 ☐   5 ☐

6 In groups or as a class, discuss the questions.

1 Do you think pet shops should be allowed to sell wild animals?

2 What do you think of John and Ace's decision to buy the cub?

3 How was George Adamson important to Christian?

4 How successful was the friends' attempt to treat a wild animal as a pet?

Speaking

7 Organise a debate between two teams of two people. One team will speak in favour of the motion. The other team will speak against it. The motion is: 'This house believes that zoos have no place in a civilised society'.

8 Brainstorm ideas for and against the motion.

The chairperson introduces the debate and the speakers ➡
First speaker for the motion ➡
First speaker against the motion ➡
Second speaker for the motion ➡
Second speaker against the motion ➡
The chairperson invites the audience to say something ➡
The chairperson takes the vote and declares the winner.

USEFUL EXPRESSIONS: holding a debate

Chairperson

We're here today to debate the motion 'This house believes that zoos have no place in a civilised society'.

I now call on Tom, who is going to speak in favour of the motion.

You have two minutes left. / Your time is up.

I'd now like to call on Kerry, who is going to speak against the motion.

I am now going to open the debate to the floor.

Speaker

Thank you very much, Mr / Madam Chairperson …

I am going to speak in favour of / against the motion.

I have three main points to make …

First of all … Secondly … / Furthermore …

Last but not least … / To sum up … / In conclusion …

The floor (= the audience)

I'd like to say …

We shouldn't forget that …

The point I'd like to make is …

Chairperson

I would now like everyone to vote.

All those in favour of the motion, please raise your hand.

All those against the motion, please raise your hand.

All those who wish to abstain, please raise your hand.

I declare the motion carried / defeated by … votes to …

 Watch a video about butterflies in Kenya. Turn to page 141.

A cub called Christian

A John, Ace and Bill went with Christian on a flight to Nairobi, in Kenya. From there they went to the remote Kora Reserve, where George Adamson took care of Christian and gradually prepared him for his return to the wild. Eventually it was time for Christian to leave, and George let him go to live the life he was meant to lead.

B A year went by. The cuddly sixteen-kilo cub was now an eighty-four-kilo lion that cost them £30 a week in food – an enormous amount of money at that time! John and Ace did not know what to do. They knew that they did not want Christian to go to a zoo. Then they had a stroke of luck! They met Bill Travers and Virginia McKenna, the famous actors from the classic wildlife film Born Free. Bill knew the legendary lion expert George Adamson and contacted him to see whether there was a chance that Christian could follow in the footsteps of Elsa and be returned to his natural habitat. George said yes! Now Christian had the chance of a real future – as a wild and free lion.

C In 1969, John Rendall and Anthony 'Ace' Bourke were looking for a special attraction for their furniture shop in Chelsea's King's Road – one of the most fashionable streets in London. They went along to Harrods, the famous department store, for inspiration. Harrods' motto is *omnia omnibus ubique* – 'all things for all people everywhere'. At that time people said that you could buy anything from a pin to an elephant at Harrods. Yes, Harrods really did sell wild animals – it was legal then.

D The story doesn't end here – almost a year later the friends returned to Kenya to find out about Christian's new life. George Adamson helped them look for Christian. It's not an easy task, finding a wild lion in an area of over 500 square kilometres, but they were in luck! By now he was a fierce-looking fully-grown male lion. At first Christian was suspicious. Did he recognize John and Ace? He watched them from a distance – uncertain…Then the most extraordinary thing happened – Christian started to walk towards them, then he started to run and then he leapt into their arms just as he used to when he was a tiny cub.

E They went to the pet section. Soon, John and Ace's attention was drawn to a cute lion cub in a cage that was for sale. They immediately fell in love with him and bought him for £210. They named the cub Christian. He became a star attraction at their shop and even lived in their flat.

'By now he was a fierce-looking fully-grown male'

Case Study 3 〉 Disaster!

1 Work in pairs. Look at the pictures and brainstorm what you already know about volcanoes.

2 Read all the information below and make notes on the following:

1 Three things that come out of a volcano
2 Places where there are a lot of volcanoes
3 A deadly volcano
4 Three different types of volcano

3 Read the information again. Decide which sentences are true and which are false. Put a tick (✓) in the correct box.

1 Volcanoes can be many kilometres high.
True ☐   False ☐

2 An eruption can destroy a town.
True ☐   False ☐

3 Active volcanoes exist in every country.
True ☐   False ☐

4 Gas or steam might mean a volcano is going to erupt.
True ☐   False ☐

5 An extinct volcano is dead and will never erupt.
True ☐   False ☐

6 People heard the Mount Tambora eruption from Europe.
True ☐   False ☐

VOLCANOES

What are volcanoes and how do they happen?
The Earth's crust is between 10 and 30 kilometres thick. A volcanic eruption is a kind of explosion that happens when gas and molten rock, called magma, breaks through this crust as lava. A big eruption can send ash and rocks many kilometres into the air. Sometimes, however, the lava comes out more slowly and, as it cools, it slowly gets hard, building up a shape like a mountain.

What kind of damage do they cause?
A major eruption can affect a large area of the land around it, destroying forests or even whole towns, as pieces of rock as big as a house can be thrown into the air. The lava that flows from the volcano will destroy buildings and anything else in its path. The ash can fill the air and make it difficult to breathe.

Do we know where or when volcanoes will erupt?
Most active volcanoes are in the area of the Pacific Ocean. The USA, Africa and Iceland have also seen volcanic activity in recent years. Sometimes, gas or steam comes out of a volcano. Although this might continue slowly for years, often it means that the volcano is going to erupt, especially if there has been an earthquake or if the volcano has been quiet for a long time.

We simply don't know if a volcano is going to erupt. Sometimes, there is gas or steam for many years without anything serious happening. However, there have been many major eruptions where people did not even realise there was a volcano there!

- **Extinct** volcanoes – active a long time ago but now not considered to be a threat. However, scientists believe that extinct volcanoes could still erupt. A volcano in Alaska erupted in 2007 after people thought it had been extinct for 10,000 years.

- **Dormant** volcanoes – not active in recent history but scientists think they will probably erupt again, although maybe not for thousands (or even millions) of years.

- **Active** volcanoes – gas or steam suggest that they are going to erupt at some time in the future.

Over 70,000 people died in the eruption of Mount Tambora in Indonesia in 1815. People could hear it thousands of kilometres away and the ash and dust blocked out the sun for days. In the following months, it changed the weather patterns as far away as the USA and Europe, where there was snow in June and icy conditions throughout the whole summer.

Volcano vocabulary

- **crust** the top surface of the Earth
- **eruption** the 'explosion' of a volcano
- **molten** when something solid, like rock, becomes liquid when heated
- **magma** extremely hot liquid rock below the Earth's surface
- **lava** extremely hot liquid rock that flows out of the ground
- **ash** burnt material
- **steam** formed when water reaches 100° Celsius

Review ⟩ Unit 5

Grammar

> extremely important / strict rule – *must*
>
> strong prohibition – *mustn't*
>
> a duty / something that is necessary – *have to* / *need to*
>
> something that isn't necessary – *don't have to* / *don't need to*
>
> something that is not permitted – *you can't* / *you're not allowed to*
>
> permit – *allow* / *let* / *don't let*
>
> force / oblige someone to do something – *make*

1 Maria is telling her friend Julia about the rules and regulations of where she works. Use the ways of talking about obligation and necessity, and rewrite the dialogue.

J = Julia, M = Maria

J   What's security like?

M   Extremely strict, we (**1**) VERY IMPORTANT RULE wear a badge at all times. They (**2**) NOT PERMIT anyone in without one. You (**3**) STRONG PROHIBITION lose your badge either. I work in a special laboratory so we (**4**) A DUTY change before we can go in.

J   What! You mean you (**5**) A DUTY take off your clothes!

M   Not exactly! But we (**6**) A DUTY put a special suit on top. You (**7**) NOT PERMITTED wear wool or cotton underneath – everything (**8**) IMPORTANT RULE be synthetic. They (**9**) NOT PERMIT us to wear jewellery either.

J   And do they (**10**) FORCE / OBLIGE you buy the suit?

M   No, they give us a fresh one every time we enter the clean room.

Vocabulary

2 Helene managed to find a job in a travel agent's. Solve the anagrams to complete the story of what happened.

1   Helene saw an _____ in a local newspaper. NADEVRTIEMEST

2   There was a _____ in a travel agent's for a French speaker. AYACNVC

3   She rang up the company and asked for an _____ form she could fill in. PAPIALCOTNI

4   They asked about her _____ and _____ and sounded interested. AULICFIAQTINOS / KLISLS

5   It didn't matter that she had no previous _____. EEXEPIRENC

6   They told her to send her CV and a _____ letter. OCVEGINR

7   A week later they called her for an _____. ITRVWNEIE

Functions

3 Terry is ringing up about a hotel receptionist job. Complete the conversation by putting the words in the right order.

R = Rebecca, T = Terry

R: Good morning. The Croft Hotel. Rebecca speaking. How may I help?

T: Hello. (**1**) the / calling / receptionist / I'm / about / hotel / job.
(**2**) Is / vacancy / the / is / available? / still

R: (**3**) Yes, / still / someone / *looking* / we're / *for*
(**4**) Let / *put* / the / you / to / *through* / manager / me. That's Karen Marsh.
(**5**) *Hold* / a / find / moment / while / *on* / I try / to / her
(**6**) I'm / that / there's / afraid / answer / no
(**7**) Would / to / you / message? / like / leave / a

T: (**8**) I / so, / think / I'll / later *call* / don't / *back*
(**9**) When / to / be / ring? / a / time / good / would / for / me

R: (**10**) Try / in / again / hour / half / an / about
(**11**) I'll / Ms Marsh / tell / call / to / your / expect

T: OK. / (**12**) I'll / half *back* / in / *ring* / hour / an

4 Think of a job that you would like to do in an English-speaking country. Complete this covering letter with words and expressions that are true for you.

> Dear Sir or Madam,
>
> Please allow me to introduce myself. My name is _____. I am a (an) _____ year-old _____ from _____. I am writing to find out if you have any vacancies for _____.
>
> I am a _____ and _____ person and I get on well with everyone. I am good at _____ and have a certificate in / experience of _____.
>
> Pleased find enclosed an up-to-date CV for your consideration.
>
> Yours sincerely,

I can ...

- ☐ speak on the phone.
- ☐ talk about jobs.
- ☐ write a covering letter and CV.
- ☐ express obligation and prohibition.

Review 〉 Unit 6

Vocabulary

1 Complete the sentences with words from the box.

> pollution   hurricane   volcanic eruption
> global warming   drought   tornado   flood

1 So much _____ comes from that chemical plant that it makes your eyes water.

2 In 1902 the _____ of Mount Pelée on Martinique killed 28,000 people. Just two people survived the explosion.

3 People are trying to beat the _____ by turning seawater into drinking water.

4 Noah built an ark to escape the _____ that covered the Earth.

5 A _____ picked up Dorothy Gale and carried her away to the land of Oz.

6 _____ is making the ice caps melt.

7 The Caribbean and Florida are _____ zones because of their geography and climate.

Grammar

2 Choose *will* or *be going to* to complete the sentences.

1 A I have to give Emma this book back.
  B I _____ (**see**) her this afternoon. _____ (**give**) it to her then if you like.

2 A Who _____ (**you invite**) to your party?
  B I _____ (**ask**) all my friends.

3 A Amy phoned while you were out.
  B Oh, did she? I _____ (**call her back**) after lunch.

4 A What _____ (**do**) this weekend?
  B We _____ (**see**) *Romeo and Juliet*. There's an extra ticket. Do you want to come?

3 Write *a / an / the / Ø* to complete the text about the mini ice age.

> Did you know that three hundred years ago there was (**1**) _____ mini ice age? (**2**) _____ river Thames in London was completely frozen – in fact (**3**) _____ ice was so thick that (**4**) _____ people walked across (**5**) _____ river and cooked (**6**) _____ whole cows on it. This mini ice age didn't completely finish until (**7**) _____ middle of the 1800s when (**8**) _____ Earth started to warm up again. So what was (**9**) _____ cause of this? It seems that (**10**) _____ increase in (**11**) _____ volcanic eruptions prevented more of (**12**) _____ sun's rays reaching us. Nowadays we are all worried about (**13**) _____ global warming. Perhaps (**14**) _____ answer is to create (**15**) _____ few more volcanic eruptions!

Functions

4 Complete the talk with words and expressions for making presentations.

> I'm now going to pass you on ...
> Thank you for coming along ...   next ...
> last but not least ...   first of all ...   To sum up ...
> As you can see ...   I am going to give you ...
> That's enough to fill a swimming pool ...

> 'Good afternoon, everyone. (**1**) _____ This afternoon (**2**) _____ some tips for saving water. (**3**) _____ from this diagram we use up to half of our water for flushing the toilet, washing up and watering the garden. You can take three immediate steps: (**4**) _____, you can change the head of your shower, (**5**) _____ you can put a brick in the toilet cistern so you use less water, (**6**) _____ you can collect rainwater to water plants and flowers. These three simple things can save on average 80 cubic metres of water a year. (**7**) _____ Incredible, isn't it? (**8**) _____ I have given you a few tips on how to save water in the home. (**9**) _____ to Tom who is going to tell you about cutting your electricity bill.'

Now I can ...

☐ present information.
☐ talk about natural disasters.
☐ write a letter to the editor.
☐ use *will* and *be going to* to talk about the future.

7

Art

In this unit you will learn

- **Communication:** expressing likes and preferences
- **Vocabulary:** art
- **Reading and Listening:** Leonardo da Vinci, the Lascaux cave paintings
- **Writing:** a thank-you letter
- **Grammar:** comparative and superlative adjectives, ability in the past

Let's get started

1 Describe the picture and answer the questions.

1 Why is the man spraying graffiti?
2 Do you think graffiti is art? Why? / Why not?

Vocabulary

2 Complete the sentences with the words in the box. Use your dictionary to help you.

> background   exhibition   foreground
> frame   gallery   landscape   masterpiece
> portrait   sculptor   Statue   still life

1 The Queen asked the artist to produce a _____ of the prince.

2 This _____ shows the hills and mountains of the north of Scotland.

3 The original painting is in a _____ in London.

4 This is an incredibly realistic _____ – it makes you want to smell the flowers and eat the fruit.

5 As well as being a painter, Michelangelo was also a wonderful _____.

6 Are you going to the Andy Warhol _____?

7 In the _____, there is a farmer working in his field. Behind him, in the _____, we can see boats on the river.

8 The _____ of Liberty is the symbol of New York.

9 The Mona Lisa is considered to be Leonardo da Vinci's greatest _____.

10 The _____ doesn't go well with the painting – it's far too heavy.

3 What is your favourite work of art? Describe it and explain why you like it.

Reading

1 Most towns and cities have at least one famous monument or statue. What about your town or city, or a place you know well?

2 Read about four statues and answer questions 1–12 by writing A, B, C or D. Each letter can be used more than once.

Which statue …

1 ☐ took 17 years to complete?
2 ☐ can we see from the sea?
3 ☐ is the most recent?
4 ☐ has a copy on the other side of the world?
5 ☐ was inspired by a poem?
6 ☐ is a venue for musical events?
7 ☐ welcomes immigrants?
8 ☐ remembers a faithful animal?
9 ☐ was a present?
10 ☐ has an existing older version?
11 ☐ can we see from trains and cars?
12 ☐ was recreated after its destruction?

3 List the different materials the artists used.

Grammar: making comparisons

4 Complete these comparative sentences from the text, and answer the questions.

a It is _____ _____ the one in New York.

b Few are _____ _____ to their local economy _____ the dog.

1 How do we form the comparative …
• with short adjectives?
• with longer adjectives?

2 What word links the two things that we compare?

5 Look back at the texts. Find the comparative forms of these adjectives.

> wide   famous   small   old   important
> big   impressive   heavy

6 Complete these sentences from the texts, which make comparisons in other ways.

a It isn't _____ _____ _____ the Statue of Liberty.

b It is _____ _____ _____ Lady Liberty.

A **The Angel of the North** stands on a hill above an old coal mine near Newcastle in the UK, and reminds us of the people who worked underground for two hundred years. At 20 metres high it isn't as tall as the Statue of Liberty, but it is wider because of its wings. It was completed in 1998 and used 200 tons of steel and 600 tons of concrete for its foundations, so it is heavier than many other statues. It is less famous than Lady Liberty, but 100,000 road and rail users see it every day.

C **The Statue of Liberty** is probably the most famous statue in the world. Situated in New York harbour, it was a gift from the people of France, and it has welcomed immigrants to the United States since it was finished in 1886. The statue is 46 metres tall, but with its foundation it measures 93 metres. It used 31 tons of copper and 125 tons of steel. Another version stands in the Luxembourg Gardens in Paris. It is smaller than the one in New York but older, as it was the model for its much bigger sister.

B **The Dog on the Tuckerbox*** is the smallest of our selection of statues. It is probably the least recognised outside Australia. It has an interesting history: in the 1850s, an explorer wrote a poem about a faithful dog that guarded its master's tuckerbox. The town of Gundagai decided to remember it with a small statue. A local stonemason carved the statue, and the Prime Minister of Australia introduced it to the public in 1932. It may be less impressive than many statues, but few are more important to their local economy than the dog, which has transformed the little town into a popular tourist destination.

tuckerbox in Australia, a box for carrying food in

7 Complete these superlative sentences from the texts, and answer the questions.

   a The Dog on the Tuckerbox is _____ _____ of our selection of statues.

   b The Statue of Liberty is probably _____ _____ _____ statue in the world.

   c It is probably _____ _____ _____ outside Australia.

   1 How do we form the superlative …

     • with short adjectives?

     • with longer adjectives?

   2 What word always comes before the superlative?

8 Find more examples of superlative adjectives in the texts.

9 Study the spelling patterns. Find an adjective in the texts for each pattern.

Comparative and superlative adjectives			
adjective	large	hot	funny
comparative	larger	hotter	funnier
superlative	the largest	the hottest	the funniest

See Grammar Reference, page 154

D Chopin's statue is one of the most famous monuments in Warsaw. The project was chosen in 1909, but because of the First World War the monument was only unveiled in 1926. The cast from which it was produced was made in France. The worst thing that happened to the statue was in 1940 during the Second World War, when the statue was blown up. Because of its importance, it was reconstructed and unveiled again in 1958. The cast consists of 116 pieces and weighs 16 tons. It is 6.4 metres high. Nowadays, in the summer there are live piano concerts by the monument. There is even a copy of it further away in Hamamatsu in Japan, where the composer has some of his biggest fans.

10 2.2 Listen and repeat the sentences. Notice how the words in **bold** are stressed, and how *than* /ðən/ and *as* /əz/ are weak.

   a It is smaller **than** the one in New York.

   b It isn't **as** tall **as** the Statue of Liberty.

11 Complete the table with the comparative and superlative forms of the words given. Three examples have been done.

	Comparative	Superlative
good		*the best*
bad		
far		
little	*less*	
many		*the most*

12 Complete the sentences using the comparative, the superlative, or *as … as*.

   1 The Dog on the Tuckerbox was certainly _____ (**expensive**) and _____ (**easy**) to make of all four statues.

   2 I think the Angel of the North is _____ (**strange**) of the statues.

   3 Chopin's statue is not _____ (**tall**) the Statue of Liberty.

   4 I'm not sure which is _____ (**heavy**) – the Angel or the statue of Chopin.

   5 At the moment the Angel isn't _____ (**famous**) the Statue of Liberty, but that is only because it is a lot _____ (**young**).

   6 Chopin's statue was _____ (**difficult**) to make than the one of the dog.

   7 Some people say that the Angel is _____ (**big**) waste of money ever.

   8 I think the one of Chopin has _____ (**interesting**) history of all.

13 Work in pairs or groups. Tell each other what you personally think of the statues you have read about. Make sentences comparing them using the words in the box.

beautiful ugly historic old
exciting important interesting

A genius called Leonardo

Reading

1 Leonardo da Vinci is one of the most famous artists and inventors in the world. Match these titles to the works of art A–D. Which do you like best?

1 ☐ *Lady with an Ermine*
2 ☐ The tank design
3 ☐ The flying machine
4 ☐ *Mona Lisa*

2 Read the text about the artist Leonardo and answer the questions.

1 Why did he become Verrocchio's apprentice?

2 According to one story, why did Verrocchio stop painting?

3 What kind of relationship did Leonardo have with …
- the Duke of Milan?
- Michelangelo?
- the King of France?

4 What strange talents did he have?

5 What did he produce in addition to his paintings?

Spotlight

on reading skills: understanding references

When we write texts, we often vary the way we refer to people and things – we use different words to avoid repeating the same ones.

1 Read this extract. How many words does it use to refer to the king?

> He spent the last few years of his life in France at the court of Francis I. The young king loved and respected Leonardo. According to legend, the artist died in the monarch's arms.

2 Read through the text and <u>underline</u> all the different words that are used to refer to …
- Verrocchio.
- Leonardo.

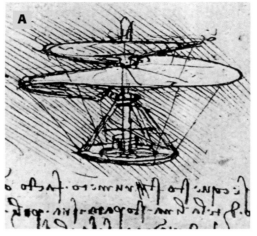

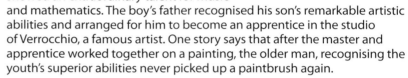

eonardo was born in 1452 in the small village of Vinci in Italy. His grandparents brought him up, but then he went to live with his father. From an early age he showed an extraordinary talent for music and mathematics. The boy's father recognised his son's remarkable artistic abilities and arranged for him to become an apprentice in the studio of Verrocchio, a famous artist. One story says that after the master and apprentice worked together on a painting, the older man, recognising the youth's superior abilities never picked up a paintbrush again.

In those days, Italy was a collection of independent city states, and artists

depended on finding a rich and powerful patron. Leonardo travelled a lot during his lifetime. The Duke of Milan was a good master and appreciated his talents, but after the Duke fell Leonardo wasn't able to stay in Milan because it was too dangerous. He returned to Florence, where he met his great rival Michelangelo. Even though they had much in common, they couldn't stand each other. Later on he worked in Rome. He spent the last few years of his life in France at the court of Francis I. The young king loved and respected Leonardo. According to legend, the artist died in the monarch's arms.

As well as being an artist, Leonardo was a mathematician, an engineer, an architect and an inventor. He was also interested in human anatomy and botany, and fascinated by flight. He loved birds so much that he often bought them just so he could set them free. He also had other peculiar talents – he could write and paint equally well with either hand, and he was able to write in mirror-writing as naturally as ordinary writing. Unusually for the time, he was also a vegetarian.

Nowadays, we remember him as one of the greatest geniuses who has ever lived. As an artist, he did not produce a lot of work, and his reputation rests on masterpieces such as *Mona Lisa*, as well as lesser-known works such as *Lady with an Ermine*. He is recognised as an incredible inventor who was far ahead of his time. There are sketches and designs for a helicopter and a tank, as well as many other machines. The

technology to turn his dreams into reality simply did not exist then. One of his designs, for a long bridge, was successfully used hundreds of years later. He also designed the fortifications and canal systems for Milan, studied human biology and botany, worked with complicated mathematical ideas and wrote poetry. All his scientific ideas were based on careful observations along with a deep understanding of the basic nature of the materials he worked with. He was truly a master of everything, a real Renaissance man.

3 All of these statements are wrong. Correct them, beginning with the words in *italics*.

1 When he was a child, Leonardo was rather stupid.
I'm not sure that's right …

2 He lived in Florence all of his life.
Really? I've read somewhere that he …

3 He loved all different kinds of meat.
I don't think that's true …

4 Verrocchio taught Leonardo how to paint.
Well actually, …

5 Michelangelo was Leonardo's best friend.
Actually, I think you'll find that …

6 Leonardo was interested in everything except the natural world.
Actually, he also studied …

7 He made lots of machines, such as a tank and a helicopter.
I'm not sure that's right …

8 Leonardo died in Florence.
I don't think so …

Grammar: ability in the past

4 Complete these sentences to talk about ability in the past.

1 Leonardo _____ write and paint equally well with either hand.

2 He _____ _____ _____ write in mirror-writing.

3 Leonardo and Michelangelo _____ stand each other.

4 Leonardo _____ _____ _____ stay in Milan.

5 Now complete the table.

can / be able to		
	can + base form	be able to + base form
present	_____	_____
past	_____	_____
past negative	_____	_____

6 Based on the topics in the box, tell each other what you could / were able to do when you were …

- three years old.
- thirteen years old.
- seven years old.

> speak   tie your laces   read and write
> swim   ride a bicycle
> play an instrument   paint   draw

Listening

7 ⏺2.3 Lucia Conti is a tour guide, showing tourists Leonardo da Vinci's *Mona Lisa* at the Louvre Museum in Paris. Read the Spotlight on listening skills box, and read questions 1–9 below. When you are ready, listen to part A of Lucia's talk and answer the questions.

Spotlight

On listening skills: reading the questions

It can be very tiring listening to to a fairly long passage. Read the questions before you listen so that you know what you have to listen for. Having these clear questions will help focus your listening, and help you listen out for key words.

1 What is *Mona Lisa*'s other name?

2 Why are many people surprised when they first see it?

3 What is special about the landscape in the background?

4 When did Leonardo start and finish it?

5 What did he paint it on?

6 How did Leonardo achieve the painting's 'smoky' appearance?

7 What does Lucia think about the theory that it was a self-portrait?

8 Who was the real Mona Lisa?

9 What two things do people often notice about the picture?

8 ⏺2.4 In part B, Lucia explains why *Mona Lisa* is so famous. Listen, and complete the notes that summarise her talk.

> It belonged to King (**1**) _____, and (**2**) _____, had the painting in his bedroom. The event that made it really famous happened in (**3**) _____, when a thief stole the painting. He took it out of its (**4**) _____ and hid it under his (**5**) _____. The police caught the thief when he tried to sell it. The painting returned to the Louvre. People only spend (**6**) _____ in front of it. Lucia believes that the painting is over-exposed. In the last century there were more than (**7**) _____ advertisements that showed it.

7C Planning a visit

Listening and speaking

1 2.5 Kathy is telephoning her aunt Julie in Liverpool. Listen to their conversation in part A. What is the reason for her call?

2 2.5 Listen again and fill the gaps.

K = Kathy, J = Julie

K   Aunt Julie, it's Kathy here.

J   Hi, Kathy! So, (1) _____ to visit me at the weekend then?

K   Yes – I hope it's still OK.

(2) _____ an interview at the university on Monday morning, so it would be a good chance to see you.

J   Of course it's still OK! How (3) _____?

K   I'm getting the coach. That's why (4) _____, actually – to tell you that (5) _____ at 7.15.

J   That's great – see you at the coach station then!

3 Which tense do they use in the gaps. When is it used to talk about now, and when is it used to express the future?

4 Ask each other about your plans for this evening / this weekend / the summer holidays.

Example:

What are you doing this summer?

I'm working on my cousin's farm.

5 Look at the picture. What is Liverpool famous for?

VISIT **LIVERPOOL**

6 2.6 It is Saturday morning. Kathy and Julie are discussing how to spend the day. Listen to part B and answer the questions.

1   Why doesn't Kathy want to go to a gallery?

2   What sport doesn't she like?

3   What do they decide to do?

7 2.6 Try to complete each sentence with two words. Then listen again and check your answers.

1   So, what do you _____ doing this afternoon?

2   I'm not sure. What do _____?

3   Well, to tell you the truth, I'm not very _____ museums.

4   _____ sightseeing and being outside to being indoors.

5   Well, I'm not a big _____.

6   I think _____ take the bus tour.

7   _____ could stop off and go to the Beatles' Story on the way.

8   Yes, _____ fun.

9   I'd _____ do that.

Pronunciation: intonation

8 🔊 2.7 Listen to the sentences in Exercise 7 and repeat them, copying the speakers' intonation.

9 Study the Useful Expressions box below. Expand the sentences to form a conversation.

A What / you do / this evening?

B I / not do / anything special. How about you?

A Well, I / like / see *Lethal Force* at the cinema. What about you?

B Well, to tell / you / truth I / not very keen / action movies. / I / rather / do something else.

A OK what / you / rather do?

B I think / I / rather / order a pizza and watch TV.

A That / sound / fine, too. What's on?

USEFUL EXPRESSIONS

Talking about preferences

I *prefer* tea **to** coffee.
I *prefer playing* computer games **to watching** television.
I'd prefer to go out than stay at home.
I'd rather drink tea **than** coffee.

Saying what you like and don't like

I (don't) like films based on comic books.
I'm (not) keen on / fond of abstract art.
I don't like / I'm not keen on going around galleries.

Expressing strong likes and dislikes

I love / adore / really like going to the cinema.
I really hate / detest / can't stand watching sport.

Being diplomatic

I'm not that keen on pizza / going to the theatre.

10 Work in pairs. Look at the pairs of options in the box and tell each other which one you prefer in each case.

> tea / coffee   horror films / comedies
> cats / dogs   classical music / pop music
> fast food / traditional food
> science subjects / arts subjects
> languages / literature

11 Choose two things you would like to do in Liverpool, and two things you wouldn't like to do. With a partner, create a similar conversation to the one between Julie and Kathy.

See Grammar Reference, page 154

Writing: a thank-you letter

12 Read Kathy's letter to Julie. Why is she thanking her?

> Dear Aunt Julie,
>
> It was lovely to see you when I came to Liverpool last week. It was kind of you to meet me at the station.
>
> I just wanted to write a few words to thank you for looking after me and showing me around the city. The bus tour was really interesting – I never knew that Liverpool had so much to offer. I've even become more interested in Liverpool Football Club!
>
> It was thoughtful of you to buy me the Beatles Experience poster. Every time I look at it, it reminds me of the lovely afternoon we spent together.
>
> I hope to see you next time you come down to London.
>
> Lots of love,
>
> Kathy
>
> PS I'm still waiting for the result of the interview. Fingers crossed!

USEFUL EXPRESSIONS: thanking someone

Thank you for taking such good care of me.
It was kind of you to meet me at the station.
I just wanted to tell you / write / say …

13 You spent a holiday with some distant relatives in England. Write a thank-you letter of 120–150 words covering the following points.

- Thank them for looking after you and say something nice about their welcome.
- Write about the food and accommodation.
- Write about at least two of your best memories of the holiday.
- Thank them for the goodbye present they gave you and say what it means to you.

Reading

1 Quickly read the text 'The find of the century' and complete the notes with dates and numbers.

> (1) It's been _____ years since the discovery of the caves. The cave paintings are from (2) _____ years ago. Altogether there are over (3) _____ images. The images of (4) _____ bulls are probably the most impressive. The biggest is over (5) _____ long. After the (6) _____ World War, (7) _____ people visited the site each day. In (8) _____, they had to close the cave to visitors. Fortunately, Lascaux II was opened in (9) _____.

2 Imagine you are interviewing an expert about the caves. Read the text again and write answers to the questions. Work in pairs and take it in turns to be the interviewer and the expert.

Y = you, E = Expert

Y How exactly were the caves discovered?

1 E _____

Y How amazing! What are the paintings of?

2 E _____

Y Are there any men in the paintings?

3 E _____

Y Do you have any idea who painted the pictures?

4 E _____

Y So why do you think they painted them?

5 E _____

Y Oh, really! That's interesting. And was it really necessary to close the caves?

6 E _____

Y That's a pity. But are they safe from danger now?

7 E _____

Y Oh dear. Let's hope that they can find a solution. Thanks very much for talking to me today.

3 Read the text again and decide which sentences are true and which are false. Put a tick (✓) in the correct box.

1 The boys noticed a new hole in the ground.
True ☐ False ☐

2 At first there wasn't enough light to see properly.
True ☐ False ☐

3 Scientists and historians have identified the main artist.
True ☐ False ☐

4 A number of the paintings are technically advanced.
True ☐ False ☐

5 The atmosphere outside the caves caused the first damage to the caves.
True ☐ False ☐

6 Scientists have completely established the reason for the fungus.
True ☐ False ☐

7 Very few people now enter Lascaux I.
True ☐ False ☐

8 Lascaux II reproduces all of the caves.
True ☐ False ☐

4 Work in groups. Choose one of the archaeological sites below. Research and prepare a short description of it. Include maps and diagrams as necessary. Why is the site important to historians?

- Sutton Hoo, England
- El-Amarna, Egypt
- Knossos, Crete
- Wonderwerk Cave, South Africa

Sutton Hoo, England

The find of the century

Near the town of Montignac in southern France there are some of the most extraordinary paintings in the world – the Lascaux cave paintings. In September 1940, four teenage boys and a dog called Robot were playing in the woods when they found a recent hole beneath a tree and decided to explore. They couldn't see very much, so they returned with a light. When they entered the first cave. they couldn't believe their eyes. Its walls were covered with paintings of ancient animals from 16,000 years ago. It was the find of the century. It contains more than 2,000 images painted by prehistoric man.

The most popular subject of the paintings is horses, but there are also prehistoric cats, bison and even a rhinoceros. Many of these creatures are now extinct. Some of the pictures showed men hunting them for food. Undoubtedly, the most striking images are those of four bulls. In the Great Hall of the Bulls there are four black bulls. One of them is over five metres long – the biggest animal ever discovered in cave art so far. It is not clear who painted them, although some people think that a 'shaman' – a sort of priest and magician – did the work. Maybe he painted them to bring them luck with the hunt. Some of the paintings are extremely skilful and use techniques that weren't used again until the Renaissance.

After the Second World War, the caves became an enormous tourist attraction, with a thousand people visiting them each day. Unfortunately, the carbon dioxide from visitors' breath damaged the paintings so badly that in 1963 they had to close the caves to the public. Experts have managed to restore the pictures to their original state but they have to check them constantly because of environmental dangers. The most recent threat is from a fungus*. This may be due to the air-conditioning in the caves. Only individual scientists can enter the cave on rare occasions. However, even if we can't see the real thing, we can visit a replica* of two of the caves and their paintings just 200 metres away. Lascaux II opened in 1983 and receives many thousands of visitors without a risk to the precious originals. Obviously it is not the same as visiting the originals, but it gives us a very good idea of what the paintings are like and their setting*.

'The most popular subject of the paintings is horses, but there are also prehistoric cats, bison and even a rhinoceros.'

fungus an area of tiny plants that can grow on an old or wet wall

replica an exact copy

setting the place where something is found

Paris

FRANCE

Montignac

A scientist studies the prehistoric cave paintings at Lascaux

A day in London

Listening and speaking

1 Describe the picture and answer the questions.

   1 Why are they taking an open-top bus tour?

   2 What is your opinion of open-top bus tours?

2 2.8 Daisy and Helena are in London and have decided to take a tour on an open-top bus. Listen to their conversation and mark the places they talk about on the map.

Welcome to London's original and best open-top bus tour

- Trafalgar Square
- St Paul's Cathedral
- The Monument
- The Tower of London
- Imax Cinema
- Shakespeare's Globe
- HMS Belfast
- Tower Bridge
- London Eye
- Big Ben and the Houses of Parliament

3 2.8 Listen again and answer the questions.

   1 Why doesn't Daisy want to join Helena and Caroline?

   2 When and where do they decide to meet in the afternoon?

   3 What do they agree to do?

   4 What do they agree to do if there's a problem?

   5 Why is Helena jealous?

USEFUL EXPRESSIONS

1 **a** *Shall we have a look at the map?* ☐
    b *Let's look at the map.* ☐

2 **a** *Yes, good idea.* ☐
    b *Yes, let's.* ☐

3 **a** *Where would you like to go?* ☐
    b *Where do you feel like going?* ☐

4 **a** *Why don't we take this route …?* ☐
    b *Perhaps we could take this route …?* ☐

5 **a** *That's a good idea.* ☐
    b *Yes, let's do that.* ☐

6 **a** *What shall we do this afternoon?* ☐
    b *What are we going to do this afternoon?* ☐

7 **a** *I'm going to meet Caroline …* ☐
    b *I'm meeting Caroline …* ☐

8 **a** *Why don't we meet in front of …?* ☐
    b *How about meeting in front of …?* ☐

9 **a** *I fancy going along the river.* ☐
    b *I'd like to go along the river.* ☐

10 **a** *I'll text you if there's a problem.* ☐
     b *If I have a problem, I'll text you.* ☐

4 2.8 Study the Useful Expressions box, then listen again. Tick (✓) the expressions you hear.

5 Work in pairs. Arrange a time and a place to meet your partner in London today.

Fitness and health

Let's get started

1 Describe the picture and answer the questions.

1 Why do you think the man in the picture is doing this activity?

2 Which sports or activities do you enjoy doing? Why?

Vocabulary

2 Match the verbs to the sport or activity.

1 ☐ go   a t'ai chi

2 ☐ play   b jogging

3 ☐ do / practise   c volleyball

3 Put the sports and activities with the right verb.

| squash | yoga | horse riding | tennis | chess |
| swimming | handball | running |

go	do / practise	play

In this unit you will learn

- **Communication:** giving advice, in hospital
- **Vocabulary:** sport, medical problems
- **Reading and Listening:** alternative medicine, sport in Britain
- **Writing:** a note
- **Grammar:** zero and first conditionals, *unless*

4 Work in groups. Think of as many sports as you can that use the following.

| club   racquet   bat   ball |
| board   net   basket   goal |

5 Read the description. Which sport is the person talking about?

'In the summer we go down to the beach and put up a net and have a game, you know just between friends for fun.'

6 Work in groups. Take it in turns to describe a sport.

Reading

1 Rates of obesity are growing in many developed countries, leading to an increase in health problems such as heart disease and diabetes. What is the situation in your country?

2 BMI stands for Body Mass Index. It is a way of finding out if you are the correct weight for your height. Follow the steps.
- Take your weight in kilograms.
- Multiply your height by itself.
- Divide your weight by your height.

3 Read the article 'Healthy body, healthy mind'. Do you think it gives good advice? Is there anything that you think is untrue or difficult to prove?

4 Study how the zero conditional is used, and answer the questions.

*If I **don't exercise** regularly, I **feel** terrible.*

1 Does it describe a situation that is …
- always true?
- only true in the future?

2 Which tense does it use in each part of the sentence?

Grammar: zero and first conditionals

5 Read the information and examples in the box, then complete the sentences.

The zero conditional

We use the zero conditional to make statements about things that are usually true. We often use the impersonal 'you' form to make a general point:
People who are good at a sport start when they are young.
If you want to be good at a sport, you need to start when you are young.

1 Top athletes have to be careful about what they eat and drink.
If you're a top athlete, _____.

2 Professional footballers risk hurting themselves.
If you're a professional footballer, _____.

3 Olympic-level swimmers need to train for four hours a day.
If you're an Olympic-level swimmer, _____.

4 First-class tennis players need excellent hand–eye coordination.
If you want to be _____.

Healthy body, healthy mind

Sitting around in front of the TV or computer all day makes you **put on** weight and feel tired. Regular physical activity burns calories and gives you more energy. Personally, if I don't go running two or three times a week, I feel terrible.

When teenagers exercise, they notice that their school work improves because they are prepared mentally. So exercise can improve your grades, too!

Which activity to choose?

The key to success is to **take up** something that challenges you and that you can still imagine yourself doing in the future. If you want to be good at anything, from playing a musical instrument to learning a foreign language, you have to work hard and practise. Sport is no different, so if you **go for** a sport you like, then there's a good chance that you'll **carry on with** it. Resist pressure from your parents to play their dream sport. In nine cases out of ten you'll **give** it **up** if you don't enjoy it.

Team or individual

Most sports build physical ability, strength and coordination, but team sports can teach a sense of fair play and develop leadership and other social skills. But if you can't stand the idea of teams, choose an individual sport like swimming, gymnastics or weightlifting.

Preventing sports injuries

If you **warm up** properly, you'll be less likely to get hurt or pull a muscle. You won't ever eliminate risk, but if you wear the right protective equipment, you'll **cut down** the chances of an unlucky injury. This means helmets for cycling, goggles for squash, and elbow and knee protection for skateboarding or hockey. And if you hurt yourself, remember to stop until you feel better. If you force yourself, you won't improve – your injury will simply get worse.

6 Study how the first conditional is used, and answer the questions.

*If you **follow** these steps, you'**ll feel** more energetic.*

1 Which half of the sentence expresses a condition?
2 Which part expresses the result?
3 Which tenses does it use in each half of the sentence?
4 Is the sentence talking about now, or the future?

The first conditional

We don't use *will* in the 'if clause' of first conditional sentences.
We usually put a comma after the 'if clause'.

7 Which form talks about a real possibility in the future – the zero or the first conditional? Find more examples of the zero and first conditional in 'Healthy body, healthy mind'.

See Grammar Reference, page 155

8 Use *if* + present simple and *will / won't* + base form to complete the sentences.

1 If you <u>exercise</u> (**exercise**) for 20 minutes a day, you '<u>ll feel</u> (**feel**) fitter and happier.
2 If he _____ (**train**) a lot, he _____ (**get into**) the school team.
3 He _____ (**feel**) tired for school tomorrow if he _____ (**stay up**) late.
4 If we _____ (**not hurry up**), we _____ (**not see**) the beginning of the match.
5 You _____ (**not play**) well if you _____ (**not eat**) breakfast.

9 Give advice to these teenagers based on the article you have just read. Use the zero or first conditional.

1 I feel tired all the time – the only thing I want to do is watch TV.
2 My tennis isn't improving. I think I'll give it up and try something different.
3 My ankle still hurts, but I think if I do some exercise it will soon get better.
4 I play football to please my dad, but I'd prefer to play basketball.
5 I love the freedom of skateboarding. Helmets and knee-protectors take the fun away.
6 Let's start playing straight away – I don't want to waste time warming up.

Vocabulary

10 Match the phrasal verbs in **bold** in the article on page 82 to definitions a–h.

a to begin a new hobby or activity
b to continue
c to do nothing; to waste time
d to do gentle practice exercises before doing sport
e to choose something
f (used about weight) to add, increase
g to reduce
h to stop an activity or habit you did before

11 Complete the sentences using the phrasal verbs from Exercise 10.

1 You need to _____ on the time you spend at the gym – schoolwork is important, too.
2 It was a difficult choice, but in the end she _____ basketball instead of volleyball.
3 He had to _____ football after he injured his knee.
4 A lot of people _____ golf when they retire.
5 He _____ weight after he stopped training.
6 We can't just _____ all day – let's have a game of tennis.
7 When it stopped raining, they _____ with their game.
8 We'd better _____ before we start playing – we don't want to hurt ourselves.

Reading

1 Look at the list of traditional 'folk' remedies and match them to the problems. Do you think they work? Are there different remedies in your country? Can you think of any others?

1 ☐ honey and lemon   a a nosebleed
2 ☐ an ice pack / frozen peas   b a sprained ankle
3 ☐ a cold key on the back   c sleeplessness
4 ☐ camomile tea   d a sore throat
5 ☐ a sudden shock   e hiccups

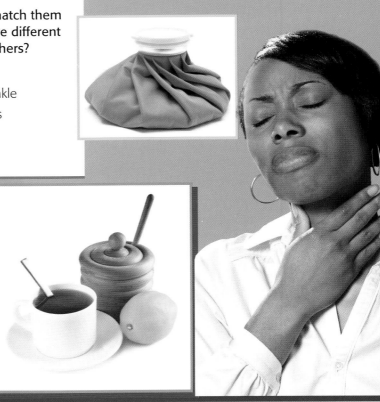

2 Read the interview about a new treatment called 'cryotherapy'. Match questions A–I to answers 1–8. There is one extra question.

A How long can people stay inside the chamber?

B How does cryotherapy work?

C What do you wear in the room?

D What are its dangers?

E So it doesn't actually **cure** patients?

F So tell me, how does it actually feel?

G Goodness! But it must be a terrible shock for your body?

H Who can it help?

I What is cryotherapy?

1 ☐
Whole-body cryotherapy involves exposing your body to a temperature of minus 120 degrees. To give you an idea of just how cold this is, the lowest recorded natural temperature is minus 90 degrees, in Antarctica.

2 ☐
Extreme cold makes the molecules in your body smaller. When you leave the cold, they expand, increasing the flow of blood, which helps reduce the pain from **swollen** joints and injuries.

3 ☐
Some experts say it can **relieve** the **symptoms** of everything from rheumatism to very serious nervous diseases. It is used a lot with athletes and sportspeople who have injured themselves. It accelerates recovery time and helps with general aches and pains. But it doesn't help with cuts or broken bones.

4 ☐
Not really, but it can help with the symptoms of the illness and give long periods of relief between each **treatment**. I **suffer from** painful rheumatism. A course of half a dozen sessions relieves it and keeps the symptoms under control.

5 ☐
Almost nothing! You take off all your normal clothes and put on cotton underwear. Unless you wear natural fibres like cotton, your clothes will instantly freeze solid. A face mask protects your nose from freezing.

6 ☐
First-timers only do two minutes. Afterwards, sessions can increase to a maximum of four minutes. That way it only cools down the outside of the body. You're OK unless the extreme cold reaches your internal organs. You need to leave before eight minutes, otherwise you can die.

7 ☐
Yes it is. That's why you have a **check-up** with a nurse before they accept you for the treatment. There are also two rooms – the first is 'only' minus 90. You stay in there for ten seconds and then they open up the door to the next chamber.

8 ☐
Well, it's an unusual sensation. At first it's a bit like needles. Then you notice a kind of burning sensation, and then you can't feel anything – you know, like after an **injection** at the dentist's!

3 Complete the sentences using the words in **bold** on page 84.

1 You should ask the doctor to give you a _____ to see that everything is OK.

2 Oh dear, your knee looks very _____ – is it painful when I touch it?

3 In spring she _____ _____ different allergies.

4 Can you describe your _____? For example, do you have a headache?

5 Can you roll up your sleeve? I'm going to give you an _____ to help you sleep.

6 I'm afraid that we can't _____ the illness, but regular _____ can control it.

7 If you put a bag of frozen peas on your ankle, it will help to _____ the pain.

Grammar: *unless*

4 Study the sentence from the interview and <u>underline</u> the correct way to complete the rules.

> *Unless you wear natural fibres like cotton, your clothes will instantly freeze solid.*
>
> 1 *Unless has the idea of* **if / if not.**
> 2 *The* **'condition' / 'result'** *clause follows unless.*
> 3 *Unless is followed by* **will / the present simple.**

5 Choose between *if* and *unless* to complete the sentences.

1 You'll be ill **if / unless** you stop worrying.

2 **If / Unless** she goes out without a coat, she'll catch a cold.

3 You won't get better **if / unless** you take your medicine.

4 They'll never find a cure **if / unless** they don't spend more on research.

5 The infection will spread **if / unless** he doesn't take his antibiotics.

6 Continue the sentences in your own words.

1 If you don't buy a pair of good running shoes, …

2 Unless you warm up before playing tennis, …

3 If you don't cut down on cakes, …

4 Unless you give up playing, …

Listening

7 2.9 Hannah is talking to her brother Daniel about her sore shoulder. Listen to their conversation and circle the correct answer, A, B or C.

1 Hannah …
   A hasn't been to the doctor yet.
   B has had different treatments.
   C thinks her shoulder can get better on its own.

2 Hannah doesn't want to try acupuncture because …
   A she doesn't know what it is.
   B she doesn't believe in it.
   C she's afraid of needles.

3 According to Daniel, acupuncture works by …
   A making the forces in your body work in harmony.
   B putting needles in certain nerves.
   C making you feel relaxed.

4 Cupping …
   A is totally different from acupuncture.
   B removes the air from the cups.
   C is a new treatment.

5 According to Daniel, the disadvantage of cupping is …
   A it can burn you if you aren't careful.
   B it leaves bruises on your skin.
   C it's painful.

8 Are 'alternative' therapies such as cryotherapy and acupuncture easily available in your country? Do you think they work?

8C Medical problems

Listening and speaking

1 How often do you visit the doctor? How easy is it to make an appointment in your country?

2 ⊙2.10 Three patients are visiting the doctor or the chemist. Listen to their conversations and complete the table.

	Patient 1	Patient 2	Patient 3
symptoms			
diagnosis			
treatment / suggestions			

3 ⊙2.10 Listen to Patient 1 again and write the complete sentences.

D = Doctor, B = Benjamin

D Hello, Benjamin. So what / matter today?

B Well, I / cold / temperature / throat / really hurts.

D Mm, let's / look. Open wide. Say 'aah'. Mm, it / sore. Right – here / prescription for / course / antibiotics.

B Can I / school? / important test.

D No / better stay / home / next three days. I / write / note / your teacher.

USEFUL EXPRESSIONS

Asking what's wrong
What seems to be the trouble?
What's the matter?

Saying what's wrong
I've got a sore throat.
I've hurt my ankle.
My throat hurts.
My foot is painful.

Making a diagnosis
It looks sore.
It sounds like gastric flu.
It feels swollen.

Giving advice
You'd better have an X-ray.
You should make an appointment.
You ought to see a doctor.

4 ⊙2.10 Listen to Patients 2 and 3 again and complete the sentences.

1 So, what _____?

2 Well, _____ my ankle.

3 _____ a look at it.

4 Mm, yes, it _____ very swollen.

5 Well, I don't think it's broken but _____ have an X-ray.

6 _____.

7 Well, _____ stomach ache and I _____ sick.

8 _____ like gastric flu.

9 You _____ see a doctor.

10 _____ this three times a day.

11 But if you don't feel better in two days, you _____ definitely see the doctor.

Pronunciation: sentence stress

5 ⊙2.11 Look at the first sentence in the Useful expressions box. The underlined words carry the most important meaning and are stressed. Listen to the other sentences and underline the words that are stressed.

Vocabulary

6 Match problems 1–6 to pictures A–F.

1 ☐ a sore eye

2 ☐ a broken arm

3 ☐ a swollen ankle

4 ☐ a painful cough

5 ☐ an upset stomach

6 ☐ a high temperature

7 Match each of the problems in Exercise 6 to one of the following treatments.

> a bandage   antibiotics   eyedrops   an X-ray
> a plaster   medicine   an ice pack
> cough medicine   plaster   painkiller

8 Work in pairs. Take it in turns to be the doctor and the patient. Choose a problem and suggest a treatment. Use the conversations as a model and follow the flow chart.

Ask about the problem. → Say what the problem is. → Make a diagnosis. → Ask what to do next. → Give an instruction.

Writing: a note

9 Malcolm is in bed with a bad cold. His sister Susie has left him a note. Read the note and answer the questions.

1 When we leave a note, we often miss words out. Which words are missing?

2 Imagine you are speaking to Malcolm. What would you say to him?

> Malcolm – Didn't want to wake you up. Here's some medicine. Two tablets every six hours after meals. Drink a lot – honey & lemon in hot water best. Keep warm & stay indoors.
>
> Call me this evening to tell me how you are. Hope you slept well.
>
> Love, Susie xxx

10 You planned to go with your English flatmate to the theatre tonight. Write a note to …

- cancel your plans because you are ill.
- tell him/her what you have to do.
- suggest going to the theatre some other time when you get better.
- say you need to rest and don't want anybody to wake you up.

Reading and writing

11 Read the health advice on a website for travellers. Underline the different ways that the writer uses to tell us what to do / what not to do.

File   Edit   View as   Tools   Help   Links

Before you travel:

✈ Make sure that you have all the right vaccinations.
✈ Don't forget to check which ones you need.
✈ Remember to buy health insurance. You should also take a basic first aid kit. It's a good idea to include basic medicines, e.g. aspirin, painkillers, etc.

While you're there:
Food and drink
☻ Avoid eating salads or anything uncooked.
☻ Don't eat street food – it can make you ill.
☻ Be careful of very spicy food.
☻ Never drink tap water or ice cubes – stick to bottled water or soft drinks.
☻ Don't accept drinks unless you know they are made from boiled water.

Out and about
☻ Be careful of where you swim.
☻ Mind how you cross the road.
☻ Watch out for dogs – don't stroke them.
☻ Be suspicious of strangers who want you to change money, or who ask you to follow them into unfamiliar places.

Have a really great time …
but remember – 'Better safe than sorry'.

12 Using the website advice as a model, create a page for visitors to your country. Use the useful expressions in the box below.

USEFUL EXPRESSIONS: giving advice

Checking
Make sure that + verb phrase
Remember to / Don't forget to + verb

Advice
You should + verb   *It's a good idea to* + verb

Prohibition
Never + verb   *Don't* + verb
Avoid + verb + *-ing*

Warning
Mind how you + verb   *Watch out for* + noun
Be careful of + noun/adverbial clause

8D Sporting world

Reading

1 Sport is an important part of British life and culture. Many of the sports that are played around the world today originated in Britain. Read these extracts from a cultural guide to Britain and complete as much of the table as you can.

		Place of origin	When it was invented	Risks and injuries
1	Tennis			
2	Golf			
3	Rugby			
4	London Marathon			
5	Cricket			
6	Highland Games			
7	Horse racing			
8	Rowing			

2 Works in pairs. Student A, turn to page 145 and find out about horse racing. Student B, turn to page 147 to learn about rowing. Exchange information and complete the rest of the table.

Listening

3 2.12 Stella is a foreign student staying in London. She is discussing sport with her landlord, Jerry. Listen to the discussion and answer the questions.

1 Which is the most popular pastime in Britain overall?

2 How do adults participate in football?

3 What happened in 1863?

4 What was a big problem in the 1970s and 1980s?

5 Complete the saying 'Football is a _____ played by _____; rugby is a _____ played by _____.'

6 According to Jerry, why are big English clubs so successful in European football?

7 Why isn't he happy with this situation?

8 Why does he like the FA Cup?

Project

As a class, make a list of important sporting events. Are there any sports or activities that are special to your country or region?

4 Work in groups. Each group should choose a sport or activity and find out about …

- its history.
- where it's played.
- the names of any famous players.

5 Produce a paragraph about your sport or activity.

6 Combine the different paragraphs to create a page called 'Sporting _____'. Illustrate it with pictures of famous people and places from your country.

Sporting Britain

The earliest form of **tennis** was the *jeu de paume* – or 'palm game' – in France, where players hit a ball over a net with their hands. In 1873 an officer in the British army introduced a version of the game close to the one that is played today. At some point most players suffer from twisted knees and ankles and tennis elbow! Wimbledon in south-west London is home to one of the world's major tennis tournaments. Matches are played on grass courts. Although tennis is still popular in Britain, British players have won very few major championships.

Golf was invented in Scotland around 600 years ago. Golf is an expensive sport – you have to buy a set of golf clubs and pay a lot to join a club. Your body often pays with sprained wrists and painful shoulders! The closest most people get to playing golf is a game of 'crazy golf' when they go on holiday to the seaside!

Rugby was invented at Rugby School in 1823 when a schoolboy called William Webb Ellis picked up the ball during a soccer game. The big annual tournament between European countries is the Six Nations' Championship, where teams from England, France, Scotland, Wales, Ireland and Italy play each other. Commonwealth countries like South Africa, New Zealand and Australia also play rugby, and Argentina has a good team. By and large, teams from the southern hemisphere are better than their European rivals.

Every year, thousands of people take part in the **London Marathon**, which starts in Greenwich and finishes in Westminster. Since 1981, world-class able-bodied and disabled athletes have competed alongside ordinary people who train hard for the event and compete against themselves, often in fancy dress. It took an ex-soldier who had been badly wounded two weeks to finish the 42 km course on crutches. Many people who participate try and raise money for charity. Before the race, doctors' waiting rooms fill up with patients with sprained ankles and pulled muscles acquired during training.

Cricket is the most English game. You can see matches in country villages every Sunday. Professional teams from different counties compete against each other. People started playing it in the 1300s, but its written rules were fixed in 1788. They are so complicated that many people find matches a complete mystery. Critics of cricket think it is slow and boring – international matches can last up to five days! The sport can be dangerous, as the small ball is very hard, and sprained and broken fingers are common. The most famous cricket ground is Lord's in London. Commonwealth countries play cricket, too, and regularly beat the English team.

The most famous traditional sporting events in Scotland are the **Highland Games**, where people from different clans compete against each other. These ancient games are held in different places in Scotland, the best-known being the Braemar Gathering. It is an outdoor festival that mixes sport with music and dancing. Participants wear their own special tartans – clothes with traditional patterns that show which clan they belong to. 'Tossing the caber' (throwing an 82-kilo wooden log) is a test of skill and strength which causes a lot of bad backs! Sword dancing allows competitors to demonstrate their speed and agility. Watch out for cut feet!

'Your body often pays with sprained wrists and painful shoulders!'

Case Study 4 > A natural alternative

1 Read the text about Native American medicine and match the underlined words to the definitions.

1 _____ the part of a plant that grows underground

2 _____ the fruit of a tree

3 _____ cuts or injuries

4 _____ biting with the teeth

5 _____ what happens if you cut your skin

6 _____ the outer 'skin' of a tree

7 _____ small branches of a tree

8 _____ the green part of a tree

2 Read the information again and find:

1 plants that would help with a sporting injury _____

2 the plant which seems to cure the most problems _____

3 trees which we can use the bark from _____

4 a cure which could be deadly _____

5 what the Cherokee did after a battle _____

6 leaves which are hot when we put them on the skin _____

7 something that might help you even if you don't drink it or touch it _____

8 something you might use if a snake bites you _____

3 What plant remedies do you know? Do you think they are a good alternative? Discuss with a partner.

NATIVE AMERICAN MEDICINE

If we are ill, we usually go to a doctor or a chemist to get medicine. The native people of North America could not do this, of course, but they were very close to nature and they found many uses for the trees and plants where they lived. Native Americans discovered hundreds of years ago that <u>chewing</u> the <u>bark</u> of the willow tree could help cure pain. Eventually, people found that the willow bark contained something called salicylic acid. These days, if you take an aspirin for a headache, you will probably feel better. That's because the main ingredient in aspirin is salicylic acid!

Some Native American plant cures

PLANT	USED FOR
Arnica	bruises / back pain

The Catawba Indians used arnica on the skin for bruises. They also made a tea from the <u>roots</u> for back pain. This can be dangerous, though, and if you drink too much, it can kill you.

Echinacea (also known as purple coneflower)	stomach problems / toothaches / sore throats / insect bites / stings / snakebites

The Sioux Indians and the Comanche Indians chewed the roots of this plant to help with pain. The plant has many other uses and is very popular today.

Juniper	stomach problems / colds / aches / sores / bleeding

Many Native Americans drank tea from juniper <u>twigs</u> for stomach problems. They used boiled twigs and <u>berries</u> to put on aches and sores. They used the berries to stop <u>bleeding</u>.

Sage or Sagebrush	killing germs

Indians often burned sage to keep an area clean and healthy. Breathing the smoke will kill germs and bacteria to help keep you healthy.

Wild cherry	coughs and colds

The Flambeau Ojibwa made a tea from the bark of wild cherry.

Witch hazel	bruises

The Iroquois poured hot water over fresh witch-hazel leaves. They then placed the hot <u>leaves</u> on bruises.

Yarrow	pain / bleeding / injuries / skin problems

The Navaho knew that this flower could stop pain and bleeding. The Cherokee bathed in water containing the leaves of this plant after a battle to help with their <u>wounds</u>.

Yellow-spined thistle	burns

The Kiowa Indians boiled the flowers and put the liquid on burns and skin sores.

Using plant cures: a warning

Although in many ways plant cures are safer than normal medicines, they can be dangerous or deadly if you use them incorrectly. Unless you are really sure, get the advice of an expert.

Aspen bark

Wild cherry

Echinacea

Review > Unit 7

Vocabulary

1 Write the words that the definitions describe.

1 It goes around a picture. **f**_____
2 street art **g**_____
3 a form of a person in stone or metal **s**_____
4 a picture of a person **p**_____
5 a building where you can see paintings
   g_____
6 to create a picture with a pencil **d**_____
7 someone who creates number 3! **s**_____
8 a picture show **e**_____
9 the front part of a picture **f**_____
10 a picture of a country scene **l**_____

Grammar

2 Use the words in brackets to make sentences using the comparative or superlative form.

John Constable is _the most famous_ (famous) landscape painter England has produced.

1 I prefer abstract art to traditional art – I find it _____ (interesting).
2 She bought _____ (heavy and expensive) frame she could find for his portrait.
3 Martin's work is _____ (good) than Heather's, but Maria's is _____ (good).
4 The documentary about Vincent van Gogh is one of _____ (fascinating) programmes I've ever seen in my life.
5 There isn't a _____ (new) edition of *Jane Eyre* than this one – the others we have are even _____ (old).
6 As far as I'm concerned, Caravaggio is _____ (great) painter who has ever lived.

3 Continue the second sentence so that it is similar in meaning to the first.

1 *Mona Lisa* is much smaller than I imagined.
   Mona Lisa isn't as _____ I imagined.
2 This is the best book about art for children.
   There isn't a _____ about art for children than this one.
3 I've never seen such a dramatic painting as Goya's *The third of May*.
   The third of May is _____ I have ever seen.
4 No twentieth century artist was as famous as Picasso.
   Picasso is _____ artist of the twentieth century.
5 Gauguin worked fast, but Van Gogh worked even faster.
   Gauguin wasn't _____ as Van Gogh.

Functions

4 Mandy and Julia are staying in Liverpool. Expand the prompts to create their conversation.

J = Julia, M = Mandy

J (1) What / you feel like / do this afternoon?
M (2) Well I not / have / plans. What / you suggest?
J (3) Well, you / like / go / the Walker Gallery?
M (4) To tell you / truth, I / be / not / keen on / stay inside / on such / lovely day.
    (5) I prefer / walk around / to / visit museums.
J (6) So what / you rather do? you / got / suggestion?
M (7) I think I / rather explore / city, or / go / Beatle's bus tour.
J (8) I / not mind / do / that, but let's do something!

Now I can ...
☐ express likes and preferences.
☐ talk about art.
☐ write a thank-you letter.
☐ use comparative and superlative adjectives.
☐ talk about ability in the past.

Review 〉 Unit 8

Vocabulary

1 Join the beginnings of sentences 1–6 with endings a–f.

1 The nurse gave her an *injection* …

2 I'm putting your *ankle* in *plaster*, …

3 They took an *X-ray* of his *wrist* …

4 The doctor checked her *symptoms*…

5 As part of your *check-up* …

6 I can see you've *twisted* …

a … but it was only a *sprain*.

b … and *prescribed* a course of *antibiotics*.

c … your knee – it looks very *painful*.

d … we're going to give you a *blood test*.

e … to help her sleep.

f … and you're going to be on *crutches* for a month.

2 Match the completed sentences to the pictures.

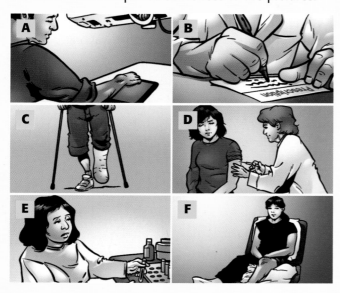

Grammar

3 Complete the sentences using the zero or first conditional.

1 I _____ (**lend**) you my tennis raquet if you _____ (**help**) me with my maths.

2 If she _____ (**go to bed**) late she always _____ (**feel**) tired the next morning.

3 People _____ (**have to**) train hard if they _____ (**want**) to get into the team.

4 If you _____ (**not do**) your homework, you _____ (**not be able to**) watch the match.

5 We _____ (**wait**) here until the rest of the team _____ (**arrive**)

4 Rephrase these sentences using *unless.*

1 If it doesn't rain we'll play tennis.

2 You'll hurt yourself if you don't warm up.

3 Dan won't come if Karl isn't there.

4 They'll never win if they don't create a better team spirit.

Functions

5 A patient is having an appointment with her doctor. Put their conversation in the correct order.

D = Doctor, P = Patient

a ☐ D Yes, make sure you drink a lot of liquids, black or herbal tea is good.

b ☐ P Well, I ate a lot of seafood while I was away. I really love it.

c ☐ D Please, come in and sit down. So what seems to be the trouble?

d ☐ P About four days ago, after I came back from holiday.

e ☐ P Thank you, doctor. I hope that won't be necessary.

f ☐ D You have probably caught a stomach bug. Did you eat or drink anything unusual?

g ☐ P I'll take it to the chemist. Is there anything else I ought to do?

h ☐ D If it's not better in three days come and see me again.

i ☐ P Well, I've got a terrible stomach ache and I keep being sick.

j ☐ D Well, it doesn't like you very much! Anyway, here's a prescription for something that will stop the problem.

k ☐ P What should I do if it doesn't get better?

l ☐ D Oh dear. When did it begin?

Now I can …

☐ give advice.
☐ talk about medical problems.
☐ write a note.
☐ use the zero and first conditionals.
☐ use *unless.*

Shops and shopping

9

In this unit you will learn

- **Communication:** making a purchase, making a complaint
- **Vocabulary:** shopping, advertising
- **Reading and Listening:** attitudes to shopping, *Charlie and the Chocolate Factory*
- **Writing:** a letter of complaint
- **Grammar:** second conditional, *too* and *enough* with adjectives

Let's get started

1 Describe the picture and answer the questions.

1 What things can you buy at a place like this? Can you buy them at a good price?

2 Where do you like to do your shopping? Why?

Vocabulary

2 Match the words in the box to the definitions.

market ☐   supermarket ☐   mail order ☐
shopping centre ☐   chain store ☐
boutique ☐   corner shop ☐
department store ☐   online shopping ☐

1 a large shop with separate sections on several floors

2 a shop with branches in different parts of the country

3 a street or square where traders sell fruit and vegetables and other goods

4 a large self-service shop that sells food, drink, goods used in the home, etc.

5 a way of buying goods where you order from a catalogue and they are sent through the post

6 a way of buying goods where you order over the Internet and they are delivered by courier

7 a small shop where you can buy exclusive fashions

8 a small shop close to home where you can buy food and groceries, often family-run and open until late.

9 a large covered shopping area

3 What kind of shops do you have near your home?

Shopping choices

Listening

1 Do you think carefully before you buy something?

2 What is your favourite kinds of shop?

3 What are your favourite brands for …

- clothes?
- sportswear?
- perfume?
- music players?
- computers / game consoles?
- mobile phones?

4 2.13 **Candice Bryant** is carrying out some market research among teenagers. Listen to the interviews and complete the table.

	Who they go shopping with	Types of shop they go to	How they pay	How they would spend €500
Gemma				
Steve				
Sally				
Me				

Grammar: second conditional

5 Study Candice's question and Steve's answer.

1 Identify the tenses in **bold**.

2 Are they discussing …

☐ something that happened in the past?

☐ an imaginary or unlikely situation in the future or present?

Candice   *If someone **gave** you five hundred euros, how **would** you **spend** it?*

Steve   *If I **had** a lot of money, I **would buy** one of the latest game consoles.*

3 Complete the rule.

The second conditional

If + subject + _____ simple,   subject + _____ / *could* + base form
CONDITION   CONSEQUENCE

See Grammar Reference, page 155

6 Work in pairs. Find out how your partner would spend a surprise €500.

7 First or second conditional? The conditional we choose depends on how likely (= possible) we think the result is. Study sentences a and b. Which one is more optimistic? Which is more pessimistic?

a *If you work hard, you'll pass your exams.*
  (= I think that you are ready to work hard).

b *If you worked hard, you'd pass your exam.*
  (= but I don't think you want to work hard).

8 Complete the sentences using either the first or the second conditional. Study the note first.

> ### If I were …
>
> When we use the verb *be* with *I* in the second conditional, it is considered more correct to use *If I **were** …* instead of *If I **was** …*
>
> Examples:
> ***If I were** a rich man, I'd never work again.*
> ***If I were** you, I'd put the money in the bank.*

1 If I _____ (**have**) a lot of money,
   I _____ (**buy**) a car.

2 If we _____ (**book**) our tickets now, we
   _____ (**spend**) less. So let's book them.

3 What _____ (**you say**) if I _____
   (**ask**) to borrow your camera?

4 I know you want to go by train, but we
   _____ (**save**) a lot if we _____
   (**take**) the bus.

5 If you _____ (**not spend**) so much money
   on clothes, you _____ (**can go**) on holiday.

6 If I _____ (**be**) you, I _____
   (**not get**) a credit card.

Speaking

9 Think about your favourite shop. Think of five ways in which you would improve it if you were the manager. Consider things such as …

- location
- opening times
- staff
- service
- goods
- prices
- sales and special offers
- advertising

10 Work in pairs or groups. Imagine you had the opportunity to open a shop.

- What would you sell?
- What would you call it?
- Where would it be (e.g. in the city centre / in a large shopping centre)?
- What would it look like?
- How would you encourage people to come to your shop?

11 Present your decisions to the rest of the class.

9B Down with shopping

Reading

1 Read about 'Buy Nothing Day' and discuss the questions.

Once a year people in some countries join in 'Buy Nothing Day'. On Buy Nothing Day people decide not to buy anything to protest against the consumer society.

1 Do you think Buy Nothing Day is a good idea?

2 What would happen if every day became Buy Nothing Day?

Spotlight

on reading skills: titles and first sentences

- Before you read an article, take a moment to think about its title as this will give you an idea of what the article is about.

- Always read the first sentence of a paragraph carefully as it often summarises the whole paragraph.

2 Read the title of the newspaper article. What do you think it will be about?

3 Read the article 'To buy or not to buy?' Match sentences A–F with paragraphs 1–5. There is one extra sentence.

A Businesses would rapidly close down.

B In many parts of the world, people don't have enough food, and are too poor to own basic items such as a refrigerator or a washing machine.

C Shoppers want value for money.

D This constant pressure to spend and consume has gone too far.

E The people who would be most affected would probably be the poor, or those in less rich countries.

F Is there an alternative to the consumer society?

4 Discuss the questions.

1 How do you think the author feels about Buy Nothing Day?

2 How well do you think Buy Nothing Day would work in your country?

To buy or not to buy?

1 ☐ Yet in the richer countries people throw away appliances that can be repaired, and change cars or computers just to have a more up-to-date model. Everywhere we go, advertisements create the desire for things that we don't really need, and encourage us to consume.

2 ☐ So we can understand why some people in the rich world show their disapproval of this consumerism by deciding not to buy anything for a day. But what would happen if we took this idea to its logical conclusion and everyone gave up buying things, not just for a day, but for months, or even a year? At first it may appear an attractive course of action, but if we think more closely, the consequences could be terrible.

3 ☐ First of all the shops would close, followed by the factories that supplied them. The people who worked in them would lose their jobs. All the service industries that depend on people

having money to spend would disappear, too – thousands of restaurant workers and hairdressers would find themselvesunemployed. Customers could stop worrying about having the latest fashion or household appliance, because we would end up with nothing to buy.

4 ☐ They are the ones who make and supply most of the everyday consumer goods. Soon, their citizens wouldn't be able to afford to buy food or other basic necessities. By not buying anything we would make them even poorer.

5 ☐ Perhaps the best thing is to shop more wisely – that way we can help the poorest among the global population. But it is essential that we carry on shopping and consuming. In fact, it's the only thing that keeps the world's economy going. So go out and spend. Take up a sport that needs lots of equipment. Buy that dishwasher and throw away anything more than three years old. If we do these things, we'll keep each other in work.

Vocabulary

5 Join the phrases together to make five sentences.

1 We got lost and **ended** ⋯ **up** yoga – then ⋯ that went into a forest.
2 You should **take** ⋯ **away** that old shirt – ⋯ and stop talking.
3 Carry ⋯ **up** on a small road ⋯ you'd feel less stressed.
4 Please don't **throw** ⋯ **on** with your work ⋯ it's my favourite.

6 Which of the phrasal verbs in **bold** means ...

1 to continue? _____
2 to begin a new activity? _____
3 to finally be in a place or situation that you did not plan to be in? _____
4 to put something you no longer need in the rubbish bin? _____

Pronunciation

7 2.14 Notice how these phrasal verbs 'link up'.

Example: take up → /ˌteɪˈkʌp/

Listen and repeat the list. Then read the sentences from Exercise 5, making sure that you link up the phrasal verbs.

Listening

8 Fiona Spicer is talking about Fairtrade and how to be a better shopper. Before you listen, compare what you know about Fairtrade with a partner.

9 2.15 Listen to Fiona's talk and number the topics in the order she talks about them.

a ☐ better than charity
b ☐ feeding the family
c ☐ more profit for growers
d ☐ health and education
e ☐ farmers
f ☐ big brands and supermarkets

Look for this Mark on Fairtrade products www.fairtrade.org.uk

10 2.15 Listen to the talk again and put a tick (✓) in the correct box.

1 Fiona thinks that value for money is the most important thing.
True ☐ False ☐
2 Cotton and coffee growers don't receive a fair price.
True ☐ False ☐
3 The families of cotton and coffee farmers are often hungry.
True ☐ False ☐
4 Fairtrade can help farmer organisations process the coffee they grow.
True ☐ False ☐
5 Fairtrade improves the lives of farming communities.
True ☐ False ☐

Grammar: *too, enough*

11 In sentences a–c, which word in *italics* comes
- before a noun?
- before an adjective?
- after an adjective?

What form of verb do we use after the words in **bold**?

a He will often be *too* **poor** to buy the basic necessities of life.
b He may not earn *enough* **money** to educate his children.
c Farming communities become **rich** *enough* to build schools.

See Grammar Reference, page 155

12 Rearrange the words to form sentences.

1 the / was / too / question / answer / to / difficult
2 coat / enough / had / I / money / buy / if / I / would / a / new
3 he / not / old / was / to / enough / drive
4 not / buy / could / I / it / too / because / it / expensive / was
5 a / enough / rich / if / were / they / school / they / build / could / new

13 Use *too* and *enough* to talk about some difficult experiences you have had involving shopping / sport / emotions / travel.

9C Shopping around

Listening and speaking

1 Study sentences 1–6 and make pairs of opposites with the words in *italics*.

1 I'm going to *take off* my tie – it feels so uncomfortable.
2 You'd better *put on* a coat – it's cold outside.
3 My jeans are so *tight* that I can't close the zip.
4 If you wash that pullover in hot water, it'll *shrink*.
5 These trousers are far too *loose* since I lost weight.
6 Don't sit with your knees under your sweater – you'll *stretch* it.

2 2.16 Adriana is looking for some new trousers. Listen to her conversation with a shop assistant.

1 What is the first problem with the trousers?
2 What does the shop assistant say?
3 What is the second problem?
4 What does Adriana ask?
5 What does the shop assistant offer to do?

3 2.16 Listen again and fill in the missing words.
S = Shop assistant, A = Adriana

S Hi. (1) _____ some help?

A Yes, please, I'd like to (2) _____ these trousers.

S Certainly. The (3) _____ is at the end. You (4) _____ great. They really suit you.

A Do you think so? They're not (5) _____ round the middle and they (6) _____ look fat. Have you got (7) _____ up?

S (8) _____ these are our last pair, but I'm sure that they'll stretch when you wear them.

A They're also (9) _____ in the leg.

S Well, we can shorten them for a small extra charge.

A If I (10) _____ would you (11) _____ for free?

S (12) _____ talk to the manager. (13) _____ what I can do.

USEFUL EXPRESSIONS

Welcoming a customer
Can I help you?
Do you need / Would you like some help?

Asking about size
Do you know your size?
What size do you take / are you?

Asking about and commenting on clothes
How does that feel?
You look great. They suit you.
It's too large / loose / tight / long.
They're not big / long enough.
They make me look fat.
They don't fit. / They fit very well.

Making a decision
I'll take them.
I'll leave it, thanks.
I need to think about it.

4 Work in pairs. Student A – you are the shop assistant. Student B – you need some smart shoes for work. They can be either black or brown.

Student A

Welcome the customer.

Ask the customer's size.

Show the customer the shoes and ask if he/she would like to try them.

Reassure the customer and ask for a decision.

Offer 20 per cent discount for both pairs.

Student B

Explain what you want.

Respond.

Try them on and say why you're not sure about the look.

Say you can't decide between colours.

Make a decision.

Writing: a letter of complaint

5 Have you ever complained in a shop, or returned an item to the shop where you bought it? What happened?

6 Read Adriana's letter to the Head Office of Topmark. What was her reason for writing?

introducing the complaint →

background to the complaint →

what happened to the thing you bought →

what happened when you took it back →

how you feel →

the action you would like →

closing comments →

Dear Sir or Madam,

I am writing to complain about the treatment I received in your Rickwood branch two weeks ago.

I tried on a pair of trousers I liked but found that they were too tight. Your sales assistant assured me they would stretch, so I purchased them. When I washed them, they shrank and the zip broke.

I returned to the shop and asked for a refund. The manager told me you never give refunds on damaged goods. The trousers were expensive, so you will appreciate that I was extremely disappointed with this reply.

Under the circumstances, I think you should refund in full what I paid for the trousers. Furthermore, it is important to train everyone to give your customers honest professional advice. Please find enclosed the trousers and the receipt.

I look forward to a positive response to this letter.

Yours faithfully,

Adriana Williams (Ms)

7 Imagine that Adriana is writing an email to a friend telling her what happened in the shop. What would she write?

USEFUL EXPRESSIONS

Complaining

I am writing about / to complain about …
As you can imagine, … / You will appreciate that …

Diplomatic language

I was angry. → *I was not at all happy.*
I was angry and fed up. → *I was extremely displeased and disappointed.*

8 Read the reply from Topmark. Do you think Adriana is satisfied? Why?

Dear Ms Williams,

Following your letter, I have discussed the matter with the manager of the Rickwood branch.

In our view, she acted correctly, as we never give refunds on items that have been altered or damaged. We are therefore unable to agree to your demand for a full refund.

However, we can understand that you are dissatisfied with the advice that you received. I hope you will accept the enclosed £20 voucher. You can spend it in any of our stores. We hope that you find this satisfactory and that you continue to shop at Topmark.

Yours sincerely,

Cheryl Jackson

Cheryl Jackson, Customer Services Manager

acknowledgement of letter

investigation

recognition of client's point of view

compromise solution

closing comments

9 Find more examples of more formal vocabulary and expressions in the two letters.

10 Study the situations. One half of the class write a letter of complaint based on situation A and the other half write a letter based on situation B. Then exchange letters with a partner from the other group and write your reply.

Situation A

During a sale you bought a pair of shoes. You only tried on one of the shoes in the shop. When you got home you tried on the other one. Unfortunately, it feels much bigger than the shoe you tried on in the shop, and you think that the wrong size is marked on the shoe. When you took it back to the shop, the shop assistant said they could not exchange items bought in the sale.

Situation B

You bought a hairdryer. The first time you used it, it got very hot and smoke started coming out. When you unplugged it, you got an electric shock. Fortunately you are OK, but you think that the hairdryer was dangerous. You want a full refund.

Reading and listening

1 Read the short biography of Roald Dahl on page 101 and explain his unusual name. Why is he famous?

2 2.17 One of Dahl's most famous books is *Charlie and the Chocolate Factory*. Listen to the summary and complete the notes.

Charlie Bucket is the (1) _____ of the story. He lives in a small house with his parents and his (2) _____ very old (3) _____. Their town is famous for its (4) _____, which is owned by Mr Willy Wonka. Charlie's family is so (5) _____ that they can only eat (6) _____ and margarine, and cabbage and (7) _____. Each year on his birthday, Charlie has a (8) _____ bar of Wonka's (9) _____. One day there is an announcement that causes a (10) _____. Inside five of the wrappers of Wonka's chocolate there are five (11) _____. The lucky winners will have a (12) _____ of the factory and chocolate for the (13) _____ of their (14) _____! The first ticket winner is Augustus Gloop, a very (15) _____ and greedy boy. The second winner is Veruca Salt, who is (16) _____ and spoilt. The third winner, Violet de Beauregard, (17) _____ all the time, and the fourth ticket is won by Mike Teavee, who is obsessed by (18) _____.

Reading

3 In the extract on page 101, Charlie has some exciting news for his family. Read the extract and answer the questions.

1 What was Charlie's family doing when he got home?
2 How did Charlie get the money to buy the chocolate bars?
3 Where was the golden ticket?
4 What was the reaction of the people in the shop?
5 How did Charlie's family first react to his news?

4 What stages did Grandpa Joe go through from hearing Charlie's news to celebrating his good luck?

Vocabulary

5 Placing golden tickets inside chocolate bars is a form of marketing. Read the text below and match the **bold** words to definitions 1–10.

When companies want to **promote** a new product, they have to organise a **marketing campaign** to go with it. You need to choose a good name for your product and a short, memorable **slogan**. You can even ask a composer to write a **jingle** that will stick in people's minds. Then you can put posters on the underground or on huge **billboards**. You can hire somebody to give out **flyers** on the street.

A TV **commercial** is an effective, but expensive way of reaching a mass audience, or you can **sponsor** a sporting event. A clear **logo** can help to create your **brand image**.

1 a symbol that represents a company
2 to advertise a product
3 to support an event by providing money and help
4 a short, memorable saying that describes a product
5 an advertisement on television
6 all the different activities businesses use to encourage people to buy a product
7 a very big noticeboard where you stick posters
8 a short song or piece of music that goes with the product or business
9 the feelings and picture in people's minds when they think about a company
10 a sheet of paper with the information about a business or product

Speaking

20 per cent extra free!!

A **superhero** in every packet

BUY ONE GET ONE FREE

Three people travel for the price of two

Buy now and **pay nothing** for **SIX MONTHS**

Money off the next time you buy with **this packet**

6 Do you think these promotions are a good idea
• for companies?   • for customers?
Is it fair to encourage people to consume more than they really need?

7 Look again at page 95, Exercise 10. Working with the same partner, think about an advertisement, slogan and logo for your shop. Plan your marketing campaign.

Roald Dahl

(1916–1990) is one of the most popular authors of books for young people. He was born in Wales, but his parents were Norwegian. He was an airman in the Second World War and was badly wounded. Afterwards he became a writer. He is famous for his short stories for adults and his stories for younger readers such as *James and the Giant Peach*, *Charlie and the Chocolate Factory*, *The BFG* (Big Friendly Giant) and *Matilda*. All of these stories have been made into films.

Roald Dahl

The Golden Ticket

Charlie burst through the front door shouting 'Mother! Mother! Mother!' Mrs Bucket was in the old grandparents' room, serving them their evening soup. 'Mother!' yelled Charlie, rushing in on them like a hurricane. 'Look! I've got it! Look, Mother, look! The last Golden Ticket! It's mine. I found some money in the street and I bought two bars of chocolate and the second one had the Golden Ticket and there were crowds of people all around me wanting to see it and the shopkeeper rescued me and I ran all the way home and here I am! IT'S THE FIFTH GOLDEN TICKET, MOTHER, AND I'VE FOUND IT!'

Mrs Bucket simply stood and stared, while the four old grandparents, who were sitting up in bed balancing large bowls of soup on their laps, all dropped their spoons with a clatter and froze against their pillows.

For about ten seconds there was absolute silence in the room. Nobody dared to speak or move. It was a magic moment.

Then, very softly, Grandpa Joe said, 'You're pulling our legs, Charlie, aren't you? You're having a little joke?' 'I am *not*!' cried Charlie, rushing up to the bed and holding out the large and beautiful Golden Ticket for him to see. Grandpa Joe leaned forward and took a close look, his nose almost touching the ticket. The others watched him, waiting for the verdict.

Then very slowly, with a slow and marvellous grin spreading all over his face, Grandpa Joe lifted his head and looked straight at Charlie. The colour was rushing to his cheeks, and his eyes were wide open, shining with joy, and in the centre, in the black pupil, a little spark of wild excitement was slowly dancing. Then the old man took a deep breath, and suddenly, with no warning whatsoever, an explosion seemed to take place inside him. He threw up his arms and yelled 'Yippeeeeeeee!'

And at the same time, his long bony body rose up out of the bed and his bowl of soup went flying into the face of Grandma Josephine, and in one fantastic leap, this old fellow of ninety-six and a half, who hadn't been out of bed these last twenty years, jumped on to the floor and started doing a dance of victory in his pyjamas.

'He threw up his arms and yelled 'Yippeeeeeeee!'

Making a purchase

Listening and speaking

1 Describe the picture and answer the questions.

  1 Why do you think the man in the picture is smiling?

  2 How good are you at negotiating? Why do you think so?

2 2.18 Vanessa wants to buy a new laptop computer. Listen and answer the questions.

  1 Does she get a discount?

  2 What deal does she make with the salesman?

3 2.18 Listen again and fill the gaps.

  S = Salesman, V = Vanessa

S Hello. Can I help you?

V Yes, I'm interested in this Contrix laptop. But is €499 (1) _____?

S Well, it's the latest model so I can't (2) _____, but I (3) _____ you an extra battery worth €60. How (4) _____?

V Mm … is (5) _____ you can do?

S I'm afraid so. But (6) _____ cash I (7) _____ you an extra year's guarantee.

V OK, that sounds fair enough, (8) _____ right away with the cash.

4 An elderly person doesn't know how to operate a cash machine. He is asking Dave for help. Put their conversation in the correct order.

  D = Dave, E = Elderly man

  a ☐ **D** That's right. And you select how much cash you want. Well done. Now take your card out and finally take your money. Don't forget your receipt!

  b ☐ **D** You're welcome.

  c ☐ **E** Excuse me, but I'm not sure how to operate this machine. Could you help me?

  d ☐ **E** Like this?

  e ☐ **E** Thanks very much!

  f ☐ **D** No problem. Well, first of all put your card into the machine. Now you type in your PIN number – I promise I won't look – and press 'Enter'. Good, now choose what you want to do by pushing one of these buttons.

5 2.19 Listen and check your answers. Note down any expressions you think are useful. List the words and expressions that Dave uses to order his instructions.

6 Work in pairs. Student A, turn to page 145. Student B, turn to page 147.

Food

In this unit you will learn

- **Communication:** talking about food, recipes and menus, at a restaurant
- **Vocabulary:** food
- **Reading and Listening:** regional dishes, Burns' Night
- **Writing:** a recipe
- **Grammar:** present perfect with *for* and *since*, causative *have*

Let's get started

1 Describe the pictures and answer the questions.

  1 How are the two situations in the pictures different?

  2 What do you feel about eating in these ways? Why?

Vocabulary

2 Read about the Slow Food movement. Do you think it's a good idea?

Since its beginnings in Paris in 1989, more and more people have joined the Slow Food **movement**. The organisation's **principles** have been based upon the idea of **encouraging** people to eat food which has been produced in environmentally and socially **responsible** ways, which tastes good, and which protects **traditional** ways of cooking and eating. The movement is also keen to **promote** food for which **customers** have paid a fair price, and for which producers have worked under **fair** conditions and have received a fair price. A worldwide **network** has been set up, and there are now more than 100,000 **members** in 153 countries. This network consists of small groups of consumers and producers who meet, discuss food, organise food-related **events** and develop local projects to encourage a healthy and responsible attitude to food, which respects the **environment** and local traditions.

3 Match the words in **bold** to the definitions.

  1 helping and attracting

  2 people who buy things

  3 the way things have always been done

  4 an organisation for change

  5 advertise and support

  6 a connected group

  7 nature and everything in it

  8 reasonable

  9 the basic ideas behind something

  10 answerable and accepting an obligation

  11 people who belong to a group

  12 public exhibitions or conferences

Reading

1 Look at the cover of the book and answer the questions.

   1 What kind of book is it?
   2 Who is it by?
   3 Who is the book for?

2 Is this the kind of book you would like as a present? Why?

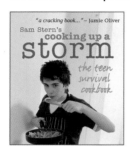

3 Before you read about Sam Stern, the teenage chef, discuss what the following are:

   • fast food.
   • takeaways.
   • ready meals.

Teenage chef Sam Stern has cooked for more than 14 years and doesn't get scared easily in the kitchen

He has just finished off mixing the ingredients for his sister Polly's wedding cake. 'It will be a nightmare to decorate,' he says. Sam is the youngest of five children. He has been a keen cook since the age of four. His mother helped him write his first book, *Cooking up a Storm*. She thought it would sell about ten copies. In fact people all over the world have bought more than half a million copies since it appeared. When the book came out, Sam received offers from TV companies to make his own series. He turned them down because he wanted to concentrate on his schoolwork, playing football and cooking. His latest book is based around his friends' favourite ingredients of pasta, cheese, tomatoes and chocolate. His mother is shocked that so many people appear to live off ready meals and takeaways. Sam wants to improve the eating habits of schoolchildren. He has come up with recipes so that families can eat more healthily. The idea is to encourage families to have a meal they have cooked together at least once a week.

4 Read the article and answer the questions.

   1 When did Sam start cooking?
   2 Who helped Sam with *Cooking up a Storm*?
   3 Why was Sam's mum surprised?
   4 Why hasn't he had his own TV series?
   5 What other hobbies does Sam have?
   6 What project is he currently working on?
   7 What does Sam's mum find shocking?
   8 What is the aim of Sam's latest book?

Speaking

5 In groups or as a class, discuss these questions.

   1 Was Sam right to turn down offers from TV companies?
   2 How important do you think it is for teenagers to learn how to cook?
   3 Who make better cooks – boys or girls?
   4 Who is responsible for preparing meals in your family?
   5 How important is it for families to eat together?
   6 How much do you depend on ready meals and takeaways?

Grammar: present perfect with *for* and *since*.

6 Study the sentences and answer the questions.

   *He has cooked **for** more than 14 years.*
   *Sam has been a keen cook **since** the age of four.*

   1 When did Sam start to be interested in cooking?
   2 Does he still cook now?
   3 Which preposition (*for* or *since*) goes with a period of time, and which one a specific date?

7 Complete the 'time line' by writing *for* or *since* in boxes 1 and 2.

the past		now
14 years ago	cooking	still cooking

[1 _____] 14 years.
[2 _____] the age of four.

8 Study the question and answer forms, then answer questions 1 and 2.

> **Present perfect questions**
>
> Has he been a cook for a long time?
> Yes, he has.
> How long has he been a cook?
> Since the age of four. / For more than 14 years.

1 How do we make the *yes / no* question? What is the short answer?

2 Which question words ask about duration?

9 🔊 2.20 **Listen to sentences a and b and answer the questions.**

a *Sam has been a keen cook since the age of four.*

b *He has cooked for more than 14 years.*

1 Where are the contractions?

2 How do the 'weak' forms of *for* and *been* sound?

10 🔊 2.21 **Imagine that you are interviewing Sam. Listen and repeat the question.**

How long have you been a keen cook?

11 Complete the interview with the present perfect and the past simple.

Y = You, S = Sam

Y How long (1) _____ (be) a cook, Sam?

S Well, I (2) _____ (cook) for more than 14 years. I (3) _____ (start) when I was four years old.

Y That's great! (4) _____ (you write) your book on your own?

S No, I didn't. My mum (5) _____ (help) me.

Y How many copies (6) _____ (sell) since it was published?

S I think sales (7) _____ (reach) half a million so far.

Y Wow! What an amazing achievement.

12 Make questions from prompts 1–3. Invent two other questions of your own.

1 How long / you live / this town?

2 How long / you know your best friend?

3 How long / you play your favourite sport?

4 _____

5 _____

13 Work in pairs and ask and answer the questions in Exercise 12. Where you can, create conversations by asking follow-up questions.

Examples:

How long have you lived in this town?
Do you like it here?
Would you like to live somewhere else?

Reading

1 Read the text 'Protecting the name' and answer the questions.

   1 Identify these products and their country of origin.

   2 What is PDO recognition?

   3 Which two countries have registered the most products?

2 Read the text again and put a tick (✓) in the correct box.

   1 Food is an important part of European heritage.
      True ☐   False ☐

   2 The idea behind PDO wasn't very original.
      True ☐   False ☐

   3 Americans can still call cheese made in the US 'camembert'.
      True ☐   False ☐

   4 Feta is only eaten raw.
      True ☐   False ☐

   5 The Danes used to make a cheese called Apetina®.
      True ☐   False ☐

   6 Producers within a country can object to PDO status, too.
      True ☐   False ☐

   7 All Cornish pasty makers want PDO recognition.
      True ☐   False ☐

   8 The PDO system covers all EU countries.
      True ☐   False ☐

Protecting the name

Heritage isn't just about the places, culture and traditions of a country – it's also to do with what we eat and drink. In 1993 the EU set up the PDO system that gives particular places the exclusive right to give their name to a product. PDO stands for Product of Designated Origin. The principle behind the PDO system was borrowed from France's way of classifying wines from different regions. In practice this means that you can only call a cheese 'camembert de Normandie' if it is from there. This restriction does not apply to non-EU countries, so you can find American brie and camembert cheeses.

People who produce imitations often object when original products win recognition. For instance the Greek cheese *feta*, made from sheep's milk, is a central part of Greek salads and an essential ingredient of the delicious spinach and feta pie called *spanakopita*. Yet for many years Denmark had produced its own version of feta made from cow's milk. In 2005, Greece finally won the fight to keep the name for their own cheese. The Danish have since changed the name of theirs to *Apetina®*.

PDO status can cause problems within countries, too. The EU has just awarded membership of this exclusive club to the Cornish pasty. Producers from the English county of Cornwall had the pasty declared a PDO. There has been a feud between Cornwall and its neighbouring county Devon over the origin of this English delicacy for years. The pasty is made from a mixture of beef and vegetables wrapped in pastry and baked in the oven. Historians from both counties have been battling it out to discover the origins of the oldest written recipes in order to settle the argument. However the EU ruling has now banned any pasty made outside Cornwall from claiming to be 'Cornish'.

It may come as no surprise to learn that Italy and France have more products on the PDO list than any other country – France has registered 42 cheeses. PDO status doesn't just cover dairy products. One of Spain's greatest delicacies is its *turrón* – a sweet made from almonds, honey and egg whites. Turrón from the town of Alicante, and *Castanha de Marvão* – Portuguese chestnuts – are two further products that have won PDO recognition. This shows that, while a Europe of 27 countries is huge, a unique product from a smaller EU member can protect its identity.

A mixture of meat and vegetables inside a pastry case. Original pasties come from Cornwall, in south-west England.

Grammar: causative *have* (*have something done*)

3 Study the sentence and answer the questions.

Producers from the English county of Cornwall had the pasty declared a PDO.

1 Did the producers declare the pasty a PDO?
2 Did someone else declare the pasty a PDO?
3 Who wanted / caused this to happen?

4 Study the structure of the example sentence, then complete the second sentence of 1–3 using causative *have*.

*Producers from the English county of Cornwall **had** the pasty declared a PDO.*

Someone + form of ***have*** + something / someone + past participle

1 A cook made Pamela's wedding cake.
   Pamela had _____.
2 A photographer took the author's picture for the book cover.
   The author had _____.
3 A chef made the Thanksgiving dinner for them.
   They had _____.

Causative *have*

We do not contract ***have / had*** when we use causative ***have***. We use the full form:

They had the pasty declared a PDO.

See Grammar Reference, page 156

Listening

5 Sophie is visiting her cousin Marc in France. Marc is introducing her to *Roquefort* cheese. What do you know about it? Do you like it?

6 ⊙ 2.22 **Listen to their conversation and complete the details.**

Name:
_____

Geographical origin:
_____

Tradition:
_____

Type of milk:
_____

Production method:
_____

7 Work in pairs or groups. Choose another famous product from your country. Make sure it is different from the products chosen by the other groups. Make notes about …

- its name / history.
- its ingredients.
- the manufacturing process.

Project

Look at the map of some British special foods and produce a similar map for your country.

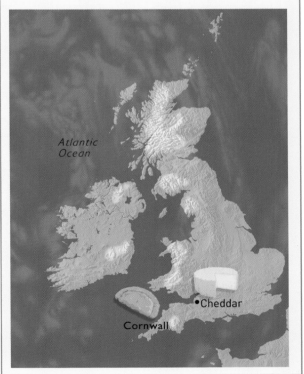

Atlantic Ocean

•Cheddar

Cornwall

10C Exotic tastes

Listening and speaking

1 How often do you eat …

- in the school canteen?
- in a fast-food restaurant?
- traditional 'street food'?
- in an expensive restaurant?

2 Where do you like to eat on a special occasion?

3 2.23 Hazel is backpacking in Vietnam. She is going to have some typical Vietnamese 'street food' with her friend My Hanh. Listen to their conversation and answer the questions.

1 What kind of meat is in the soup *pho*?
2 What can you order *mi xao* noodles with?
3 What is the main ingredient of *cha ca*?
4 What meat is cooked with lemon leaves and ginger?
5 What do My Hanh and Hazel decide to order?

4 2.23 Listen again and complete the conversation.

M = My Hanh, H = Hazel

M Let's stop here.

H Wow, yes. It all _____, and it _____.

M Yeah. I often come here. So what _____ to eat?

H Well, what _____?

M Well, _____ There is *pho*. That's a soup with noodles – it's served with beef or chicken.

H Mm, _____. How is the beef cooked? I don't like it rare.

M Don't worry, it's well done. And there's *mi xao*. _____ crispy noodles _____ meat, seafood and vegetables. You _____ *cha ca*.

H *Cha ca*. _____?

M Well it's made of fish, peanuts, onions and herbs, mixed and fried into a patty shape.

H Mm, you're making _____.

M Or if you want to be adventurous, _____ snail with lemon leaves and ginger.

H Mm, I'm not _____ snails. But there's so much to choose from – I can't _____.

M Well, we're both hungry, so _____ a selection of dishes and share?

H Yeah, that sounds great!

5 Think of the different kinds of street food that you can have in your country. Create a conversation between you and a visitor.

Writing: a recipe

6 Read about Chinese spring rolls below and answer the questions.

1 Why are they called spring rolls?
2 How is Chinese New Year different from New Year on the Gregorian calendar?
3 What did spring rolls traditionally contain?

Spring rolls are a popular Chinese appetiser, but how did they get their name? It's because this tasty and filling snack was originally cooked for the annual Chinese Spring Festival. Traditionally the Spring festival was a holiday which started on the first day of the Chinese New Year (between 21st January and 21st February on the Gregorian calendar) and lasted for 15 days, ending with the Lantern Festival. Spring rolls contained fresh vegetables which were collected at the first harvest of the spring and were a truly vegetarian dish. Later, someone had the idea of adding meat to the vegetables to make them a more substantial meal.

7 You are going to find out how to make spring rolls. Read the list of ingredients. Where could you find them?

Chinese spring rolls

Ingredients

2 cups bean sprouts
2 teaspoons soy sauce
6 dried black mushrooms
½ red bell pepper
salt/pepper to taste
1 medium carrot

18–20 spring roll wrappers
50g tinned bamboo shoots
1 egg, lightly beaten
2 tablespoons oil for stir-frying
5 cups oil for deep-frying

23

Vocabulary

8 Match the different ways of cooking to the definitions.

1 ☐ fry   3 ☐ boil   5 ☐ roast
2 ☐ grill   4 ☐ bake

a to cook in the oven (for bread, cakes, etc.)
b to cook directly over or under a hot flame
c to cook in the oven with a little oil or fat
d to cook in water
e to cook in oil or butter on top of the oven

9 🔊 2.24 We use a lot of action verbs when we cook. Read and listen to the verbs and mime the actions.

a   stir

c   slice

b   chop

d   mix

10 Work in pairs. Take it in turns to mime the action. Your partner has to say what you're doing.

11 Create the recipe by putting sentences a–k in the correct order.

a ☐ Fold the left and right sides of the wrapper over the vegetables, and roll up the wrapper into a cylinder.

b ☐ Heat the stir-frying oil in a frying pan, then add and stir-fry the vegetables.

c ☐ Add the spring rolls and cook them until they are golden brown and crispy (3–4 minutes).

d ☐ 7 First of all, wash and drain the bean sprouts 30 minutes before you start, so they can dry.

e ☐ Add salt/pepper and soy sauce to the vegetables, then remove them from the heat and leave to cool.

f ☐ Then put two tablespoons of the vegetables into the middle of the wrapper in a rectangle shape, but not touching the edges.

g ☐ At the same time put the dried mushrooms into water to soften for around 30 minutes.

h ☐ Heat the oil for deep-frying to 150°C.

i ☐ When you have almost finished rolling, brush the final part of the wrapper with beaten egg before you seal it.

j ☐ Next, chop the bell pepper and carrot finely, and slice the bamboo shoots and mushrooms.

k ☐ To make the rolls, take each spring roll wrapper in turn and brush the edges with the beaten egg.

12 Underline the words and expressions that are used to put the recipe in order.

13 Work in pairs or groups. Select a traditional recipe from your country. Make a list of ingredients, then write the different steps for making the dish.

e   drain

g   add

f   pour

h   sprinkle

Listening and reading

1 🔘 2.25 *Babelphile*, a magazine for language learners, ran a competition for an essay on the topic of food and culture. The winning entry was by Eliana Romano, who spent a year at St Andrews University in Scotland. Listen to the introduction of her essay and complete the notes.

Robert Burns is considered to be Scotland's _____ _____.
He was born on _____ 25th _____. Burns' Night is held on the anniversary of his birthday. He came from a _____ _____ family. He didn't have much formal education and _____ himself. He collected _____ and wrote _____ and _____. His most famous poem is 'Tam O'Shanter', which is about a man who is chased by _____. He supported the _____ revolution. He died a poor man when he was just _____ years old.

2 Read the article about Burns' Night on page 111 and complete the menu, then answer the questions.

Starter
_____
_____

Main course
_____
_____
_____

Dessert
_____
_____

1 What do you think of the menu? Would you like to try everything on it?

2 Is there anything in your country similar to haggis?

3 Put the events of the evening into the correct order.

a ☐ speeches   e ☐ cut open the haggis
b ☐ 'Auld lang syne'   f ☐ dance display
c ☐ bagpiper   g ☐ arrival of the haggis
d ☐ 1 poem about the haggis

4 Read the poem 'In praise of haggis'. How does the writer feel about haggis?

In Praise of Haggis

Haggis is my favourite dish
It satisfies my every wish
My **grandmother's** recipe can't be beaten
Her **haggis** is the best I've eaten
Sheep's meat is the main ingredient
For a perfect culinary experience
Chop and mix it – don't be in haste
The more care you take the better the taste
Add some **spices** to adjust the flavour
For later it'll be the better to savour
Boiled slowly in a pan is how it's best prepared
Make sure there's enough so it can be shared
Neeps and potatoes are the ideal accompaniment
And pay the **haggis** a perfect compliment
For me it beats **French** cuisine
A **more delicious** dish there has never been
Bagpipe music sets the mood
To best enjoy this **sublime** food.
And **Burns' Night** is the ideal time of year
So make sure you keep your diary clear!

5 Read the poem again and answer the questions.

1 When is the best time to eat it?
2 What are the main things in it?
3 How do you cook it?
4 Who makes the best haggis?
5 What should you eat with it?

6 Work in pairs. Choose a food and change the words in **bold** to create your own poem!

Project
You want to produce a magazine article about an event in your country where food plays a part. Work in groups and choose an event to research.

Describe …
- the background to the event / its history
- famous people associated with the event
- food / drink / clothes
- the different stages of the event.

 Watch a video about a cheese-rolling competition. Turn to page 142.

Burns' Night

The Burns' Night celebration I attended was held in the dining room of a farmhouse near the famous golf course at St Andrews. Our hosts the McDougals and their fifteen guests were smartly dressed – some of the men wore kilts and the ladies wore evening dress. Before the meal, Mr and Mrs McDougal's children and nephews and nieces performed some traditional Scottish dances. Then we sat down to eat at the long, beautifully decorated table. To start we had soup made from chicken, leeks and potatoes. Everyone was waiting for the main event – the arrival of the haggis.

Haggis is made from sheep's meat mixed with herbs and spices and various other things that go into it. It is then boiled slowly for a long time.

A friend of the family came in playing the bagpipes, then our host brought in the haggis on a plate. Bryan McFarlane, a teacher, recited Burns' famous poem about the haggis. He said something about it being the 'great chieftain of the puddin' race'. Then, in the middle of one verse, he took a knife and cut open the haggis. The air was filled with its wonderful smell. It was served with mashed potatoes and a yellow vegetable the Scots call 'neeps'. The haggis tasted delicious and was definitely waiting for!

'Piping in' the haggis

Afterwards people read and recited more of the poet's work or gave speeches about what Burns meant to them. The meal ended with *cranachan*, an absolutely heavenly dessert made from oatmeal, honey, cream and raspberries. Finally, at the end of the very long evening everyone stood up, linked arms and sang a song that is known all around the world. Here are just the opening words and the chorus. I am sure that you know how the music goes!

Auld lang syne (The good old days)
Should old acquaintance be forgot
And never brought to mind?
Should old acquaintance be forgot
And auld lang syne?
CHORUS:
For auld lang syne, my dear,
For auld lang syne,
We'll take a cup of kindness yet
For auld lang syne.

'Everyone was waiting for the main event – the arrival of the haggis.'

This is a song about friendship and remembering the past. People all over the English-speaking world hold hands and sing it at midnight on New Year's Eve. It was already a traditional song when Robert Burns wrote the version that most people sing now.

A haggis

Case Study 5 › Our daily bread

STAPLE FOODS

A *staple food* is the term we use to refer to the basic food which a country or community eats most days. Staple foods can be stored for use all year round and are also usually cheap to produce or buy, so they form the basis of a **daily diet** in the poorest of homes, often with recipes for using the same staple at every mealtime, in sweet and **savoury** dishes as well as drinks.

Staple foods have existed since the time of the first people. As farming methods developed, people began to choose foods that they knew would be a reliable source of energy all year round. Of course, a staple food like bread or rice is not enough on its own to make up a **balanced diet**, and people add things like meat and vegetables depending on how **freely available** they are.

One problem with staple foods is that if something goes wrong, poorer people are vulnerable and might **starve**. A drought one year could mean that there is nothing to eat the next year. In Ireland, in the 19th century, around one million people died, and another million **emigrated**, because their staple food – the potato – had been affected by a disease and people had nothing to eat.

Below are some of the main staple foods that people eat around the world.

Cereals

Some people have claimed that rice is the main staple food for over half of the world's population. In Asia, people have eaten it for thousands of years, and it continues to feed some of the world's poorest populations. Today, rice is a popular food all over the world and people also use it to make noodles, sweets and cakes.

Other cereals include wheat, barley, maize (corn) and oats. We can use cereals in soups, as porridge, to make pancakes or crepes, as well as many different kinds of bread. Around the world, people also make many different kinds of pasta (such as spaghetti and macaroni) from cereals.

Potatoes

Potatoes and other root vegetables are popular in many parts of the world because they help you feel full after you have eaten and you can keep them for a long time. They can be boiled, roasted, fried or baked.

Beans

Beans can be stored for a very long time and they can be a meal in themselves. They have more protein than most staples and are most popular in Africa and Latin America, although their use has spread all over the world.

Milk and dairy products

Milk, cheese and yoghurt are used almost everywhere, with some countries producing hundreds of different kinds of cheese. Although milk and yoghurt do not last a long time, cheese does. They are all high in protein and contain other things, such as calcium, which are important for our health.

Types of bread

Many countries use some kind of bread as a staple. Here are a few you might know:

- *Tortilla* – thin, flat bread popular in South America, where they often eat it with different fillings
- *Pitta* – flat bread used throughout southern Europe and the Middle East
- *Naan/Chapati/Paratha* – flat bread which is fried or dry-cooked and served with many meals in India and Pakistan
- *Rye bread* – dark, heavy bread from northern Europe and Scandinavia which has become popular in the USA
- *White/Wholemeal bread* – which is used all over the world in sandwiches and for making toast

And not forgetting … *buns, bagels, croissants, rolls* and, of course, *pizza!*

---

1 In pairs or small groups, discuss the following questions.

How many different kinds of bread can you name?

What kind of food do you eat the most of?

Have you ever travelled to another country? How was the food different?

2 Read the first part of the text and, with a partner, discuss what you understand by the words and phrases in bold.

1 daily diet   3 balanced diet   5 starve

2 savoury   4 freely available 6 emigrated

3 Now read all of the information and answer the questions.

1 What kinds of bread are popular in India? _____

2 Where do people eat the most beans? _____

3 Which foods contain a lot of protein? _____

4 Where do people eat tortilla? _____

5 What do we make spaghetti from? _____

6 Which staple feeds the most people? _____

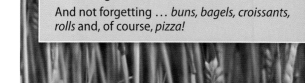

Review > Unit 9

Vocabulary

1 Complete the sentences about different types of shop with words from the box.

> chain store   street market
> department store   corner shop
> online shopping   shopping centre

1   I do a lot of _____ _____. A credit card and a click of the mouse are all you need.

2   If you go to the _____ _____ towards the end of the morning, you can buy some really cheap fruit and vegetables.

3   I'm going to buy some milk from the _____ _____ at the end of the street.

4   I love going to the _____ _____ because all the shops are under one roof.

5   There is a branch of this _____ _____ in every town.

6   It's probably the most famous _____ _____ in the world, where you can buy everything you can imagine.

Grammar

2 Continue the 'logic chain' by writing sentences with the second conditional.

1   If we stop buying things / factories have to stop making them

   Example: *If we stopped buying things, factories would have to stop making them.*

2   If factories stop making goods / shops have nothing to sell

3   If shops have nothing to sell / they have to close down

4   If shops and factories close down / people lose their jobs

5   If people lose jobs / they not able to go to restaurants or have their hair cut

6   If nobody work any more / we not able to buy food and necessities

3 Decide where *too*, *very* and *enough* belong in these sentences.

1   These trousers are much tight.

2   You're not old to wear make-up, Jenny.

3   We were pleased to see you again.

4   Sorry to keep you waiting.

5   Have you had to eat?

6   This skirt is expensive, but I'm going to buy it anyway.

Functions

4 Bridget is in an electrical goods shop. Complete her conversation with the salesman with the words and phrases from the box.

> you bought it   just for today   would be so
> you would be one of   isn't it
> you can unlock it   if you slide your finger
> how much would this cost me
> how does it   download all your favourite
> I'll let you have it   could give you
> that's so cool   far too expensive

S = Salesman, B = Bridget

S   I see you're looking at the brand new Delta phone. It's beautiful, (1) _____?

B   Mm, yes, so (2) _____ work?

S   Well, (3) _____ across the screen (4) _____.

B   Wow, (5) _____! And there are lots of icons!

S   This one's for email, and this one's for the Internet. It's even a camera and music player. You can (6) _____ songs.

B   That's amazing. So (7) _____?

S   Well, it's just €300. But just think! (8) _____ the first to have one. Your friends (9) _____ jealous.

B   But €300! That's (10) _____.

S   But if (11) _____ today, I (12) _____ a €50 discount.

B   That sounds interesting.

S   And if you sign up to our phone operator, (13) _____ for just €99! But this is a special offer, (14) _____.

B   Wow. Let me ask my dad – he's paying!

Now I can ...

- [ ] buy things and make a complaint in a shop.
- [ ] talk about shopping and advertising.
- [ ] write a letter of complaint.
- [ ] use the second conditional.
- [ ] use *too* and *enough* with adjectives.

Vocabulary

1 Choose the right word to complete the sentences.

1 Every evening they eat a three-*course / starter* meal.

2 This is delicious. Can you give me the *receipt / recipe*? I'd love to make it myself.

3 He's our best *chief / chef* – his *cuisine / kitchen* is world-famous.

4 What's your favourite *plate / dish*?

5 My favourite *desert / dessert* is raspberries and meringues with fresh cream.

6 Is your boyfriend a good *cook / cooker*?

7 That was a delicious meal. Could we have the *menu / bill* please?

2 Match the different ways of cooking to the pictures.

boil   roast   bake   grill   fry

Grammar

3 Belinda Ferguson is a travel journalist who writes books about cooking around the world. Complete the interview by changing the verbs into the present perfect or the past simple.

I = Interviewer, B = Belinda

I How (**1**) *long / you be /* a food journalist?

B (**2**) *I / be / one / ten years.* (**3**) *I / start* at university where *I write / articles* for a student magazine.

I (**4**) *How many countries / you visit / since you / start*?

B (**5**) *I / be / more than thirty*, but (**6**) *we / be / in* Adelaide since 2003, which is when my son Ben was born. (**7**) *We all / go /* to Indonesia for a family holiday last year, where (**8**) *we / eat / some* delicious and unusual food.

I (**9**) *How many books / you write*?

B (**10**) Well, *I / write / about six* myself, but (**11**) *I / edit* another dozen or so.

I I see. And what are you doing now?

B Well, recently (**12**) *I / finish /* a guide to the cuisine of South-East Asia. (**13**) It *start /* just with Thailand, but since then (**14**) *it / grow* to include the whole region.

I So tell me, Belinda, (**15**) *what / worst thing / you ever eat*?

B That's difficult to say, (**16**) *I / eat / all sorts of* terrible things in the past ten years. Sometimes it's best not to think too much about the ingredients!

Functions

4 Who says what? Write *W* for waiter or *C* for customer.

1 Are you ready to order? ☐

2 The roast lamb with blackcurrant jelly is very good. ☐

3 And for the main course? ☐

4 If you'd like to follow me, there's a table by the window. ☐

5 Could I have a table for two, please? ☐

6 I think I'll start with the onion soup. ☐

7 What would you like to drink? ☐

8 Could I have the bill, please? ☐

9 Good evening, sir, madam. ☐

10 What would you recommend? ☐

11 Would you like to look at the dessert menu? ☐

12 Just a bottle of sparkling mineral water, please. ☐

5 Put the statements and questions in order as they would happen during the meal.

Now I can ...
☐ talk about food, recipes and menus.
☐ write a recipe.
☐ use the present perfect with *since* and *for*.
☐ use the causative *have*.

English around the world

Let's get started

1 Describe the picture and answer the questions.

1 Why are there so many people in the street?

2 In which country would you like to learn English? Why?

Vocabulary

2 Complete the text about Joseph Conrad with the words in the box. Use your dictionary to help you.

> accent   jargon   bilingual   mother tongue
> native speaker   catch   picked up

England's Polish genius

Joseph Conrad, the famous English writer, was actually a Pole, so his (1) _____ _____ was Polish. In fact English was his third language after Polish and French, was (2) _____! Sailing on English ships in his youth, he (3) _____ _____ a lot of English, including the special (4) _____ spoken by sailors. Conrad's Polish (5) _____ was so strong that it was sometimes difficult to (6) _____ what he was saying. However, when he wrote, no one could tell that he wasn't a (7) _____ _____.

Joseph
Conrad
(1857–1924)

3 🔊 2.26 Listen and check your answers.

4 Tick (✓) the things that you hope to use English for. Compare your list with a partner and ask each other for more details.

- ☐ travelling in English-speaking countries
- ☐ speaking to other non-native speakers
- ☐ working in an international company
- ☐ teaching English
- ☐ reading novels in English
- ☐ living in an English-speaking country
- ☐ listening to songs in English
- ☐ finding information on the Internet

In this unit you will learn

- **Communication:** asking polite questions, describing things
- **Vocabulary:** language
- **Reading and Listening:** EU translators, varieties of English
- **Writing:** presenting information
- **Grammar:** reported speech, question tags

By word of mouth

Slip carefully

SPECIAL TODAY
No ice cream

We take your bags and send them in all directions

• Visitors are expected to complain at the office between the hours of 9 and 11 a.m. daily.

English well talking.

Here speaching American.

Please do not feed the animals. Give food to the zoo keepers.

Reading

1 Look at the signs and notices, and answer the questions?

1 What did each one mean to say?

2 Have you ever had to translate for somebody? How easy was it?

2 Tara is an exchange student from Ireland. She is meeting her exchange friend Sylvie's family for the first time. Look at how Sylvie reports what her grandmother says and work out what the grandmother says in English.

G = Grandmother, S = Sylvie, T = Tara

G *Enchantée. Je te souhaite la bienvenue.*

S My grandmother says she's pleased to meet you and wishes you welcome.

T Thank you very much. I'm pleased to meet her, too.

G *C'est la première fois que tu viens en France?*

S She's asking if this is your first visit to France.

T Tell her it is and that I'm very pleased to be here.

G *Assieds-toi.*

S She's telling us to sit down.

T Thank you very much.

G *Veux-tu du thé ou du café?*

S She's asking if you want tea or coffee.

T Tea, please.

G *Prends une madeleine.*

S She's asking you to take a sponge cake.

T It's delicious.

G *D'où viens-tu en Angleterre?*

S She wants to know which part of England you come from.

T Actually, tell her I don't come from England – I'm from Dublin, in Ireland.

Grammar

3 Complete the table with information from the conversation.

Reported speech

Reporting statements

I am very pleased to meet you. →	She says she (1) _____.

Reporting orders

Please sit down. →	She's telling you (2) _____.
Have a sponge cake. →	She's asking you to (3) _____.

Reporting questions

Note that when we report a question, we do not use the same word order as the question:

How are you? →	She's asking / She wants to know how you are. (**Not** … ~~how are you~~)
Where do you live? →	She's asking / She wants to know where you live. (**Not** … ~~where do you live~~)
Do you want tea or coffee? →	She's asking (4) _____
What part of England do you come from? →	She wants to know (5) _____

See Grammar Reference, page 157

4 Put these sentences using reported speech into the correct order.

1 city / she / a / says / beautiful / is / Oxford
2 if / asks / you / ever / food / she / eaten / Mexican / have
3 is / try / chocolate / you / to / telling / she / a / biscuit
4 she / France / visit / know / to / wants / your / if / this / is / to / first
5 you / is / she / telling / that / Madrid / she / has / in / cousins
6 that / she / hair / you / lovely / have / says / red
7 she / if / any / asks / you / know / expressions / Spanish / words / or
8 know / if / wants / she / to / again / you / come / will / week / next

5 Put the sentences from Exercise 4 into direct speech.

6 Tara is sending an email to her parents in Dublin. Read what she says. What extra information do you find out?

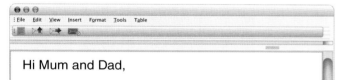

Hi Mum and Dad,

I'm having a great time here. Sylvie has introduced me to some of her family. Yesterday we visited her grandmother. She's a really nice lady – you would like her. She asked lots of questions! She wanted to know if I had been to France before. She asked me if I had ever eaten French food. She told me to try a sponge cake – it was heaven! She said I could take the rest of the box. She wanted to know what part of England I came from, so I told her that I was from Dublin in Ireland. She said she had some cousins who lived in London. She said she had written to them last week. She said she was a big fan of English detective stories. She said she was reading a book by Agatha Christie – she told me she had read all of her detective stories. She asked me if I had read any books by French writers – I had to say I hadn't. Sylvie said she would give me something in translation.

Love,

Tara

7 Use the information to complete the table. What do you notice about the reporting verbs, and the tenses that follow them?

Direct speech	Reported speech
Oxford is a beautiful city. → tense = present simple →	She told me _____ tense =
Which part of England are you from? → tense = present simple →	She wanted _____ tense =
I'm reading a book by Agatha Christie. tense = present continuous →	She said _____ tense =
Have you been to France before? → tense = present perfect →	She wanted to know _____ tense =
I wrote to them last week. → tense = past simple →	She said _____ tense =
You can take the rest of the box. → form = can →	She said _____ form =
I'll give you something in translation. → form = will →	Tara said _____ form =

Speaking

8 Work in pairs or small groups. Ask and answer the questionnaire.

1 Which modern languages do you study?
2 How old were you when you started to study English?
3 When do you use English?
4 Which English-speaking country would you most like to visit? Why?
5 When do you hope to travel abroad?

9 Find a partner from another group and report what your original partner said. Use the expressions below.

I asked which / if …
I wanted to know …
He/She told me (that) …
He/She said (that) …

Reading

1 Describe the picture of Kasia and answer the questions.

    1 What do you think Kasia's job is?

    2 Would you like to do her job? Why? / Why not?

2 Read the text about languages in the European Union and find out what these numbers refer to.

> 23   506   €1 billion   2 per cent   €2

The European Union is the biggest employer of translators in the world. 23 official languages provide an incredible 506 interpreting combinations! This explains how the EU now spends more than €1 billion a year on translation. However, in practice, French and English are probably the two most widely used languages.

Despite the cost, there is pressure to include even more languages. Irish Gaelic is the mother tongue of just 2 per cent of Ireland's 4 million population, yet adds €1 million to the translation bill! By contrast, Basque with over half a million speakers, and Catalan with over six million, only have semi-official status, so their translation costs have to be paid by the Spanish government rather than the EU.

Minority EU languages can cause difficulties: with more unusual language combinations there is often no one who can translate from one into the other, for example from Latvian into Maltese. One solution is 'relay' translation, where a third language, common to both parties, acts as a bridge. While there are sometimes misunderstandings, interpreting can bring benefits. Interpreters tend to make something they translate into their language more diplomatic than the original. Politicians are prepared to compromise when messages are expressed in a more neutral way. So, even though critics talk about the hospitals that could be built with €1 billion, translation costs are just €2 per citizen – which is a small price if it helps to preserve democracy.

3 Read the text again and choose the best answer to questions 1–5. Circle A, B or C.

    1 The EU employs so many translators because …

        A it wants to provide jobs.

        B it wants to promote different languages.

        C it has so many official languages.

    2 What does the writer feel about Irish Gaelic?

        A It is not logical that the EU pays its translation costs.

        B It should only be a semi-official EU language.

        C The Irish government should not pay its translation costs.

    3 'Relay' translation is used …

        A for most minority languages.

        B when there is no common language.

        C when direct translation is not possible.

    4 What is an advantage of using interpreters at the EU?

        A It can encourage agreement.

        B It encourages politicians to speak politely.

        C Meaning becomes clearer.

    5 The writer appears to think the money spent on translation …

        A costs each EU citizen very little.

        B is a terrible waste of money.

        C could be spent on better things.

4 As a class, discuss the questions.

    • Do you think this is a good use of €1 billion?

    • How would you reduce translation costs at the EU?

    • Are there any minority languages in your country? How many people speak them?

Listening

5 2.27 Kasia studied linguistics at university and now works as an interpreter at the European Commission. Listen to part A of the interview and decide if the statements are true or false. Put a tick (✔) in the correct box.

1 Kasia has been in this job for ten years.   True ☐   False ☐

2 She usually works in Brussels.   True ☐   False ☐

3 Interpreters have to have a degree.   True ☐   False ☐

4 Applicants have to take a written examination.   True ☐   False ☐

5 She works with one other colleague.   True ☐   False ☐

6 They take it in turns to interpret.   True ☐   False ☐

7 At the end of the day she is very tired.   True ☐   False ☐

8 Her job is difficult but satisfying.   True ☐   False ☐

9 She translates from Polish into English too.   True ☐   False ☐

10 The translation is instant.   True ☐   False ☐

6 2.28 Kasia talks about a misunderstanding that happened in one of the meetings she attended. Listen to her story in part B of the interview and complete the notes.

> The speaker came from Rottweil in (**1**) _____. He said his town was famous for its (**2**) _____ / _____. Kasia thought that he meant it was a kind of (**3**) _____ competition so this is how she translated it. She found it difficult to imagine because Rottweilers are (**4**) _____ and (**5**) _____. In fact the person wanted to talk about a (**6**) _____ of _____, which is not the same thing!

7 Does this story remind you of any similar misunderstandings?

Grammar: question tags

8 Study these sentences from the interview and answer questions 1 and 2.

a *You're based in Luxembourg, aren't you?*

b *It wasn't easy, was it?*

c *You enjoy it, don't you?*

1 Is the interviewer expecting Kasia to agree or disagree with her?

2 Are they real questions?

9 Complete the rules for making a question tag using the words in the box.

> statement   auxiliary   pronoun
> opposite   order

1 Identify the _____ verb and its subject.

2 Replace the subject with a _____.

3 Change their _____.

4 Change a positive or negative to its _____.

5 Put the tag at the end of the _____.

See Grammar Reference, page 157

Pronunciation: saying question tags

10 2.29 When we expect people to agree with us, or to confirm what we say, our voices fall on the question tag. Listen and repeat sentences a–c from Exercise 8.

11 Complete the sentences with the correct tag.

1 Her English is excellent, _____?

2 She works in Luxembourg, _____?

3 She studied a lot, _____?

4 She doesn't have any colleagues, _____?

5 It's a well-paid job, _____?

6 Misunderstandings sometimes happen, _____?

7 She doesn't think it's a waste of money, _____?

8 It isn't very comfortable in the booth, _____?

12 Make statements about people you know, or your home town. Add a question tag. (Expect people to agree with you!)

Example:

Oxford is a beautiful city, isn't it?

Malta

summer sun holiday brochure

Listening

1 ⊙2.30 **Luis is at a language fair. He is interested in doing an English course in Malta. He is talking to Carmelita from a language school. Listen and tick (✓) the topics that Richard asks about.**

☐ cost
☐ the advantages of Malta
☐ accommodation
☐ length of stay
☐ transport
☐ social programme
☐ specialised English

Grammar: asking polite questions

2 ⊙2.31 **Listen and complete sentences 1–5.**

1 _____ English?
2 _____ one of your brochures?
3 _____ if people speak good English?
4 _____ the social programme _____?
5 _____ where students live during their studies.

3 **Study your completed sentences and answer a–c.**

a How are sentences 1–3 different from 4 and 5?
b Which questions are more direct?
c Which questions are indirect / more polite?

Pronunciation: polite intonation

4 ⊙2.32 **Listen to sentences 1–5 again and identify which words are stressed.**

5 ⊙2.32 **Listen and repeat the sentences, copying the intonation pattern.**

USEFUL EXPRESSIONS

Asking for permission

Is it OK if I ask you some questions?
Can you spare me a couple of minutes?
Could I have one of your brochures?
Excuse me, could I …?

Examples of direct questions

Do you speak English?
What are the advantages of studying in Malta?
What's the social programme like?

Asking indirect / polite questions

Can you tell me if people speak good English?
Can you tell me how old you are?
I'd like to know where students live during their studies.
I'd like to know if you use English more with foreigners or native speakers.

Speaking

6 You are doing some research into why people study English. Imagine that you are using a street questionnaire. Work in pairs and decide how you will ask the questions in a polite way.

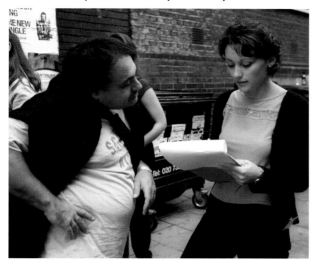

1 Languages spoken:

2 Why are you studying English?

3 Do you speak English or another language outside school?
Yes ☐ No ☐

4 Which accent do you find more difficult to understand?
☐ standard British English
☐ standard American English

5 Is it easier to understand English spoken by …
☐ other foreigners?
☐ native speakers?

7 When you are ready, ask and answer the questions with a partner.

8 Collect the results of the questionnaire for the whole class.

Writing: presenting information

9 Match expressions a–c to the percentages in the box. Some percentages are repeated.

10 per cent   25 per cent   33.3 per cent
50 per cent   66.6 per cent   75 per cent
90 per cent

a a quarter
b a third
c nine out of ten
d half
e one in four
f two out of three
g a tenth
h one in ten
i three-quarters

10 Richard decided to find out more about the different languages that people speak in Malta. Read his report and decide what language each part of the pie chart and the bar chart refers to.

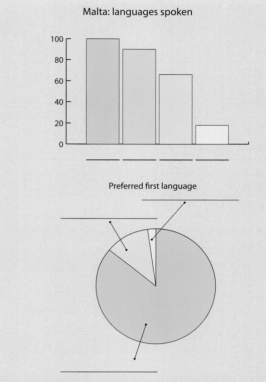

Malta: languages spoken

Preferred first language

I discovered that Malta is a really 'polyglot' society. There are two official languages, Maltese and English. They are used equally in school. Maltese is a fascinating language which reflects the island's history and the peoples that have occupied and ruled it. It uses a kind of Arabic grammar with vocabulary from Italian, French and English. Just over half of the words used are of Latin origin. Everyone speaks Maltese, and English is spoken by nine out of ten people. Nevertheless, Italian is popular, too, and two-thirds of Maltese use it as a second language. Almost a fifth of the population speak French as well, so Malta is the EU country where the most European languages are spoken. Even so, according to a questionnaire, 86 per cent of the Maltese population said that they preferred to use Maltese as their first language, with English coming second at 12 per cent, and Italian in third position with just two per cent.

11 Use the results of your questionnaire from Exercise 7. Write a summary of the results. Use expressions from Exercises 9 and 10.

11D Varieties of English

Listening

1 2.33 Damian Healy is an expert on American English. Listen and complete the tasks.

1 Complete the table with the examples that Damian gives us.

BrE	
AmE	*It's a quarter of ten.*

BrE	*What did you do at the weekend?*
AmE	

BrE	
AmE	*Did you eat?*

2 Match the British English words 1–5 to their American partners a–e.

1 ☐ flat   a cookie
2 ☐ biscuit   b hood
3 ☐ boot   c apartment
4 ☐ lift   d elevator
5 ☐ bonnet   e trunk

2 What other pairs of English and American words do you know?

3 Do you agree with Damian that some people exaggerate the differences between British and American English?

Reading

4 Read the first section of the text on page 123, 'Southern Hemisphere English', and answer the questions.

1 Why do Australians, New Zealanders and South Africans sound so similar?

2 How do Australians make the vocabulary they use sound more informal?

3 What accent did many of the early settlers in Australia have?

4 What is special about Australian intonation?

6 What does the 'fish and chips' and 'bacon and eggs' test help us do?

7 In South Africa, how many people speak English as their mother tongue?

8 How has Afrikaans affected the South African accent?

Spotlight

on reading skills: guessing meanings

Being able to guess the meaning of unknown words is a useful skill that effective readers use all the time. To do this we need to be able to use clues in the passage and have a good overall understanding of the text and the writer's intentions.

Look at the words in **bold** in the text. What do you think they mean?

1 **tell them apart**
   a understand them
   b know which is which
   c describe them

2 **settlers**
   a people who came to live there
   b sounds used in a language
   c informal words

3 **adopted**
   a changed
   b studied
   c started to use

5 Work in pairs. Student A, read about Indian English on page 123. Student B, read about Caribbean English on page 123. Find answers to these questions.

1 Why do people speak English there?

2 How do they feel about English?

3 Are there any important differences between standard English and the English that is spoken there?

4 What mixture of English and other languages exist?

5 Why can they make people upset?

6 When you are ready, exchange information with your partner.

Southern Hemisphere English

Australians, New Zealanders and South Africans sound similar. So how can we **tell them apart**? Australians are known for their informality, which shows itself in their treatment of vocabulary. They shorten words then add *-o* and *-ie* to them, so barbecue becomes *barbie*, sunglasses *sunnies* and afternoon *arvo*.

Australian English also sounds more like Cockney – the London accent – as that is where many of the original **settlers** came from. Another feature of Australian English is rising intonation at the end of statements. This makes them sound like questions. Telling a New Zealand accent from an Australian one is difficult. One way is to use the 'fish and chips' and 'bacon and eggs' test'! Someone with a strong New Zealand accent will say 'fush 'n' chups' and 'bacon and iggs.'

South Africa has eleven official languages, and only one person in ten speaks English as their mother tongue.

'South Africa has eleven official languages'

South Africans who are native speakers of English have **adopted** some of the pronunciation from Afrikaans speakers – descendants of the original Dutch settlers. Strangely, the result is very close to the New Zealand accent!

Indian English

India is a land of many languages, but Hindi and English are used across the country. Whether people speak English as a first, second or even third language depends on their social class. There are two important differences in grammar. Firstly, Indian speakers use the present continuous instead of the present simple; for example, *I am understanding you*. Secondly, the question tag *isn't it?* is used in all situations; for example *She lives in Delhi, isn't it?* rather than *doesn't she?* Of course, some people don't like using English because it reminds them that India is an ex-British colony. Even so, English words are entering Hindi, which has led to the development of 'Hindish', a mixture of Hindi grammar and English words. So *Are you hungry?* in Hindish becomes *Hungry kya?* This upsets Hindi speakers who don't want to see their language 'polluted' by English, and English

'Whether people speak English as a first, second or even third language depends on their social class'

speakers who don't like their language treated in this way.

Caribbean English

People speak English in many parts of the Caribbean because it was colonised by the British, who grew sugar there. Pronunciation is close to standard British English, but American English is having an influence, too.

'Creole is a mixture of two languages which have combined to create a new language'

This is partly because of movies and music, but also because the Caribbean is popular with American holidaymakers. We should also say a few words about Creole here. Creole is a mixture of two languages which have combined to create a new language. Many Jamaicans have ancestors who were slaves from Africa, so Creole developed and is now spoken by large parts of the population. In Jamaican Patois, someone may say *Me did eat* instead of *I ate*, or *Me a go eat* for *I am going to eat*. Some black teenagers in England copy the Jamaican style of speaking even though they grew up in England – this is mockingly called Jafaican ('faic' sounds like *fake* = 'false'). All of this, of course, is guaranteed to make parents and teachers crazy!

Describing things

Listening and speaking

1 Look at the pictures and answer the questions.

1 If a student who didn't speak your language started at your school, what help could the school and other students give him/her?

2 What advice would you give a friend travelling to a country if he/she didn't speak that country's language?

2 ⊙2.34 Natalie is visiting Jim's school on a language exchange. Listen to conversations 1 and 2 and write down the name of the thing Natalie wants in each case.

1 _____

2 _____

3 ⊙2.34 Listen to the conversations again and fill in the missing words.

1

N = Natalie, J = Jim

N Have you got one of **(1)** _____ paper together?

J What, one of these – a paper clip?

N No, it's **(2)** _____ machine. What **(3)** _____ it in English?

J Oh, you **(4)** _____ a stapler.

N A sta …? I didn't **(5)** _____. How **(6)** _____ it?

J S-T-A-P-L-E-R.

N Oh, a sta … **(7)** _____ it?

J Stapler.

2

N Have you got any of **(7)** _____?

J What? Glue?

N No, not glue. **(8)** _____ plastic ribbon. **(9)** _____ 'scotch'.

J Let me think. Oh, you **(10)** _____ sticky tape.

N Sorry, **(11)** _____ that again?

J Sticky tape.

4 <u>Underline</u> the words Natalie uses to describe the items she doesn't know the name for.

5 What expressions do the speakers use to ask for the name and give the name of the objects?

6 Work in pairs. Student A, turn to page 145. Student B, turn to page 147.

People and places

Let's get started

1 Describe the picture and answer the questions.

1 Why are the people in the picture wearing these costumes?

2 Do people in your country celebrate some events by re-enactment? What events? Why?

Vocabulary

2 Read about the English Civil War and answer the questions.

1 What was the result of the English Civil War?

2 What is 'the Sealed Knot' and what does it do?

Between 1641 and 1645, the King and Parliament fought a Civil War in England. The Parliamentarians, known as 'Roundheads' because of their round helmets, eventually defeated the Royalists, or 'Cavaliers', and King Charles I was executed. Nowadays, members of a group called the Sealed Knot **dress up** as Cavaliers and Roundheads to **commemorate** the Civil War in a regular **festival** that lasts several days. This begins with a **parade** through the town where it is held, but the **highlight** is the **re-enactment** of a major battle, which involves thousands of people and can become quite violent!

In this unit you will learn

- **Communication:** guiding and warning
- **Vocabulary:** important people and places
- **Reading and Listening:** famous architecture, Machu Picchu
- **Writing:** an informal email
- **Grammar:** the passive, relative pronouns

3 Match the words in the text in **bold** to definitions 1–6 below.

1 a day when people celebrate a special event _____

2 the most exciting or impressive part of an event _____

3 a performance that recreates an event _____

4 to wear a costume or put on special clothes _____

5 to remember an important event _____

6 an organised walk through the streets to celebrate an event _____

4 What are the most important events in your country or region? How do you celebrate them?

'Roundheads' from the Sealed Knot prepare for battle

Reading

1 Look at the statue of a black woman sitting on a bus. What do you think the story is about?

2 Read about Rosa Parks and answer the questions.

1 Where did she grow up?

2 Why were black people treated differently from white people?

3 What did this mean to the everyday lives of black people?

4 How did Rosa break the law?

5 What happened next?

Sit down for your rights

Today, the southern state of Alabama is known for its modern aerospace industry as well as its cotton. Yet two hundred years ago African Americans were used as slaves on its cotton farms. Even though they had been given their freedom in 1863 by President Abraham Lincoln, fifty years later black people were still treated as second-class citizens. This is the Alabama where Rosa Parks was born in 1913 and grew up. One day when Rosa was 11, she and her cousin went to buy a soda, but the girls were told, 'We don't serve soda to coloured people'. The two races went to different schools and drank from different water fountains. On buses

Grammar: the passive

3 Identify the verbs in the sentence and answer the questions.

*In 1955 **Rosa refused** to give her seat to a white man so **she was taken** to the police station.*

1 Which action did Rosa perform? (in other words, she was 'active')

2 Which action did someone perform on Rosa? (in other words, she was 'passive')

3 Who do you think performed the action on Rosa?

4 Complete the rule.

The passive
We make the passive with a form of the verb _____ + the _____ of the verb.

whites sat at the front and blacks at the back. If a white person needed a seat then a black person had to give them their place. In 1955 Rosa refused to give her seat on a bus in Montgomery to a white man. She was taken to the police station and treated like a criminal. Black people refused to use Montgomery buses until the law was changed. The protest was organised by Martin Luther King. In the end, Rosa and her supporters won. Rosa has been called the 'mother of the civil rights movement'. Her life has been celebrated in poetry and film, and there is a museum dedicated to her. The bus where Rosa made her protest can be seen in the Henry Ford Museum in Detroit. Fifty years after these events, an African American will be chosen as the country's president by the American people.

5 Complete the table with sentences from the text.

Active and passive forms

present simple
Active: People know Alabama for its aerospace industry and cotton.
Passive: Alabama _____.

past simple
Active: White people treated black people as second-class citizens.
Passive: Black people _____

present perfect
Active: People have called Rosa the 'mother of the civil rights movement'.
Passive: Rosa _____.

past perfect
Active: Abraham Lincoln had given them their freedom.
Passive: They _____.

can
Active: You can see the bus where Rosa made her protest in Detroit.
Passive: The bus _____.

will
Active: The American people will choose an African American as their president.
Passive: An African _____.

See Grammar Reference, page 158

6 Rewrite the biography of Barack Obama, changing as much of it as you can into the passive.

Barack Obama was born in Honolulu, Hawaii in 1961. His parents brought him up in Indonesia and Hawaii. In 1981 Columbia University accepted Obama to study political science and international relations. In 1988 the Harvard Law School admitted him to do an MA, and then the University of Chicago in the state of Illinois took him on as a Professor. In 1996 the Illinois authorities elected Obama as a State Senator, a job which he did until 2004. He changed many laws about social justice while he did that job. In 2005 they elected him to be a US Senator in Washington. He held that post until 2008, when he decided to run for President of the USA. He won the election in November 2008. In October 2009 the Nobel committee awarded him the Peace Prize for his attempts to bring different people closer together.

Speaking

7 Which causes do you associate with the people in the pictures?

votes for women ☐   end of apartheid ☐
helping the sick ☐   civil rights in the USA ☐
independence ☐

Martin Luther King

Mahatma Gandhi

Nelson Mandela

Mother Teresa

Millicent Fawcett

8 Imagine that you are the mayor of a new town or city. How will you celebrate local and international heroes and heroines? Work in groups.

1 Decide whether to dedicate a street, square, museum or school to the person, or to have a special day in their honour.

2 Decide how to organise the option you have chosen.

3 Work in pairs with someone from a different group. Tell them the details of what you have decided to do.

Stonehenge   The Taj Mahal   The White House   Sydney Opera House

Reading

1 Read the texts about four famous places and answer the questions by writing A, B, C or D. Each letter can be used more than once.

Which place …

1 do you need special permission to visit? ☐

2 is the oldest? ☐

3 uses a clever way of keeping cool? ☐

4 is a mixture of architectural styles? ☐

5 houses different artistic enterprises? ☐

6 is the result of a moving love story? ☐

7 faces environmental dangers? ☐

8 is the subject of a false legend? ☐

9 isn't made of stone? ☐

10 has a spirit who does housework? ☐

11 is not a UNESCO World Heritage Site? ☐

12 was used as an early computer? ☐

2 Which place would you like to visit the most / the least?

3 <u>Underline</u> examples of the passive in the texts.

A Stonehenge

Stonehenge is without doubt the most famous prehistoric monument in Britain. It was built between 3,000 and 1,500 BC. It stands on Salisbury Plain, and consists of two circles of standing stones, one within the other. Some of the stones were transported from 250 km away in Wales. How this was done is a mystery. Nobody knows for sure why Stonehenge was built, but it was probably used to study the stars, worship the sun or perform calculations. Some experts think that it was probably the site of human sacrifice. More recently, it inspired one of John Constable's most famous paintings, *Stonehenge* (1835), as well as the novelist Thomas Hardy, whose heroine Tess in *Tess of the D'Urbervilles* (1891) meets her destiny there. It became a World Heritage Site in 1986.

B The Taj Mahal

The Taj Mahal in Agra, India, became a World Heritage Site in 1983. It was built by Mogul Emperor Shah Jahan in memory of his wife Mumtaz Mahal, 'beloved ornament of the palace'. It was started in 1632, a year after her death, and was completed twenty years later. When the emperor died he was buried next to his wife. It was made from material from all over India and Asia. More than 1,000 elephants were used to transport it. It has four marvellous minarets and a spectacular dome made from marble. The palace combines the architecture of different cultures, and is beautifully decorated in the Islamic fashion with geometric shapes and calligraphy. The Taj can be seen in the delightful reflecting pool in its gardens. It is visited by up to four million visitors a year. The biggest modern danger it faces is from acid rain, which threatens to turn the building yellow.

C The White House

The White House, which was originally built between 1792 and 1800, is the home and workplace of US presidents. Its site and design were approved by the first president George Washington. It is the place where many of the most important decisions that affect the world are taken. Very little is left of the original building, which has been destroyed, rebuilt, extended and renovated during its two-hundred-year history. Its yellow sandstone has always been painted white, but the legend that it was repainted to hide the damage it had suffered in 1814 when British troops set fire to it is simply untrue. John Adams was the first president to take up residence there in 1800. His wife Abigail's ghost can sometimes be seen doing her laundry in the East Room! Unfortunately the general public can no longer visit the building because of security considerations, but a lucky few can have a tour if it is organised in advance by their congressional representative.

D Sydney Opera House

The remarkable building is the concert hall where the world's top artists love to perform. It is an instantly recognisable symbol of Sydney. It was designed by the Danish architect Jørn Utzon, who left the project before it was finished. It is mainly built from concrete. The roof is a series of shells which have been covered with over a million white tiles. It has some of the most complex and challenging shapes of modern architecture. It has an innovative air-conditioning system that uses water from Sydney harbour to cool the building down. It is home to the Australian National Ballet, Sydney Theatre Company and Sydney Symphony Orchestra. The building was opened by Queen Elizabeth II on 20th October 1973. The first opera, Prokofiev's *War and Peace*, had already been performed there a month earlier. It has been a UNESCO World Heritage Site since 2007.

Buckingham Palace

Windsor Castle

Grammar: relative pronouns

4 Study the sentence from the text on page 128. What word is used to join together the two clauses? What does the word represent?

*Very little is left of the original building, **which** has been destroyed, rebuilt, extended and renovated during its two-hundred-year history.*

5 Relative pronouns provide a useful way of joining clauses together. Match the pronouns in the box with the things they represent.

> that / which   when   where   who
> whose   why

1 a person _____

2 a reason _____

3 a thing _____

4 a time _____

5 the owner of something _____

6 a place _____

6 Join the following sentences with a relative pronoun. Make any other necessary changes.

1 Sydney Opera House was designed by the Danish architect Jørn Utzon. He left the project before it was finished.

2 The roof is a series of shells. They have been covered with over a million white tiles.

3 It's a concert hall. The world's top artists love to perform there.

4 Thomas Hardy was a novelist. His heroine, Tess, met her destiny at Stonehenge.

5 The White House was damaged in 1814. The English tried to burn it down then.

7 Check how these sentences are joined in the four passages you read.

Listening

8 2.35 Listen to a tourist guide talking to a group about Buckingham Palace and Windsor Castle. Put a tick (✓) in the correct box.

1 Buckingham Palace was built for a king.
True ☐   False ☐

2 The outside of Buckingham Palace is quite modern.
True ☐   False ☐

3 The visitors are in London in the summer.
True ☐   False ☐

4 The Queen has her own personal flag.
True ☐   False ☐

5 The Union flag shows the Queen is at Buckingham Palace.
True ☐   False ☐

6 Windsor Castle is under an hour away by coach.
True ☐   False ☐

7 Fire destroyed many of the trees in Windsor Park.
True ☐   False ☐

8 Queen Mary's Dolls' House is perfect in every way.
True ☐   False ☐

A place of interest

Listening and speaking: guiding and warning

1 2.36 Katie Harper is greeting a group of visitors to Shakespeare's birthplace in Stratford-upon-Avon. Listen to the recording. What safety warnings does Katie give the visitors?

2 2.36 **Try to complete each sentence from the talk with two words. Then listen again and check.**

1 Before we go in, I'd _____ say a few words about safety.

2 First of all, it's an ancient building, _____ the floor is not level and the doors are low.

3 So mind your heads, and remember _____ out when you go through doorways.

4 May I also _____ that flash photography is not allowed?

5 This is to protect the exhibits, _____ very old and precious, from strong light.

6 So if you'd like to follow me, we'll begin the tour. _____ step!

7 We are standing in the visitors' centre, _____ dedicated to Shakespeare's life and times.

8 May I draw your _____ these early editions of his plays?

9 Let's take a look at the workshop. This _____ his father made his gloves.

10 As you _____, there are examples of traditional tools and gloves.

11 Now we are going upstairs to the _____ the poet was probably born.

12 Do _____ because the stairs are very dangerous. We don't want any accidents!

3 Write down any useful expressions in Katie's talk.

Pronunciation

4 2.37 Katie sounds excited and enthusiastic because she uses her voice to stress important words, and a wide voice range. Follow Katie's introduction and notice the words that are stressed. Then listen again and repeat.

> Good **morning**, everybody. **I'm** Katie Harper and I am going to be your guide today. On behalf of Culture Tours I'd like to **welcome** you to the **birthplace** of England's **famous poet** and **playwright**, **William Shakespeare**.

5 2.38 Read Katie's farewell words and decide which words you would stress. Then listen to the recording and repeat.

> I hope that you have enjoyed today's visit. Don't forget to visit the souvenir shop, where you can find postcards and gifts. Do take the opportunity to enjoy the calm of the beautiful gardens. Enjoy the rest of your stay in Stratford. Goodbye!

6 Work in groups. Choose a place of interest in your country. Write what you would say to a group of visitors. Draw a plan of the place of interest and the route that you will take. What will you point out to your visitors? Act out your presentation in class.

Stratford-upon-Avon

London

Shakespeare's house

Writing: an informal email

7 What do you know about New Zealand? What is it famous for?

8 Rudi has gone on holiday to New Zealand. Read his email to his family and friends. Match the things he mentions with the pictures.

9 Read the email again and identify the relative pronouns and relative clauses.

Hi everyone,

Well, here I am in New Zealand! The flight was totally <u>exhausting</u> but it has certainly been worth it. So far it has been full of excitement. I did a bungee jump in the Waikato river valley which was absolutely <u>terrifying</u>: it's the highest splash-site in New Zealand.

I am also planning to go to the New Zealand Rugby Museum to find out more about the best team in the world.

You know I am a great fan of *Lord of the Rings* – well, I visited some of the locations where the films were made. The scenery here is unbelievably <u>gorgeous</u>: there are mountains, lakes and glaciers, and it is so unspoilt! You can understand why it was chosen. Our guide was a guy who had helped build the film set. He gave us a <u>fascinating</u> guided tour. I even held one of the swords that had been used in the film. I have attached some of the photos. There is one of me dressed as a Hobbit!! I look completely <u>ridiculous</u>.

For more images have a look at my blog.

Love,

Rudi

10 Find vocabulary that shows Rudi is enthusiastic about his trip.

11 Match the adjectives that have been <u>underlined</u> to the definitions below.

1 very interesting _____
2 very frightening _____
3 very beautiful _____
4 very tiring _____
5 very stupid _____

12 We can make these adjectives more interesting by introducing them with adverbs such as *totally*, *absolutely* and *unbelievably*. Find examples of these in his email.

13 Choose four or five places or activities that you think a visitor to your country should experience. Make a list and say what feelings / emotions you would expect someone to have.

Spotlight

on writing: making adjectives more interesting

- Add an adverb in front of an adjective to make it more 'colourful'. To make most adjectives stronger, you can use *so* / really / very / extremely*.

  The weather was really hot.

- To make them less strong, you can use *quite / fairly / pretty**.

  The hotel was pretty good, but not the best I've ever stayed in.

- In front of a negative adjective, you can use *a little / a bit* / too*.

  Food was a bit expensive.

- With adjectives that already have a strong meaning, add emphasis with *totally / completely / absolutely / really / unbelievably**.

  The view was absolutely amazing!
  (* = in more informal writing).

---

14 Imagine that you are a visitor to your country. Write an email to your family and friends telling them about your experiences. Use relative clauses and expressions that show your enthusiasm.

New Zealand's rugby team performing the 'haka'

Reading

1 Study the pictures of the famous Inca site of Machu Picchu. Where is it situated? What does it look like?

2 Read the information in 'About the Incas' and answer the questions.

1 How long did their empire last?
2 How big was it?
3 What caused its downfall?
4 What was special about the Incas?

3 Quickly read the article 'Heritage in danger' and complete the notes below with dates and numbers.

> Position: _____ in the Andes Mountains
>
> Built: _____
>
> Conquistadors arrive: _____
>
> Discovery by Augusto Berns: _____
>
> Hiram Bingham arrives: _____
>
> Becomes a World Heritage Site: _____
>
> Number of visitors a year: _____

4 Read the first three paragraphs of the article and answer the questions.

1 What is the weather like on Machu Picchu?
2 What is special about it according to one tour guide?
3 What happened to its population?
4 Who received recognition for the discovery of Machu Picchu?
5 How did the National Geographic Society celebrate the discovery?
6 Who probably discovered Machu Picchu first?

5 Read the rest of the article and decide who you think is speaking in A–D.

1 ☐ Julio Alvarez
2 ☐ Richard Wellner
3 ☐ Martha Gorman
4 ☐ Ana Cubillas

A 'From my point of view, the more people who come, the better. Foreign visitors bring money and open up Peru to different cultures. This kind of tourism is a great way of encouraging understanding between different cultures and people. Let's share it with the rest of the world.'

B 'Tourism is a great thing – it means that we can sell handicrafts and feed our families. It is the only way for people around here to have a better life. I have a stall where I sell things to people who take the bus to the summit.'

C 'Even though we receive a lot of visitors each year, nothing can take away the magic of Machu Picchu. Everyone I show around can feel the special power and magnetism of the place. It is a huge attraction.'

D 'So many visitors are causing damage to the site and the surrounding area. Some of the stones have been broken. There are people running around everywhere! When I first came fifteen years ago I was almost on my own.'

6 What do you think the government of Peru should do? Discuss the options as a class.

Should it …
• limit the numbers of visitors?
• improve the facilities for visitors?
• allow the situation to continue as it is?
• stop visitors in order to preserve the site?

7 Write about a place that is important for your country's heritage. How has it been affected by tourism? What can be done to encourage people to visit it, but to preserve it, too?

 Watch a video about Machu Picchu. Turn to page 143.

About the Incas

History

◆ 12th century AD: The Incas begin as a tribe in the Cuzco area.
◆ By mid-1400s most of southern Peru is under Inca control. The Incas incorporate other communities from the Andes. By 1525 the Inca Empire stretches north into modern-day Ecuador and Colombia and south into Chile.
◆ Civil war breaks out between two princes who want to become king.
◆ 1532–33: With just 180 men, 27 horses and one cannon, the Spanish conquistador Francisco Pizarro conquers the Incas.

Art

◆ The Incas were great architects and builders.

Religion

◆ The Incas worshipped different gods, but Inti the sun god was the most important. The Inca king was believed to be descended from him. Inti Raymi was the most important Inca festival in his honour.
◆ The Incas practised human sacrifice.

Heritage in danger

This beautiful quiet place is covered in sunshine and has very high mountains all around. Its name is Machu Picchu. It is sometimes called the 'Lost City of the Incas', and is nearly two and a half thousand metres up in the Andes mountains of Peru. Even in the fog many think it's wonderful to climb up the mountain and walk through the ruins of the city. The story of Machu Picchu is the story of a place where the ancient world and the modern world meet.

'The story of Machu Picchu is the story of a place where the ancient world and the modern world meet.'

Julio Alvarez is a tour guide who knows Machu Picchu very well. He thinks that it has a special quality. 'It's known all over the world that Machu Picchu is one of the magnetic centres of the world,' he says. Machu Picchu is a city with a long history; it's more than 500 years old. It was built in around 1460. Most of the population probably died of smallpox* even before the arrival of the conquistadors in 1532.

Today it's a favourite destination for tourists from all over the world. They want to step back in time and to understand the Inca civilization. When it ended, few people knew that Machu Picchu existed. For a long time Machu Picchu was lost to the outside world. Then, in 1911, an explorer called Hiram Bingham found it again. He was led to the citadel by an eleven-year old Quechua boy. It was such an important discovery that the National Geographic society dedicated the entire edition of its magazine for April 1913 to it. Even though Bingham took the credit for its discovery, a growing number of people believe that a German adventurer and businessman called Augusto Berns discovered it in 1867, and removed the remaining Inca treasure. Whatever the truth behind its discovery, in 1983 it was declared a World Heritage Site.

At first very few people visited the ruins of Machu Picchu, but now many hundreds come here each day. If this continues, there could be half a million visitors every year. Some people in Peru hope that even more tourists will come. People like **Richard Wellner** who live near the site are proud of it and the ancient culture it represents. He wants foreigners to see it and create a bridge between Peru and other cultures. They also believe it will create more business and earn money for the country. They want to make it easier for tourists to come and want to establish better, more modern services.

However, some conservationists worry that more visitors won't be good for Machu Picchu. This is the opinion shared by returning visitor **Martha Gorman.** This time she couldn't even find a place to sit and enjoy the view. She thinks that tourism is bad for the environment and the old ruins. If this continues, Machu Picchu could find itself on UNESCO's list of endangered sites. Others simply worry that the ancient city will change and lose its special quality. Hotel owner José Ramírez, on the other hand, says that Machu Picchu and Peru need more visitors. He thinks that Machu Picchu is a special place and that everyone should be able to see it.

Of course, tourism brings a lot of money to some communities. Aguas Calientes is a good example of a tourist community. People catch the bus to the summit where the city lies. Aguas Calientes has grown from almost nothing into a town. **Ana Cubillas** is grateful to foreign tourists who buy her handicrafts and have helped improve the lives of her family. Like nearly everyone in Aguas Calientes she depends on tourism as her only income.

smallpox a very dangerous infectious disease that leaves marks on the skin

Case Study 6 〉 Reach for the sky!

BUILDING THEM TALL

Modest beginnings
The record for the tallest building, long held by the Great Pyramid of Giza (146 metres), was not **surpassed** for around 4,000 years. In fact, as recently as 1884, when the Washington Monument became the tallest building in the world, the record was still only 169 metres.

A sudden rise
Until the 1880s, most tall buildings had been constructed using stone and iron. This meant that the walls at the bottom of the building had to be extremely thick to support the weight of the **structure**, so there was very little usable space on the lower floors. The use of steel in construction meant that buildings could be made taller. At the same time, lifts were invented, saving people the trouble of climbing hundreds of stairs. In the next fifty years, the height of the tallest buildings doubled. Throughout the 20th century, buildings kept getting taller and, by the time the Burj Khalifa was completed in 2010, it was not only the tallest building in the world, but it was over 300 metres higher than the previous record holder, Taipei 101.

The difficulties of constructing tall buildings
Even though many construction problems have been solved, other considerations include things like earthquakes, wind and severe storms, which must all be **overcome** at the design stage. In fact, the Burj Khalifa was **rotated** 120 degrees from its original design so that the wind put less stress on the structure (although the top of the tower still **sways** a distance of about 1.5 metres). In addition, lifts have to be designed which will carry large numbers of people quickly and safely over half a kilometre into the air. Then we have to provide water and electricity to the tens of thousands of people who live and work in the building. Despite these challenging problems, it seems that nothing will stop architects from designing higher and higher buildings. In terms of imagination at least, the sky's the limit.

1 In pairs or small groups, discuss the following questions.

Why do you think people want to build tall buildings?

What problems do you think architects and builders face when they build tall buildings?

Would you like to live on the 100th floor of a building? Why / Why not?

2 Match the words in bold from the text to the definitions.

1	surpassed	a	turned in a circular direction
2	structure	b	moves from side to side
3	sways	c	solved
4	overcome	d	building
5	rotated	e	exceeded; overtaken

3 Use all the information on this page to answer the questions below. Use your own words as much as possible.

1 Why was the height of buildings limited before the 1880s?

2 Why were changes made to the design of the Burj Khalifa?

3 What special problems do architects face when designing tall buildings?

4 What do you understand by the word 'skyscraper'?

Some of the tallest buildings in the history of the world:
- 2,575 BC The Great Pyramid of Giza, Egypt (146 metres)
- 1884 The Washington Monument, Washington DC, USA (169 metres)
- 1889 The Eiffel Tower, Paris, France (300 metres)
- 1931 The Empire State Building, New York, USA (381 metres)
- 1998 Petronas Towers, Kuala Lumpur, Malaysia (452 metres)
- 2004 Taipei 101, Taiwan (509 metres)
- 2010 Burj Khalifa (formerly Burj Dubai), Dubai, UAE (828 metres)

What is a skyscraper?
If the surrounding buildings are low, as they were in the 1890s, a building of just ten floors (or *storeys*) would be considered a skyscraper. These days 100 or 150 metres is generally recognised as the lowest height. We usually measure to the top part of the building but don't count any communications aerials or masts that are attached.

Review > Unit 11

Vocabulary

1 Join the beginnings of the sentences to their ends.

1 I'm sorry I didn't **catch** …

2 There's too much **jargon** in this manual –

3 I love her French **accent** when she speaks English –

4 On her CV she said she was **bilingual**, …

5 **Native speakers** sometimes have a poor understanding …

6 Italian was her **mother tongue**, …

a I could listen to it all day.

b but she stopped using it when she was five.

c your name; could you say it again?

d why can't they use ordinary English?

e of the grammar of their own language.

f but in fact her German was basic.

Grammar

2 Alice is telling her friends about a conversation she had on a train with a stranger called Jane. Complete what Alice says to her friends using reported speech.

A = Alice, J = Jane

1 J Is this seat free?

   She asked me if the seat next to me _____.

2 J You're not English, are you? Where are you from?

   She said I _____ and asked me where _____.

3 A I'm from the United States.

   I told her _____.

4 J You have a lovely accent. Do you come from Boston?

   She said _____, and asked me if I _____.

5 A No, I am from San Diego in California.

   So I said that _____.

6 J How long have you been here?

   Then she asked _____ in England.

7 A I've been here eight months. I'm going back home next week.

   I told her I _____ there eight months and that I _____ the following week.

3 Add question tags to the ends of the statements.

1 Spanish is your mother tongue, _____?

2 Irregular verbs are difficult, _____?

3 We can use a dictionary in the exam, _____?

4 She isn't English, _____?

5 He doesn't have a very strong accent, _____?

6 That was a hard English test, _____?

Functions

4 Megan is doing a language survey in Cambridge. Re-order the words to form questions.

M = Megan, D = Donatella

M Excuse me, (1) *minute / can / me / a / questions / you / to / answer / some / spare.*

D Yes, of course. (2) *do / know / what / you / to / want?*

M Let's begin then. So, first of all, (3) *you / nationality / are / what?*

D I'm Italian. I'm from Verona.

M It's a beautiful city. And (4) *you / old / tell / can / are / how / you / me?*

D I'm seventeen.

M Now (5) *list / you / could / look / this / at* and put your reasons for using English in order.

D Mm, the first one is for school, then it's listening to music. Then travel, and the last one is for making friends.

M (6) *it / studying / OK / if / is / I /ask / you / where / are?*

D No problem. I'm at the Peal school.

M Thanks. Finally, (7) *like / to / if / I'd / know /* you use English more with foreigners or with native speakers.

D Definitely more with other foreigners.

Now I can …

- ☐ ask polite questions.
- ☐ describe things.
- ☐ talk about language.
- ☐ present information in writing.
- ☐ use reported speech.
- ☐ use question tags.

Review › Unit 12

Vocabulary

1 Complete the text by putting the letters of the words in the correct order.

> Last year we decided that we wanted to
> _____ (**ocmemmeroat**) the 100th
> _____ (**anyinverasr**) of the foundation
> of our village school. So the parents and
> teachers decided to organise a weekend
> _____ (**fsvetial**). We had a
> _____ (**apreda**) where the children
> _____ (**rdeessd/pu**) as pupils from
> different periods of history and marched
> through the village. The _____
> (**osutemcs**) were wonderful. There was even
> a _____ (**renemactetn**) of a typical
> school day with a very strict teacher. The
> _____ (**hggihltih**) of the second day
> was a _____ (**irefkowr**) display to look
> forward to the next 100 years.

Grammar

2 Complete the exchanges by transforming a basic adjective into an extreme adjective.

Example: *Was the film good?*
Good? It was wonderful.

1 I thought the story was <u>stupid</u>.
   Stupid? It was completely _____.

2 She looked <u>beautiful</u> in her new dress.
   Beautiful? I thought she looked _____.

3 The walk was <u>tiring</u>, wasn't it?
   Tiring? It was absolutely _____.

4 I thought the documentary was <u>interesting</u>.
   Interesting? I thought it was _____.

5 He's a <u>frightening</u> driver, isn't he?
   Frightening? He's totally _____.

3 Rewrite the active sentences using a passive form.

1 People in Japan made this laptop.
   Example: *This laptop was made in Japan.*

2 Someone has decorated the classroom.

3 Someone sells tickets for these events online.

4 A teacher sent Josh home for fighting.

5 Police have arrested three men.

6 Someone has made all the beds!

Functions

4 Danuta is welcoming a group of tourists to Malbork Castle. Expand the prompts to form her introductory speech.

1 Good afternoon, everybody. My name / Danuta and I / be your guide today.

2 It / give me / great pleasure / welcome you / Malbork Castle / which have / important place / Polish history.

3 The castle / be / built entirely / brick but / be / badly damaged during / last war.

4 But / you can see, it be / restored to / former glory.

5 Now, if you / like / follow me, we / begin / tour.

5 Join the parts of the sentences that give some important details about the castle. Pay special attention to the relative pronouns.

Part 1	Part 2	Part 3
Malbork Castle is a fine example	until 1457	with a black cross over their armour.
It was built by the Teutonic Order	<u>where</u> you can find	<u>which</u> is why it is a World Heritage Site.
It remained under the order's control	<u>whose</u> members wore a white cloak	the tombs of eleven of its grand masters.
The Teutonic Knights was a military order	<u>which</u> was formed	<u>when</u> the Poles took it over.
This is St Anne's chapel	of gothic military architecture	in the 12th century.

Now I can ...

- [ ] understand a guide and safety warnings.
- [ ] talk about important people and places.
- [ ] write an informal email.
- [ ] use the passive.
- [ ] use relative pronouns.

Irregular verb list

Infinitive	Past simple	Past participle
be	was / were	been
become	became	become
begin	began	begun
break	broke	broken
bring	brought	brought
build	built	built
buy	bought	bought
can	could	been able to
catch	caught	caught
choose	chose	chosen
come	came	come
cost	cost	cost
cut	cut	cut
do	did	done
draw	drew	drawn
dream /driːm/	dreamt /dremt/ / dreamed	dreamt /dremt/ / dreamed
drink	drank	drunk
drive	drove	driven
eat	ate	eaten
fall	fell	fallen
feel	felt	felt
fight	fought	fought
find	found	found
fly	flew	flown
forget	forgot	forgotten
get	got	got
give	gave	given
go	went	gone
grow	grew	grown
have	had	had
hear /ˈhɪə/	heard /hɜːd/	heard /hɜːd/
hide	hid	hidden
hit	hit	hit
hold	held	held
hurt	hurt	hurt
keep	kept	kept
know	knew	known
learn	learnt / learned	learnt / learned

Infinitive	Past simple	Past participle
leave	left	left
lend	lent	lent
let	let	let
lie	lay	lain
lose	lost	lost
make	made	made
mean /miːn/	meant /ment/	meant /ment/
meet	met	met
pay	paid	paid
put	put	put
read /riːd/	read /red/	read /red/
ride	rode	ridden
ring	rang	rung
rise	rose	risen
run	ran	run
say	said	said
see	saw	seen
sell	sold	sold
send	sent	sent
set	set	set
show	showed	shown
sing	sang	sung
sit	sat	sat
sleep	slept	slept
speak	spoke	spoken
spell	spelt / spelled	spelt / spelled
spend	spent	spent
split	split	split
stand	stood	stood
steal	stole	stolen
swim	swam	swum
take	took	taken
teach	taught	taught
tell	told	told
think	thought	thought
throw	threw	thrown
understand	understood	understood
wear	wore	worn
win	won	won
write	wrote	written

Before you view

1 Look at the photograph. You are going to watch a video about archaeologists. Discuss these questions in pairs or small groups.

1 What do you think archaeologists do every day?

2 What do you think the study of archaeology can tell us about the past?

3 What kinds of things do archaeologists find in your country?

Word list

2 Check you know the meanings of these words.

> ancient bones carvings
> civilisation discover fossils
> pots shovels skulls spades

First viewing

3 Watch the video and write at least one more thing in each category.

Archaeologists study:

Man-made things	buildings, pots, _____
Works of art	jewellery, _____
Human and animal remains	skulls, _____

Second viewing

4 Watch the video again, and answer the questions.

1 What is archaeology?

2 What do archaeologists have to do to find things?

3 Do archaeologists work quickly?

4 Is the work boring?

5 What do the carvings tell us about the Maya?

6 Where do archaeologists work?

7 Is the work dangerous?

After viewing

5 Complete the text with the words in the word list.

Archaeology is the study of (1) _____ things. Archaeologists look at old buildings and houses and they look for things like jewellery, (2) _____ and plates. Archaeologists study paintings in caves. They also study (3) _____ (these are the (4) _____ of old animals). And they study human remains, like (5) _____. Teams of archaeologists work with (6) _____ and (7) _____. It is slow work and it is dirty, but it can be exciting. The beautiful (8) _____ in a Mayan city tell the history of the Maya and help us (9) _____ things about the Maya (10) _____.

6 Imagine you are an archaeologist. What would you like to discover?

The future of a village   4

Before you view

1 Read the facts about Essaouira. Does anything surprise you? Would you like to visit it?

> - The port has existed since the 5th century BC.
> - In the 1st century it produced the purple dye used in Roman senators' togas.
> - Different European powers tried to conquer it but never succeeded.
> - The current city was built in the 18th century. The architect was a French-born slave.
> - Essaouira used to be Morocco's main port. Caravans came from Timbuktu, to Marrakech and then Essaouira.
> - It is a UNESCO World Heritage Site as it is an 18th century fortified town.

Word list

2 Check you know the meanings of these words.

> a breadwinner   to compete
> the economy   Heritage   historic
> tourism   tourists   tourist boom   trawlers

First viewing

3 You are going to watch a video about Essaouira nowadays. Watch the first section and complete the notes about its fishing industry.

> Things look great at the fishing port of Essaouira, but in fact _____.
> There are three reasons why fishing is no longer a good job:
> 1 The number of fish _____.
> 2 Some of the work has _____.
> 3 _____ can't compete with big trawlers.
> Abdelhabdi, a typical fisherman, finds life difficult because _____
> _____.

4 Watch the second section about tourism in Essaouira and choose a, b or c.

1 The first tourist boom was in the …
   a 1950s   b 1960s   c 1970s
2 Since 1996 tourism has increased by …
   a 100%   b 200%   c 300%
3 Its 'medina' was built in the …
   a 1700s   b 1800s   c 1900s

5 Watch the rest of the video. What important choice does Essaouira have to make?

Second viewing

6 Watch the first part of the video again, and answer the questions.

1 What can you smell in the air at the port?
2 What happens if Abdelhabdi works for a week?
3 According to the narrator, tourism is the town's new _____.
4 What kind of people came to Essaouira in the first tourist boom?
5 What is the big problem facing the people of Essaouira?

7 What examples of Essaouira's past and its heritage can you see?

After viewing

8 Complete the text with the words in the word list.

Fishing is difficult in Essaouira. The small boats which leave out of this port can't (**1**) _____ with the big fishing boats. Those boats, or (**2**) _____, can simply catch more fish. Recently, this town has a new (**3**) _____ – tourism. Last year, thousands of (**4**) _____ visited Essaouira, and this tourism has brought hope and money to the town. Essaouira is experiencing its second (**5**) _____ – the first was in the 1960s. It's not difficult to see why people like the (**6**) _____ village. Essaouira's 'medina', or historic town centre, was built in the 1700s, and was recently put on UNESCO's World (**7**) _____ list. Essaouira now has a very good chance to develop tourism and help its (**8**) _____. But the 'new' Essaouira must also try not to sell out the local people, their culture and the environment.

9 Imagine Essaouira in 20 years' time. How will it look if people make …

- the right decisions?
- the wrong decisions?

5 Peruvian weavers

Before you view

1 Look at these pictures of people who live in a village in the Andes mountains, and discuss the questions.

1 How easy do you think their life is?

2 How do you think the villagers …
- clothe themselves?   • feed themselves?
- make money to buy the things they can't produce themselves?

3 How rich are they?

Word list

2 Check you know the meanings of these words.

> a coat   a cooperative   shawls   to spin
> threads   traditional   weavers   yarn

First viewing

3 Watch the video, and answer the questions by choosing a, b or c.

1 The women ….
   a are in charge of their business.
   b work for a boss in Lima.
   c would prefer a regular salary.

2 The women …
   a are working in a new industry.
   b are exploiting traditional skills.
   c needed teachers from another village.

3 How have the men of the village reacted?
   a They want to take control of the industry.
   b Some are helping more with the sheep.
   c They don't like the power their wives have.

4 Farming …
   a is a recent activity.
   b goes back to Inca times.
   c is the villagers' main source of money.

5 What effect has weaving had on the villagers' lives?
   a They can earn lots of money.
   b There is a lot more jealousy between villagers.
   c They work fewer hours.

4 Put the weaving process in the right order.

The women …
a ☐ spin the wool
b ☐ colour the yarn
c ☐ sell the finished articles
d ☐ make the yarn
e ☐ take the wool from the sheep
f ☐ weave the yarn into cloth

Second viewing

5 Watch the video again, and answer the questions.

1 How is the cooperative a mixture of the new and traditional?

2 Which animals produce the wool?

3 How many women are involved?

4 Why was Nilda sad? How does she feel now?

5 Tick (✔) the crops that the farmers grow:
   sugar cane ☐   maize ☐   quinoa ☐
   coffee ☐   wheat ☐   potatoes ☐   barley ☐

6 What is the problem with farming as a profession?

7 How has the weaving industry changed the villagers' way of thinking?

8 Why does the narrator think that weaving is more than a tradition?

After viewing

6 Complete the text with the words in the word list.

The villagers of Chinchero catch a sheep and cut off its winter (**1**) _____. The methods they use are (**2**) _____, but they are collecting wool for a new and different business – a weavers' (**3**) _____ that the women here manage.

The women (**4**) _____ the wool into (**5**) _____ for making cloth.

Now that it is difficult for men to make money from farming, these women (**6**) _____ are becoming the main economic supporters of the family. They learn basic weaving at school, and go on to weave blankets, shawls and (**7**) _____, and to prepare their own yarn. The women's cooperative hopes to prove that many (**8**) _____ together are stronger than one alone.

7 Can you think of examples of traditional crafts in your country that can be revived to help people lead better lives and overcome unemployment?

Kenya's butterflies

Before you view

1 Continue the explanation of *metamorphosis* by putting sentences a–g in the correct order.

Metamorphosis is a process in which an animal's body changes as it grows. Most insects develop through **metamorphosis**.

a ☐ This becomes a **chrysalis** (= a form covered with a hard case).

b ☐ At last the chrysalis opens and an adult butterfly comes out.

c ☐ A **butterfly** starts as an egg.

d ☐ It creates its **cocoon** (= soft covering).

e ☐ Inside the chrysalis, the **pupa** (= developing insect) changes into a butterfly.

f ☐ The female butterfly lays its eggs.

g ☐ The egg hatches into a **caterpillar**, which eats and grows.

Word list

2 Check you know the meanings of these words.

> cocoons a forest income to lay
> pupae to pupate to rear returns
> species a survival rate a threat

First viewing

3 All these sentences are false – correct them!

1 The Arabuko Sokoke forest is the biggest forest in West Africa.

2 The biggest danger the forest faces is pollution.

3 People aren't as well educated as before.

4 Only local farmers go to the butterfly project's headquarters.

5 The price of caterpillars is fixed.

6 Farmers don't see the benefits of breeding butterflies.

7 Farmers can't be bothered to learn their botanical names.

8 Farmers have to collect a new stock of pupae each time they want to breed.

Second viewing

4 Watch the first two thirds of the documentary again, and answer the questions.

1 What was the problem with catching live butterflies and transporting them?

2 What solution to the problem did farmers have?

3 Why do people cut down the forests?

4 What money-making activities can the forest be used for?

5 What was the mission of the butterfly farm project when it was first founded?

6 Why do farmers need to have a good head for business?

7 How much money had sales of pupae made the year before the documentary was made?

8 How has the project contributed to reducing unemployment?

After viewing

5 Complete the text with the words in the word list.

The Arabuko Sokoke (1) _____ is home to more than a third of Kenya's eight hundred and seventy (2) _____ of butterfly. The demand for unusual butterfly species for public and private collections has long been (3) _____ to natural environments such as this Kenyan forest. In the past, live butterflies were sold to collectors around the world, but most died before they arrived. Now, local farmers have started using their skills to (4) _____ caterpillars instead. The caterpillars are sent around the world as (5) _____ and arrive just in time to become butterflies. These butterflies have (6) _____ of nearly 100%.

First, small number of butterflies are caught. The females (7) _____ their eggs and caterpillars finally emerge. After they (8) _____, or enter their (9) _____, the caterpillars are brought to the project centre in the heart of the forest. Butterfly farming is popular because it has quick (10) _____ – just one month after starting, it is possible for a new farmer to generate (11) _____.

6 The butterfly project helps the local population have better lives while protecting nature. Do you know any other projects that do this?

10 Cheese-rolling races

Before you view

1 Think about the title of the race and answer the questions.

1 What do you imagine happens in this race?
2 Do you think the race is dangerous or just fun?
3 What do you think is the prize?

Word list

2 Check you know the meaning of these words.

> annual   cheer   keep on   route
> spectator   steep   sure   wild

First viewing

3 Watch the video and put the sentences in the correct order.

1 The competitors start running after the cheese. ☐
2 The race is repeated again a year later. ☐
3 The winner gets a prize. ☐
4 People get together at the top of Coopers Hill. ☐
5 Sometimes people get injured. ☐
6 The wheel of cheese is pushed down the hill. ☐

Second viewing

4 Watch the video again and answer the questions

1 When did cheese-rolling races start in Brockworth?
2 How fast can a wheel of cheese roll down the hill?
3 What is the prize for the race?
4 How many spectators were injured a few years ago?
5 When do competitors get injured?

After viewing

5 Complete the text with words in the word list.

Cheese-rolling is a tradition in the town of Brockworth. First the competitors come together at the top of Coopers Hill and wait. Then someone pushes a very large wheel of cheese down the (1) _____ slope. And after that, things get a little (2) _____. The first one to the bottom wins!

Many people enjoy the cheese-rolling races. However, they can be dangerous. A few years ago, one of the cheeses rolled down the hill too quickly and unexpectedly went into the crowd. Now, the competition (3) _____ has crash barriers to protect the crowd. It's not just (4) _____ who get injured, competitors do as well.

These cheese racers may be crazy, but year after year the crowds keep on (5) _____ and the competitors (6) _____ running. Is it for the fame? Is it for the fun? We may never know, but you can be (7) _____ of one thing. It's more than just cheese that makes people want to win Brockworth's (8) _____ cheese-rolling race.

6 Work in groups. Imagine you went to Brockworth and took part in the cheese-rolling race. What did you see? Did you have fun? Did you win? Were there any injuries? Prepare to tell the rest of the class about your day.

The lost city of Machu Picchu **12**

Before you view

1 What do you know about the Incas? Try this quiz.

1 The Incas lived in …
   a Venezuela.   b Peru.   c Mexico.

2 The Inca Empire was at its height in …
   a 1325.   b 1425.   c 1525.

3 The adventurer who conquered the Incas was …
   a Montezuma.   b Pizarro.   c Cortés.

4 The Incas were conquered in …
   a 1532.   b 1542.   c 1552.

5 The most important festival for the Incas was …
   a Halloween   b Inti Raymi
   c Bonfire Night.

Word list

2 Check you know the meanings of these words.

> the environment   fog   magnetic   ruins
> stalls   the summit   tourism

First viewing

3 Watch the first part of the video, and answer the questions.

1 How high is Machu Picchu?
2 What other name is it known by?
3 How old is it?
4 What happened in 1911?
5 Who was Hiram Bingham?
6 How many people visit the city each day?

4 Watch the rest of the video, and make notes. What are the arguments for and against more tourism?

+ for more tourism	– against more tourism

Second viewing

5 Watch the video again, and answer the questions.

1 Describe the opening scenes of the video. What are the different opinions about Machu Picchu?
2 Why does Julio, the tour guide, think that Machu Picchu is so special? What are his exact words?
3 How has tourism changed since Hiram Bingham's discovery of the site?
4 What do you think it is like to be a tourist at Machu Picchu nowadays?
5 What are conservationists afraid of?
6 What does the hotel owner think about limiting tourism?
7 What does life look like for the ordinary people of Peru?
8 How do you think the people of Aguas Calientes feel about tourism?

After viewing

6 Complete the text with the words in the word list.

Machu Picchu is one of the (1) _____ centres of the ancient world. Visitors from all over the world love to walk through the (2) _____. Even in the rain and (3) _____, it is spectacular. Some conservationists worry that more visitors won't be good for Machu Picchu. They say that (4) _____ may not be good for (5) _____. The town of Aguas Calientes grew suddenly near an area where visitors get on buses to travel up to (6) _____ of the mountain. The town is just a group of (7) _____ where local people sell art and things they have made to visitors. The people who survive on tourism want the visitors to keep coming to Machu Picchu.

7 How important is it to preserve historic sites?

Communication activities

Student A

1A page 7

You are Jo Lennox from Wales. You are 17. Your family are sheep farmers. You have three older brothers. One is at university studying law, the second one is a doctor and the third one is still at home. He helps your parents with the farm.

Your are at sixth form college where you study science subjects.

You are in (country) because you are visiting the countryside. You want to learn about native wildlife.

In your free time you like reading, bird-watching and orienteering (going for long walks using a map and a compass).

You would like to become a vet or do some other kind of work with animals.

1 Everyday English page 14

1 You are the youth centre officer. Your partner wants information about the mural painting course.

MURAL PAINTING COURSE

who for:	anyone
teacher:	local mural artist Chester Banks
cost:	£40 / ten two-hour sessions
time:	14.00 – 16.00 Saturdays
place:	the old cement factory
need:	old clothes, mask, not allergic to paints
don't need:	to be good at painting

2 You want to find out about the 'Build your own PC' course. Ask questions like Cindy's about the course.

5A page 51

Alex Ward – 19 years old

Job:	close-up magician (performs tricks in front of people, not on a stage)
Working day:	evenings and weekends; busiest at Christmas and New Year
Good things:	own boss; fun; not have to work in office; meet different people
Bad things:	people sometimes rude; you mustn't interrupt them
Skills:	know how to 'read' people; know when you are welcome or unwelcome
Requirements:	need to practise hours each day; have to like entertaining people
Money:	beginning £12,000 a year, up to £100,000 for someone well-known

5 Everyday English page 58

1 You are telephoning Kidcamp about their advertisement for camp counsellors. You would like to speak to Martin/Martha Green about the jobs that are available. Say you'll ring back later.

2 Ask to speak to Martin/Martha. Be yourself. Answer his/her questions about your age, skills and interests. Accept his/her offer to send you an application form.

6C page 65

Henry – Saving energy

Contrast: One hundred years ago people read by candlelight or gaslight; now you can see the lights of Los Angeles from the moon.

What to do: Turn off the stand-by button, use low-energy light bulbs, turn off lights when not needed.

Interesting fact: Altogether, all electrical appliances on stand-by use as much energy as the whole of Morocco.

Communication activities

8D page 88

Horse racing is a popular spectator sport. The most famous race is the Grand National. It was invented at Aintree near Liverpool by the Earl of Sefton. It is a long and dangerous race where horses jump over hedges and water obstacles. Horses and their jockeys can be badly injured. The first race was in 1836. Millions of people watch it on TV and bet money on the result. Another famous racecourse is at Ascot, near Windsor. Ascot Week is a big social event too, as members of the Royal family attend it. It is a great privilege to be allowed into the Royal enclosure. It is also famous for the extravagant hats that women wear on Ladies' Day.

9 Everyday English page 102

1   You are a hotel receptionist. Business is quiet and you have a lot of empty rooms. The high season price is €80 a night, and low season price is €50 a night. Low season begins in two weeks. Breakfast is extra and costs €7. You are prepared to negotiate a deal with the customer.

2   You want to know how to send an email from a friend's computer. Ask them for help and instructions.

11 Everyday English page 124

1   You need these two items but don't know what they are called in English.

1

2

2   Your partner wants these two items but doesn't know what they are called in English. Listen to their description and give them the name of the object.

1   a sticking plaster (at first you think they want a bandage)
2   a safety-pin (at first you think they want a drawing pin)

6D page 66

The mountain gorilla is found in Africa – in Rwanda, the Democratic Republic of Congo, and Uganda.

The African elephant is found in Africa.

The giant panda is found in China.

The polar bear is found in the Arctic.

The leopard is found in Asia and parts of Africa.

The giant tortoise is found in tropical islands such as Madagascar, Mauritius and the Galapagos Islands.

Communication activities

Student B

1A page 7

You are Bobby Carter from New Mexico. You are 19. Your mother is a school teacher. Your father works in a factory. Your grandparents are Irish. You have a younger sister called Jasmine.

Back home you are at art college. You want to be a jewellery designer.

You are in (country) because you want to learn about jewellery-making with silver and amber. You are staying with a jewellery maker. You are staying another three months.

In your free time you like visiting historical sites and museums.

You also enjoy snowboarding. You want to go snowboarding this winter in Italy or France.

Your ambition is to have your own design studio.

1 Everyday English page 14

1 You are interested in the mural painting course. Ask questions like Cindy's about the course.

2 You are the youth centre officer. Your partner wants information about the 'Build your own PC' course.

'BUILD YOUR OWN PC' COURSE	
who for:	anyone
teacher:	Doctor Jenny Hope (from the university)
cost:	£200 / twenty two-hour sessions £100 deposit + £100 at the end – you keep the PC
time:	19.00 – 21.00 Mondays
place:	the youth centre
need:	parents' agreement to pay the full cost of the PC to be patient to be able to follow instructions
don't need:	to be a good scientist any equipment – everything is supplied
enrolment:	this Friday evening

5A page 51

Colin Gitsam – 21 years old

Job:	department store employee; Father Christmas in Christmas season
Working day:	arrives 9.30; replies to letters children have written to Father Christmas; changes into costume; sits in armchair and waits for children to come; works until 7.30
Good things:	seeing children's faces when they pull your beard and find out it is real
Bad things:	talking to children all day can be tiring; unemployment; need another job as Father Christmas only works at Christmas!
Skills:	know how to make each child feel comfortable; be a quick thinker to answer children's questions
Requirements:	need to be big and fat and have a realistic beard; have to know all the latest toys
Money:	pay doesn't change; a self-employed Father Christmas can earn £200 a day

5 Everyday English page 58

1 You are a receptionist at Kidcamp. Answer the phone to Student A.

Try to put Student A through to Martin/Martha Green. There is no answer.

Offer to take a message. Give Student A Martin's/Martha's direct line.

2 You are Martin/Martha. Find out about Student A.

Ask about his/her age/interests/special skills.

Offer to send an application form.

6C page 65

Melanie – Saving water

Contrast: People take water for granted, but in the future it will be as scarce as oil.
What to do: Take a shower not a bath, turn off the tap while cleaning teeth, only flush the toilet when absolutely necessary.
Interesting fact: A dripping tap can fill a bath in one day.

Communication activities

8D page 88

Rowing is a minority sport. Nevertheless, there are two well-known events associated with it. The first is the University Boat Race, where crews from the universities of Oxford and Cambridge row against each other along a stretch of the river Thames. The first race took place in 1829. You have to be a good swimmer, as sometimes the boat sinks! The second event is the Henley Regatta, which consists of a series of races over five days at Henley, a town on the Thames in Oxfordshire, England. As well as being a sporting event, it is also where members of high society and the rich and famous go to meet each other and be seen.

9 Everyday English page 102

1 You want to book a hotel room for two or three nights. You want to know if there are any special offers. You want breakfast to be included in the price. You want a discount because it is almost low season.

2 Tell a friend how to send an email from your computer.

11E page 124

1 Your partner wants these two items but doesn't know what they are called in English.

   Listen to their description and give them the name of the object.

1

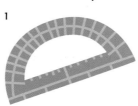

2

1 a protractor (at first you think they want a compass)
2 a tin-opener (at first you think they want a corkscrew)

2 You need these two items but don't know what they are called in English.

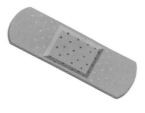

2C page 20 Quiz results

For each A answer give yourself 2 points.
For each B answer take away 1 point.
For each C answer you get 0 points.

Negative scores: You consider yourself to be an unlucky person with little or no control over your destiny. Learn to be more open and take chances. Good things can happen to you if you are prepared to take the occasional risk.

0–5 points: You are happy without taking risks. You worry a lot before taking decisions and regret bad decisions. A more positive attitude can make better things happen. Always look for the positive side of a negative experience as this can teach you how to react in a similar situation.

6–8 points: You are a fairly positive person. A bad experience or bad experiences mean you are more cautious than you used to be. Make sure that too much caution doesn't prevent you from identifying exciting opportunities.

9+ points: You are a positive and adventurous person. You do not let difficulties or failures stop you. You are someone who knows how to make the best of situations and identify lucky opportunities. Make sure that you are not over-confident.

Grammar reference

UNIT 1

present simple vs present continuous

present simple

We use the **present simple** to talk about ...

- general facts and truths:

  The verb *be*:

  Elephants are very big.

  Is snow white?

  Other verbs:

  A baker makes bread and cakes.

  The Sun does not go round the Earth.

- personal information:

  My sister Jackie plays the piano.

- routines – things which happen regularly:

  My father always goes to work by train.

- states, senses, possession and emotions, using stative verbs:

  I believe you.

  This soup does not taste very nice.

  Does this bike belong to Paul?

  Jane hates maths and history.

Affirmative

I/You/We/They	like	swimming.
He/She/It/	likes	

Negative

I/You/We/They	do not (don't)	eat meat.
He/She/It/	does not (doesn't)	

Interrogative

Do	I/you/we/they	run fast?
Does	he/she/it	

Short answers

Yes,	I/you/we/they do.	No,	I/you/we/they don't.
	he/she/it does.		he/she/it doesn't.

adverbs of frequency

never	**sometimes**	**often**	**usually**	**always**

0%   100%

We use adverbs of frequency with the **present simple** to show how often something happens. They go before the verb, but after the verb *be* and modal verbs (e.g. *can, must*):

They usually play football on Saturday morning.

She is always late for school!

I can't often come out in the evenings.

present continuous

We use the **present continuous** to talk about ...

- actions which are happening now:

  Look! The baker is making some bread.

  The Sun is not shining at the moment.

- temporary actions:

  Jackie is not playing the piano this week because she's hurt her left hand.

- changes to routines and habits:

  My father is going to work by bus today because the railway line is closed.

- actions which are happening around now:

  We are travelling through Europe.

- processes which increase (often using the verbs *grow* and *get*):

  It is getting very dark. There's a storm coming.

Affirmative

I'm	(I am)	walking to the park.
You're/We're/They're	(You/We/They are)	
He's/She's/It's	(He/She/It is)	

Negative

I'm not	(I am not)	playing in the garden.
You/We/They aren't	(are not)	
He/She/It isn't	(is not)	

Interrogative

Am I		
Are you/we/they	going home now?	
Is he/she/it		

Short answers

Yes,	I am.	No,	I'm not.
	you/we/they are.		you/we/they aren't.
	he/she/it is.		he/she/it isn't.

UNIT 2
past simple vs past continuous
past simple
We use the **past simple** to talk about ...

- a completed single event in the past:

  The verb *be*:

  I was happy to see her yesterday.
  Were you angry about the result?

  Regular verbs:

  We watched the match in the afternoon.
  They didn't play football last Saturday.

  Irregular verbs:

  She made that dress herself.
  Did she make the trousers, too?

- a sequence of completed events in the past:

  She walked home, made tea and read a book.

time expressions with the past simple
- yesterday
- last week/year/Friday/summer/weekend etc.
- two days/a week/an hour ago
- in 1998/in the 18th century
- when I was young/in my childhood

Affirmative		
I/He/She/It You/We/They	was were	at home last night.
I/You/He/She/ It/We/They	watched ate	a film yesterday. a great pizza last night.

Negative		
I/He/She/It You/We/They	wasn't weren't	happy yesterday.
I/You/He/She/ It/We/They	didn't work didn't sleep	at home last weekend. well last night.

Interrogative		
Was Were	I/he/she/it you/we/they	there on Sunday?
Did	I/you/he/she/ it/we/they	play in the park on Friday? Fly to Paris last summer?

Short answers				
Yes,	I/he/she/it was. you/we/they were.	No,	I/he/she/it wasn't. you/we/they weren't.
Yes,	I/you/he/she/it/ we/they did.	No,	I/you/he/she/it/we/ they didn't.

past continuous
We use the **past continuous** to talk about ...

- actions in the past which continued for a period of time:

  I was swimming in the river from 10 to 12 yesterday.
  Were they working in the garage all afternoon?

- actions in the past which continued at the same time:

  While I was cooking lunch, my sister was watching TV.
  He wasn't studying maths while we were writing our essays.

- an interrupted continuous action in the past:

  I was watching the film when he arrived .
  Were you having a shower when the phone rang?

time expressions with the past continuous
- this time last year
- while, when

subject and object questions
subject questions

Who saw you ?	John saw me.
Which film won the prize?	Space Dog won the prize.
Whose bike hit you ?	John's bike hit me.

object questions

Who did you see?	I saw John.
Which film did you watch?	We watched a space film.
Whose bike did you clean?	I cleaned Mary's bike.

When *who, which, what* or *whose* is the subject of the question, we don't use the auxiliary verb *do/does*.

When *who, which, what* or *whose* is the object of the question, we use the auxiliary verb *do/does*.

UNIT 3

past perfect

We use the **past perfect** to talk about ...

- actions which happened before a more recent action in the past:

  After he had finished his work, he went home.

  They had not left home before the rain began.

- actions in the past which prevent a more recent past action:

  By the time I got to the station, the train had left.

  They had not opened the park gates when I arrived.

Affirmative

I/You/He/She/It/We/They	had watched the film had eaten everything	before we arrived.

Negative

I/You/He/She/It/We/They	hadn't cleaned done	it when she got home.

Interrogative

Had	I/you/he/she/it/we/they	finished gone out	when he telephoned?

Short answers

Yes, No,	I/you/he/she/it/we/they	had. hadn't.

used to

We use **used to** ...

- to talk about actions we did in the past and don't do now, or didn't do in the past, and do now:

  They always used to play tennis but they don't play any more.

  She didn't use to like swimming when she was a girl, but she swims every day now.

- to show that something has changed, without actually mentioning it:

  My father used to smoke when I was a child.

  I didn't use to eat cauliflower then.

Affirmative

I/You/He/She/It/We/They	used to	go to the cinema every week.

Negative

I/You/He/She/It/We/They	didn't (did not) use to	talk very much.

Interrogative

Did I/you/he/she/it/we/they	use to	wear glasses?

Short answers

Yes, No,	I you/he/she/it/we/they	did. didn't.

would

We can use **would** as a substitute for **used to** in the situations described above.

We would We used to	go to Wales every summer when I was young.
Did you used to	read in bed with a torch as a boy?
I wouldn't I didn't use to	get home until very late after school.

UNIT 4

present perfect

We use the **present perfect** to talk about ...

- past experiences where the time is not important, with *ever* and *never*:

  Have you *ever been* to the UK?

  They have never seen *an elephant.*

- past experiences which refer to the time up to the present moment, with *so far, this week/month/year/ century etc, the first/fifth time*:

  The new James Bond film came out last week, but I haven't seen *it so far.*

  He has been *to the dentist's twice* this week.

  It's the third time it has rained *today!*

- past experiences related to a period of time or to a point in time, with *How long...?, since* and *for*:

  How long have you lived *in Manchester?*

  We have worked *here* since 1995.

  She has known *him* for *ten years.*

- recently completed past events, with *just, already, not yet* and *yet*:

  Have they arrived *home* yet?

  He hasn't finished *his homework* yet.

  My mother has already prepared *lunch.*

  They have just started *secondary school.*

Affirmative

I/You/We/They	have watched	this film before.
He/She/It	has drunk	all the water.

Negative

I/You/We/They	haven't (have not) been	here since 2008.
He/She/It	hasn't (has not) tried	it for two months.

Interrogative

Have I/you/we/they	lived	here for a long time?
Has he/she/it	worked	here for many years?

Short answers

Yes,	I/you/we/they have. he/she/it has.	No,	I/you/we/they haven't. he/she/it hasn't.

UNIT 5

modal verbs

Verb	Meaning	Present	Past	Future
have to	an external obligation, a duty	He **has to** start work at 7.30.	He **had to** start work at 6 a.m. last week.	He **will have to** start work at 8 a.m. next week.
need to	a requirement	She **needs to** find a new job.	She **needed to** find a new job when she got fired.	She **will need to** find a new job when her current contract ends.
must	an internal obligation, an order to oneself	I **must** read this book before the exam.	I **had to** read this book before the exam.	I **will have to** read this book before the exam.
don't have to/ need to	lack of necessity and obligation	We **don't have to** go to school tomorrow – it's a holiday.	We **didn't have to** go to school yesterday – it was a holiday.	We **won't have to** go to school next week – it's a holiday.
mustn't	a prohibition	You **mustn't** use mobile phones in class.	You **weren't allowed to** watch films at night.	You **won't be allowed to** wear jeans at work.

make and let

Verb	Meaning	Present	Past	Future
make somebody do something	to force to do, to cause to do	They **make us work** ten hours a day. He often **makes her laugh**.	They **made us work** ten hours a day. He often **made her laugh**.	They **will make us work** ten hours a day. He **will** often **make her laugh**.
let somebody do something	to allow, to give permission	My mother **lets me sleep** late on Saturdays.	My mother **let me sleep** late last Saturday.	My mother **will let me sleep** late next Saturday.

UNIT 6
future: 'will' vs 'be going to'
will

We use *will* to talk about …

- personal predictions about the future:

  I think he will be a famous actor one day.

  We don't need the umbrellas – it won't rain this afternoon.

- spontaneous decisions about future actions:

  A: There isn't any sugar left.

  B: I will get some when I go into town.

- definite facts about the future:

  The fast train for London will leave from platform 3.

- offers and promises of future actions:

  I will collect you at ten o'clock.

  I won't tell him anything about it.

Affirmative

I/You/He/She/It/We/They	'll (will)	do it tomorrow.

Negative

I/You/He/She/It/We/They	won't (will not)	eat it later.

Interrogative

Will	I/we you/he/she it/they	like it?

Short answers

Yes,	I/you/he/she/it/we/they	will.	No,	I/you/he/she/it/we/they	won't.

be going to

We use *be going to* to talk about …

- definite future facts:

  She is going to have a baby in July.

  The English team is not going to win the match.

- sudden future plans:

  There's no food in the house so I am going to order a pizza.

- longer term future plans:

  We are going to France next summer.

  She is not going to visit them tomorrow.

Affirmative

I	'm (am)	
He/She/It	's (is)	going to eat it soon.
You/We/They	're (are)	

Negative

I	'm (am)	
He/She/It	's (is)	not going to be there tomorrow.
You/We/They	're (are)	

Interrogative

Am	I	
Is	he/she/it	going to win?
Are	you/we/they	

Short answers

Yes,	I am. he/she/it is. you/we/they are.	No,	I'm not. he/she/it's not. you/we/they're not.

definite article 'the'

We use the definite article *the* to talk about …

- something we are mentioning for the second time:

  I talked to a policeman yesterday. The policeman told me what the law about cycling was.

- something of which there is only one:

  The moon is very beautiful tonight.

- certain geographical names:

  the (River) Danube, the Atlantic Ocean, the English Channel, the Alps, the Sahara Desert, the Solomon Islands

- certain countries, especially those with *Kingdom* or *Republic* in their name:

  the United Kingdom, the United States, the Czech Republic, the Netherlands, the Bahamas, the Gambia

- superlatives:

  Everest is the highest mountain in the world.

- ordinal numbers:

  It was the second time I had met him.

UNIT 7
comparative and superlative adjectives

Adjective	Comparative	Superlative
one- and two-syllable words: **long, nice, narrow**	adjective + *er* **longer, nicer narrower**	adjective + *est* **longest, nicest narrowest**
two-syllable or longer words ending *in:* *-ing, -ed, -ful:* **intelligent, exciting, worried, forgetful**	*more* + adjective **more intelligent, more exciting, more worried, more forgetful**	*most* + adjective **(the) most intelligent, (the) most exciting, (the) most worried, (the) most forgetful**
irregular adjectives:		
good **bad** **far** **little** **many/much/a lot of**	**better** **worse** **farther (further)** **less** **more**	**best** **worst** **(the) farthest (furthest)** **least** **(the) most**

Spelling rules

- when the adjective ends in -y, the -y changes into an -i + -er/-est:

  happy – happier – happiest

- when the adjective ends in single vowel + single consonant, the final consonant is doubled:

  hot – hotter – hottest

- when the adjective ends in -e, we just add -r/-st:

  wide – wider – widest

constructions with adjectives, comparatives and superlatives

- comparing two things using *as ... as*:

  Tom is as talented as his father.

- comparing two things using comparative + *than*:

  Tina is taller than Donna.

- using superlatives:

  Hugh is the youngest painter in this contest.
  Jane was the most beautiful girl in our class.

preferences: 'would rather' and 'prefer'

- When we compare preferences we can use **would rather** + **than**:

  He would rather visit a gallery than a museum.

- We can also use **would rather** + **not** in the negative form:

  She would rather not go to the cinema tomorrow.

- We can ask questions about preferences using **would rather** + **or**:

  Would you rather eat chicken or turkey?

- When we compare preferences of actions using **prefer** we add **than**:

  They would prefer to come on Friday than on Saturday.

- We can also use **prefer** + **to** to compare preferences about things:

  She prefers sculpture to graphics.

- We can also compare preferred actions using **prefer** + **-ing** + **to**:

  They prefer swimming to running.

UNIT 8

zero conditional, first conditional, second conditional

0 conditional	1st conditional	2nd conditional
Form: *If* + present simple, present simple	**Form:** *If* + present simple, *will* future	**Form:** *If* + past simple, *would/could* conditional
If the temperature drops below 0°C, water freezes.	*If he takes these pills, he will feel better soon.*	*If she won the lottery, she would travel around the world.*
If you buy three tickets, you get a discount.	*If you buy three tickets, you will get a discount.*	*If you bought three tickets, you would get a discount.*
Meaning: this presents true facts or information	**Meaning:** this presents an action which can happen and which is likely to happen.	**Meaning:** this presents an action which can happen, but which is not very likely to happen.

UNIT 9

too / enough

- **too** + adjective/adverb:

  You are too short *to sit in the front seat.*

  He works too slowly.

- **enough** + noun:

  I don't have enough time.

- adjective/adverb + **enough**:

  You aren't tall enough *to sit in the front seat.*

  You don't work quickly enough.

UNIT 10

causative 'have': 'have something done' and 'get something done'

Tense	Personal pronoun	Appropriate form of verbs *have/get*	Object	Past participle of verb	Time expression
present simple	He	has gets	his flat	redecorated	every five years.
present continuous	He	is having is getting	his flat	redecorated	right now.
present perfect	He	has (just) got has (just) had	his flat	redecorated.	
past simple	He	had got	his flat	redecorated	last month.
past continuous	He	was having was getting	his flat	redecorated	When I saw him last week.
past perfect	He	had had had got	his flat	redecorated	before he moved in.
will future	He	will have will get	his flat	redecorated	next week.
going to future	He	is going to have is going to get	his flat	redecorated	during the holidays.
modal verbs	He	must have must get	his flat	redecorated	immediately.

UNIT 11
reported speech

Direct speech	Reported speech
John: *This is a great film.*	*John says (that) this is a great film.*
John: *I saw a great film last night at this cinema.*	*John said that he had seen a great film the previous night at that cinema.*
present simple present continuous present perfect past simple past perfect will can have / has got haven't / hasn't got	past simple past continuous past perfect past perfect past perfect would could had didn't have
now today tonight tomorrow yesterday next week / year last month / night / year ago / so far this / these here	then that day that night the next / following day the day before / the previous day the following week / year the previous month / night / year before that / those there

reported questions

if/whether and yes/no questions	
John: *Have you been here before?*	*He enquired whether I had been there before.*
Mary: *Will we meet these people tomorrow?*	*She wanted to know if we would meet those people the following day.*
Wh- questions	
Mary: *Why did you wake me up at 5 a.m. yesterday?*	*She wanted to know why he had woken her up at 5 a.m. the day before.*
John: *Where does your mum work?*	*He asked me where my mum worked.*

question tags

- *Linda is late, isn't she?*
- *His parents don't live here, do they?*
- *Mr Ross left for Rome, didn't he?*
- *I am your best friend, aren't I?*

reported orders, promises and requests

Direct speech	Reported speech
Officer: *Run!*	*The officer ordered us to run.*
Mary: *Don't be late again.*	*She told us not to be late again.*
Mary: *Please pass me the salt.* Ann: *Could you pass me the salt, please?*	*She asked me to pass her the salt.*
John: *Please don't touch the glass.* Tom: *Could you not touch the glass?*	*He asked us not to touch the glass.*
Plumber: *I'll call you next week.*	*The plumber promised to call me the following week.*

UNIT 12

passive voice: affirmative and negative

Tense	Subject	Appropriate form of the verb *be*	Past participle of the main verb
present simple	I The books My room	am (not) are (not) is (not)	finished. printed. cleaned.
present perfect	The books My room	have (not) been has (not) been	printed. cleaned.
past simple	The books My room	were (not) was (not)	printed. cleaned.
past perfect	The books My room	had (not) been has (not) been	printed. cleaned.
will	The books My room	will (not) be will (not) be	printed. cleaned.
going to	The books My room	are (not) going to be is (not) going to be	printed. cleaned.
modal verbs	The books My room	cannot be can be	printed. cleaned.

passive voice: interrogative

Tense	Appropriate form of the verb *be* or auxiliary	Object	Form of verb *be* if auxiliary in column 2	Past participle of the main verb
present simple	Are	the books	–	printed?
present perfect	Has	my room	been	cleaned?
past simple	Were	the books	–	printed?
will	Will	my room	be	cleaned?
going to	Are	the books	going to be	printed?
modal verbs	Can	my room	be	cleaned?

Pronunciation guide

Vowels	
/iː/	meet
/i/	study
/ɪ/	middle
/e/	end
/æ/	catch
/ɑː/	hard
/ɒ/	hot
/ɔː/	sport
/ʊ/	put
/uː/	school
/u/	influence
/ʌ/	up
/ɜː/	learn
/ə/	never
/eɪ/	take
/əʊ/	phone
/aɪ/	price
/aʊ/	now
/ɔɪ/	boy
/ɪə/	here
/eə/	where
/ʊə/	pure

Consonants	
/p/	pen
/b/	bag
/t/	table
/d/	dog
/k/	cat
/g/	get
/tʃ/	chair
/dʒ/	jump
/f/	fill
/v/	very
/θ/	thing
/ð/	this
/s/	sit
/z/	zoo
/ʃ/	ship
/ʒ/	treasure
/h/	hat
/m/	man
/n/	no
/ŋ/	sing
/l/	long
/r/	ring
/j/	yellow
/w/	well

CREDITS

Photos

The publishers would like to thank the following sources for permission to reproduce their copyright protected photographs:

Cover: (Benjamin Albiach Galan / Shutterstock.com)

Inside: pp 5 (Siri Stafford/Getty Images), 6a (JenDen2005/iStockphoto), 6b (lisafx/iStockphoto), 6c (Shutterstock), 6d (Shutterstock), 8a (John Terence Turner/Taxi/Getty Images), 8b (track5/iStockphoto), 8c (sjlocke/iStockphoto), 8d (gaspr13/iStockphoto), 9 (New York Times/eyevine), 10a (Shutterstock), 10b (Shutterstock), 11a (Shutterstock), 11b (monkeybusinessimages/iStockphoto), 11c (Shutterstock), 11d (AFP/Stringer/Getty Images), 11e (aabejon/iStockphoto), 11f (Shutterstock), 12a (Bob Watkins/Photolibrary), 12b (Action Press/Rex Features), 12c (Mitchell Funk/Photographer's Choice/Getty Images), 13a (Hemis/Alamy), 13b (Marka/Alamy), 13b (stevenallan/iStockphoto), 14a (clearviewstock/iStockphoto), 14a (Hill Street Studios/Blend Images/Getty Images), 15 (Barry Bishop/National Geographic Image Collection), 16a (courtesy of Wayne Mushrow), 16b (National Maritime Museum/National Geographic Image Collection), 16c (Bill Curtsinger/National Geographic Image Collection), 16d (Nick Caloyianis/National Geographic Image Collection), 18a (evemilla/iStockphoto), 18b (stocksnapper/iStockphoto), 18c (Doug Baines/Fotolia), 19a (Brown Brothers/National Geographic Image Collection), 19b (St Mary's Hospital Medical School/Science Photo Library), 20 (Stephen St. John/National Geographic Image Collection), 21 (Atlantide Phototravel/Corbis), 22 (Amerigo Vespucci) (U.S. Government Library Of Congress/National Geographic Image Collection), 23a (Mark Thiessen/National Geographic Image Collection), 23b (Photo Archive Submitter/National Geographic Image Collection), 23c (Newell Wyeth/National Geographic Image Collection), 23d (Bob Sacha/National Geographic Image Collection), 24a (Shutterstock), 24b (Shutterstock), 25 (Tullio M. Puglia/Getty Images Sport), 26 (AndreasWeber/iStockphoto), 27a (Trinity Mirror/Mirrorpix/Alamy), 27b (Trinity Mirror/Mirrorpix/Alamy), 30a (Daisy Images/Alamy), 30b (eMC Design), 32a (eyecrave/iStockphoto), 32b (vnlit/Fotolia), 32c (wwing/iStockphoto), 32d (Peter Macdiarmid/Getty Images News), 33a (eurobanks/iStockphoto), 33b (MsInferno/iStockphoto), 33c (Shutterstock), 34 (The Print Collector/Alamy), 35a (John Kellerman/Alamy), 35b (Todd Gipstein/National Geographic Image Collection), 36 (Kirsty Wigglesworth/Getty Images), 37 (Reuters/NASA TV), 38a (Anthony Devlin/PA Archive/Press Association Images), 38b (Shutterstock), 40b (Carl Court/PA Archive/Press Association Images), 40c (Shutterstock), 40d (Shutterstock), 40e (Shutterstock), 41 (Shutterstock), 42a (Shutterstock), 42b (SoopySue/iStockphoto), 42c (Selcuk Arslan/Fotolia), 42d (StockImages/Alamy), 43 (Andrew Barker/Alamy), 44a (Jonathan Littlejohn/Alamy), 44b (David Lochhead/Fotolia), 44c (John McKenna/Alamy), 45 (Shutterstock), 46a (Shutterstock), 46b (Eric Rohr), 49 (Reuters/China Daily/National Geographic Image Collection), 50 (Rune Hellestad/Corbis), 51a (David Turnley/Corbis), 51b (plastique/BigStockPhoto), 52 (@ Ricochet.co.uk), 53a (Stuart Forster/Alamy), 53b (Shutterstock), 54 (Briss/iStockphoto), 55 (Per Winbladh/Corbis), 56a (ChrisCrafter/iStockphoto), 56b (Ariel Skelley/Corbis), 56c (Shutterstock), 56d (technotr/iStockphoto), 57a (Jonathan Utz/Getty Images), 57b (Romko_chuk/iStockphoto), 57c (Jason Edwards/National Geographic Image Collection), 58 (Jeff Greenberg/Alamy), 59 (Mike Theiss/National Geographic Image Collection), 60 (Carsten Peter/National Geographic Image Collection), 61 (yegorius/Fotolia), 62a (salihguler/iStockphoto), 62b (Copit/iStockphoto), 62c (Volker Wierzba/Fotolia), 62d (LeggNet/iStockphoto), 62e (CostinT/iStockphoto), 63 (Tomasz Paczos/PAP/Corbis), 64a (jophil/iStockphoto), 64b (millraw/iStockphoto), 65 (tfoxfoto/iStockphoto), 66a (Duncan Noakes/Fotolia), 66b (Gary Scott/Fotolia), 66c (Kitch Bain/Fotolia), 66d (MOKreations/Fotolia), 66e (Clarence Alford/Fotolia), 66f (Thomas Barrat/Fotolia), 67a (Bill Travers from Christian The Lion At World's End www.bornfree.org.uk), 67b (Bill Travers from Christian The Lion At World's End www.bornfree.org.uk), 68a (Carsten Peter/National Geographic Image Collection), 68b (Shutterstock), 70 (JulienGrondin/iStockphoto), 71 (ranplett/iStockphoto), 72a (konradlew/iStockphoto), 72b (laurent dambies/Fotolia), 72c (Iconsinternational.Com/Alamy), 72d (Mike Theiss/National Geographic Image Collection), 73 (HP_Photo/Fotolia), 74a (Shutterstock), 74b (The Gallery Collection/Corbis), 74c (PoodlesRock/Corbis), 74d (Bettmann/Corbis), 74e (Edimédia/Corbis), 75 (Chad Ehlers/Alamy), 76a (tmacphoto/iStockphoto), 76b (holicow/iStockphoto), 76c (Pictorial Press Ltd/Alamy), 76d (Daniel Tackley/Fotolia), 76e (ilbusca/iStockphoto), 76f (Vehbi Koca/Alamy), 78 (The National Trust Photolibrary/Alamy), 79 (Sisse Brimberg/National Geographic Image Collection), 80 (Justin Kase ztwoz/Alamy), 81 (David Madison/Corbis), 82 (Shutterstock), 83 (Gmosher/iStockphoto), 84a (LionHector/iStockphoto), 84b (egal/BigStockPhoto), 84c (Vladiro9/iStockphoto), 84d (Marc Dietrich/Fotolia), 84e (Custom Medical Stock Photo/Photolibrary), 85 (Yuri_Arcurs/iStockphoto), 87 (Luedke and Sparrow/Digital Vision/Getty Images), 88a (TheDman/iStockphoto), 88b (imagewerks/Getty Images), 89a (Gannet77/iStockphoto), 89b (Shutterstock), 89c (Creativel/iStockphoto), 89d (Chris Young/AFP/Getty Images), 89e (Image Source/Corbis), 89f (mikedabell/iStockphoto), 89g (coopder1/iStockphoto), 89i (johnwoodcock/iStockphoto), 90a (Shutterstock), 90b (iStockphoto), 90c (Shutterstock), 91 (FrankyDeMeyer/iStockphoto), 93 (Shutterstock), 94a (Yuri_Arcurs/iStockphoto), 94b (AnnettVauteck/iStockphoto), 94c (dsharpie/iStockphoto), 94d (theboone/iStockphoto), 95a (Andrew Watson/Photolibrary), 95b (Richmatts/iStockphoto), 96a (carlosalvarez/iStockphoto), 96b (Shutterstock), 96c (Shutterstock), 96d (Shutterstock), 97a (ranplett/iStockphoto), 97b (Fairtrade Foundation), 99 (Shutterstock), 100 (Shutterstock), 101a (Ian Cook/Time & Life Pictures/Getty Images), 101b (Warner Bros./The Kobal Collection/Mountain, Peter), 101c (Shutterstock), 101d (Shutterstock), 101e (Warner Bros./The Kobal Collection/Mountain, Peter), 102a (Radius Images/Alamy), 103a (Mel Yates/Photolibrary), 103b (Shutterstock), 104a–b (Cover image © 2005 Walker Books Ltd. Photograph by Trish Gant. From Sam Stern's *Cooking Up A Storm*. Reproduced by permission of Walker Books Ltd, London SE11 5HJ, www.walker.co.uk), 104c (twohumans/iStockphoto), 105 (caracterdesign/iStockphoto), 106a (Eric Egea/Fotolia), 106b (Brasil2/iStockphoto), 106c (Nimbus/Fotolia), 106d (NZG/Fotolia), 106e (Paperboat/iStockphoto), 107 (Shutterstock), 108a (imagebroker/Alamy), 108b (Bon Appetit/Alamy), 108c (shoutforhumanity/iStockphoto), 109 (CollinsChin/iStockphoto), 110a (Shutterstock), 110b (luapeed/Fotolia), 110c (Shutterstock), 111a (Tony Harris/PA Archive/Press Association Images), 111b (blackjake/iStockphoto), 111c (Joff Lee/Photolibrary), 112a (Shutterstock), 112b (Shutterstock), 112c (Shutterstock), 112d (Shutterstock), 115 (David Boyer/National Geographic Image Collection), 118a (courtesy of Nowa Era), 118b (Shutterstock/gezik), 118c (Shutterstock/gezik), 119a (Elizabeth Dalziel/AP/Press Association Images), 120a (cenix/iStockphoto), 120b (MichaelUtech/iStockphoto), 120c (tobiasjo/iStockphoto), 120d (Cassianus12/iStockphoto), 120e (miralex/iStockphoto), 120f (Mlenny/iStockphoto), 121 (Janine Wiedel Photolibrary/Alamy), 122 (fstop123/iStockphoto), 123 (Shutterstock), 124a (SteveStone/iStockphoto), 124b (track5/iStockphoto), 125 (Detail Heritage/Alamy), 126a (Raymond Gehman/Corbis), 126b (David R. Frazier Photolibrary, Inc./Alamy), 126c (AP/Wide World Photos/National Geographic Image Collection), 126d (William Philpott/Reuters/Corbis), 127a (Bettmann/Corbis), 127b (Dinodia Images/Alamy), 127c (Gideon Mendel/Corbis), 127d (Tim Graham/Alamy), 127e (Michael Nicholson/Corbis), 127f (Rex Features), 128a (The Gallery Collection/Corbis), 128b (ratluk/iStockphoto), 128c (nojustice/iStockphoto), 128d (iam5tv/BigStockPhoto), 128e (ratluk/iStockphoto), 129a (waiheng/BigStockPhoto), 129b (Shutterstock), 130b (Niall McDiarmid/Alamy), 130c (Shutterstock), 131a (Shutterstock), 131b (Mark Boulton/Alamy), 131c (New Line Cinema/The Kobal Collection), 131d (David Gray/Reuters/Corbis), 132 (Gina Martin/National Geographic Image Collection), 133a (rest/iStockphoto), 133b (Shutterstock), 133c (Shutterstock), 134a (Shutterstock), 134b (Shutterstock), 138 (stuart emmerson/Alamy), 139 (Robb Kendrick/National Geographic Image Collection), 140a (Chris Rainier/National Geographic Image Collection), 140b (Chris Rainier/National Geographic Image Collection), 141 (Thomas Marent/Minden Pictures/National Geographic Image Collection), 142 (Stephen Dorey ABIPP/Alamy), 143 (Michael Hanson/National Geographic Image Collection)

Text

We are grateful to the following for permission to reproduce their copyright protected material:

National Geographic for material about Kenya Butterflies adapted from National Geographic Digital Motion Video Site; and an extract adapted from 'Q&A With Enric Sala, Marine Ecologist and National Geographic Fellow' http://kids.nationalgeographic.com/Stories/PeoplePlaces/Interview-with-enric-sala, copyright © National Geographic, reproduced with permission; *Charlie and the Chocolate Factory* by Roald Dahl (Puffin, 1973) Text Copyright © Roald Dahl Nominee Ltd, 1964 Reproduced by permission of Penguin Books Ltd.

The Publisher would also like to thank The Born Free Foundation, especially Will Travers for his invaluable help. The Born Free Foundation is an international wild animal charity in action worldwide to save lives, stop suffering and rescue individuals. Born Free works to phase-out zoos and protect lions, elephants, gorillas, tigers, wolves, bears, chimpanzees, marine turtles and many more species in their natural habitat. www.bornfree.org.uk.

Illustrations by Nigel Dobbyn (Beehive Illustration) pp 86, 92, 109, 114; Javier Joaquin (The Organisation) pp 28, 29, 38; Tim Kahane pp 39, 80, 145, 147; The Map Specialists Ltd p 79; Martin Sanders (Beehive Illustration) pp 22 (map), 107